POSTCARD HISTORY SERIES

Collinsville

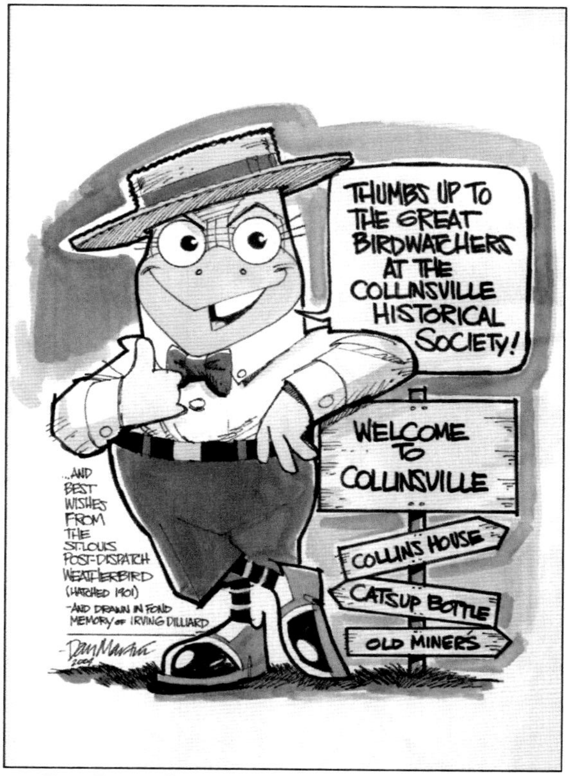

The sketch of the *St. Louis Post-Dispatch* Weatherbird was done by artist Dan Martin. After dedicating the drawing to Irving Dilliard, Martin donated it to the Collinsville Historical Museum.

The Collinsville Historical Museum was founded in 1965 when librarian Myrtis Bowers displayed two glass cases of historical items. In 1972, Irving Dilliard, a member of the Collinsville Library Board of Directors, acquired the Collins family trunk of memorabilia and placed it in the library. Since then, the museum has accumulated over 10,000 artifacts that have been housed in a temporary fashion on the lower level of the Collinsville Memorial Public Library.

Since 1976, members of Friends of the Collinsville Historical Museum have volunteered as attendants, office workers, and researchers and have served on various committees to help improve the museum and its artifacts.

A permanent home for the museum has been a long-awaited project. Members of the Friends of the Collinsville Historical Museum are currently engaged in finalizing plans to construct a museum on the property of the Collinsville Memorial Public Library.

POSTCARD HISTORY SERIES

Collinsville

Collinsville Historical Museum
Neal Strebel, Editor

ARCADIA
PUBLISHING

ISBN 978-0-7385-3366-7

Published by Arcadia Publishing
Charleston, South Carolina

Printed in the United States of America

Library of Congress Catalog Card Number: 2001012345

For all general information contact Arcadia Publishing at:
Telephone 843-853-2070
Fax 843-853-0044
E-mail sales@arcadiapublishing.com
For customer service and orders:
Toll-Free 1-888-313-2665

Visit us on the Internet at www.arcadiapublishing.com

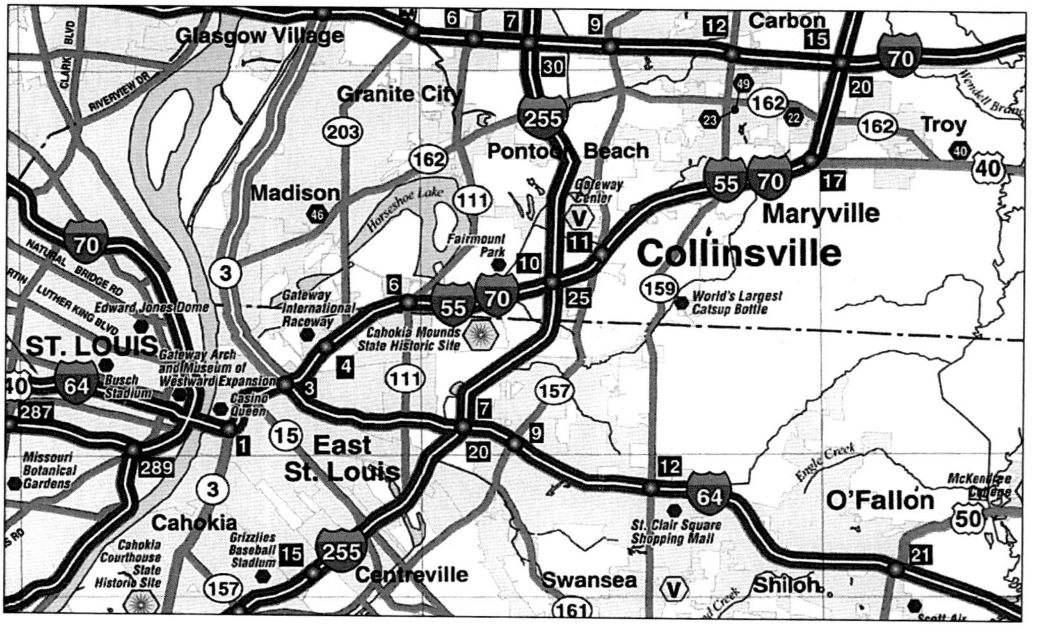

Contents

ACKNOWLEDGMENTS

Without the assistance of a number of people, assembling this book would not have been possible. I would like to thank Floyd Sperino for his assistance and for his confidence in asking me to do the book. A special thanks goes to Lois Metzger, Doris Bauer, and Janet Albertina for their role in this project. Ralph and Marian Haury provided invaluable assistance for scanning 100 photographs and postcards and enhancing via computer over 50 of the damaged Marshall postcards. The book would not have been completed without the assistance of Elaine Hartley, who provided encouragement, technical advice, and help with developing and composing the text. I certainly appreciate the support of the people who provided information, loaned pictures and postcards, and generally embraced the project.

For what is, basically, a book of pictures, this book also contains quite a bit of data. I am sure that there are mistakes within the book, but I hope they are minor ones. After consulting many periodicals and books, I found that the single best source of basic information about the city is Lucille M. Stehman's comprehensive overview *Collinsville, A Pictorial History*. Unfortunately, the book is out of print.

EDITOR'S NOTES:

Because of my interest in postcards, Floyd Sperino, Curator of the Collinsville Historical Museum, approached me about doing a book based on the museum's postcards. The museum's collection includes postcards randomly accumulated through the years, the collection of nearly 350 cards that I contributed a few years ago, and the Henry J. Marshall group that were removed from the post office cornerstone in 1964. Collinsville postcards are generally scarce, and quality views of early Collinsville are difficult to find.

I took the project on as a fundraiser for the museum, to preserve the Marshall collection, to share early views of Collinsville with others, and to publicize the fascinating hobby of postcard collecting.

The first picture postcards were published in this country in 1893. Collecting postcards had become widespread by 1905. The golden age of postcards in the United States was generally from 1904 to 1918. In 1906, there were nearly 800 million postcards sent through the mail in the following categories: expositions and minor events, political and social history, sets, signed artists, patriotic and greetings, novelties, topicals, and views. This book presents primarily view cards. City and especially small town views portray poignant aspects of American life as it was in earlier years. Appreciation of the past tends to generate pride in who we are and where we come from.

A fascinating feature of vintage postcards is that they can be found on virtually any topic. Stamp collectors can consult a catalog or list to find what stamps were issued and the number printed. Postcard collectors do not have this advantage or limitation as their source is vast. Therefore, the postcard collector may search through many thousands of postcards and will usually find a card that he or she hasn't seen before.

INTRODUCTION

Much of the City of Collinsville is located on the bluffs overlooking the American Bottom. The vast flood plain of the American Bottom was carved from glacial melt water during the Ice Age and the route changes of the Mississippi River. Seasonal flooding of the lowlands produced fertile soil and lush vegetation that attracted Native Americans who occupied this region for several thousand years. French settlers first documented the historic occupation when they traveled up and down the Mississippi River.

John Cook, born in Germany in 1769, came to America during the Revolutionary War. Cook's family moved from Pennsylvania to Virginia and then West Virginia. Late in the 18th century, Cook joined a group of people in Sharpsburg, Maryland. They were going west, with St. Louis as a possible destination. In 1810, after a stay in St. Louis, Cook built the first cabin in what was to become Collinsville.

When John Cook lived in this cabin, the area had no official name. Later it was known as Downing Station in recognition of James Downing's home and an adjoining small business at a nearby crossroads. On November 20, 1819, a post office was established, and the Downing Station name was registered in Washington, D.C. By this time, other families had moved to the area, and a few businesses had been established. However, when John Cook settled, there were no other homes within the boundaries of the plat that later became Collinsville.

For an unrecorded reason, the name of the first post office was changed to Unionville in 1822. By this time, John Cook had sold his cabin to three brothers, Augustus, Anson, and Michael Collins. The Unionville post office was discontinued in 1823, and mail was channeled to the community by way of Edwardsville. Residents petitioned the U.S. government for restoration of the Unionville office. The settlers were notified that their request had been granted except for the name. They were told that there was another Unionville post office in Illinois. A subsequent search failed to locate another Unionville. The name was changed to Collinsville effective December 31, 1825. Augustus Collins was appointed postmaster, and the office was in his general store. The three Collins brothers had been joined by their father, Deacon William Collins and two more brothers, William Burrage and Frederick. Their signatures, along with those of other residents, influenced the United States Postal Department to reestablish the post office in the community. Perhaps the large number of Collins signatures on the petitions affected the naming of the settlement.

The first three Collins brothers had started a sawmill, tannery, wagon shop, and distillery. They had also built a house of worship for all denominations. William Burrage and his wife Elizabeth Wilt Hertzog Collins, along with other family members, were strong supporters of temperance. They were also interested in platting the settlement. Realizing the conflict between the ideas of religion and ownership of the distillery, Augustus, Anson, and Michael demolished the distillery. They, however, relocated and pursued business ventures in other locations.

William Burrage and Elizabeth Collins became religious leaders in Collinsville. They also acquired land and moved towards platting the area. After William's death from typhoid fever in 1835, Elizabeth, with the help of others, continued the project of platting the region. She attempted to tie land ownership to temperance, but the courts ruled the restriction invalid.

When the survey was officially recorded at the Madison County Courthouse in Edwardsville on May 12, 1837, the population of the Collinsville area was estimated to be between 400 and 500 persons. It was not until February 15, 1850, that it was incorporated as a village and registered at the Secretary of State's office in Springfield. A special election on the proposal to organize a city was held in 1872. At that time, the population was a bit over 1,800. Many citizens seemed not to care one way or another, but the proposition to switch to a city carried by a vote of 101 to 78.

When the Wonderly brothers sank a mine at the foot of Mill Hill in 1859, the coal mining era began in Collinsville. Dr. Octavius Lumaghi envisioned the industrial potential of the area after he learned that Collinsville was to have rail service. He sank the Lumaghi Mine No. 1 in 1869. By 1880, Collinsville became a commercial center providing goods and services to a growing population who came to work in the mines and other industries. By 1922, coal miners and their families made up almost a third of the 9,800 residents of the city. More mines were opened during the next half-century. Other industries including lead and zinc works, a knitting mill, cowbell factory and canning plant also flourished. Due to competition and the Great Depression, most of these businesses were closed by 1950. Because St. Louis is only ten miles to the west, the city developed into a "bedroom" community.

Today, the City of Collinsville is still a fast-growing suburb with a population of 24,800. One of the exciting current developments is the popular and growing hospitality district that includes a convention and visitors' complex. For over 175 years, Collinsville has grown and changed by adapting to new developments and ideas.

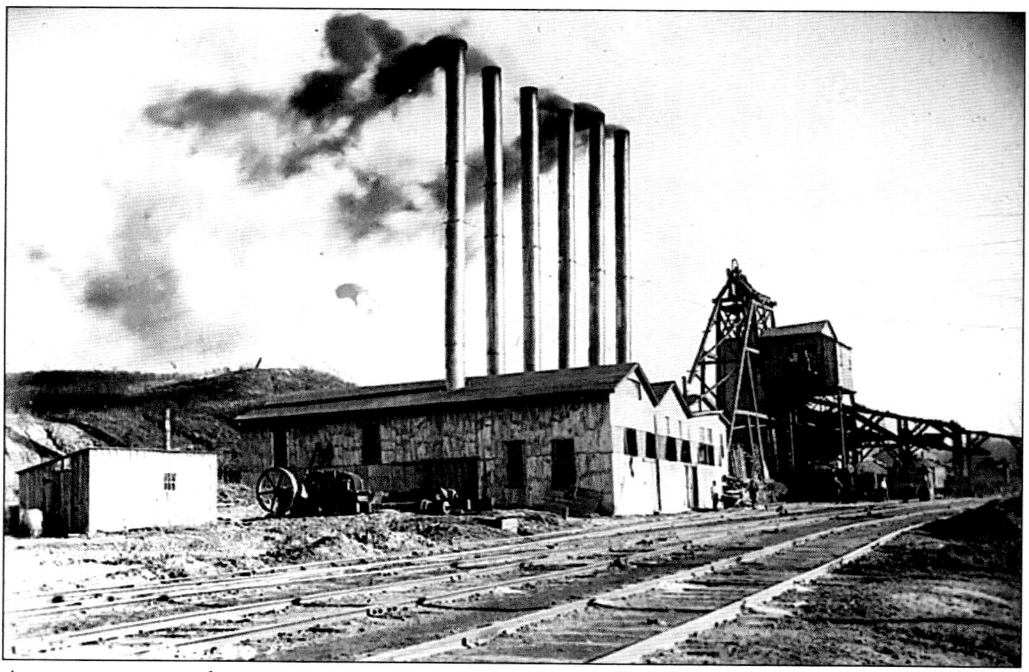

At varying times from 1860 to 1964, there were about 20 coal mines in operation in the Collinsville area. In 1921, Collinsville mines had 1,786 employees, and about 2,000 area miners resided there. This is the Lumaghi No. 2 Mine that was active from 1899 to 1951. It was on the north side of Lebanon Road just west of the railroad trestle.

One

Public Places, Public Services

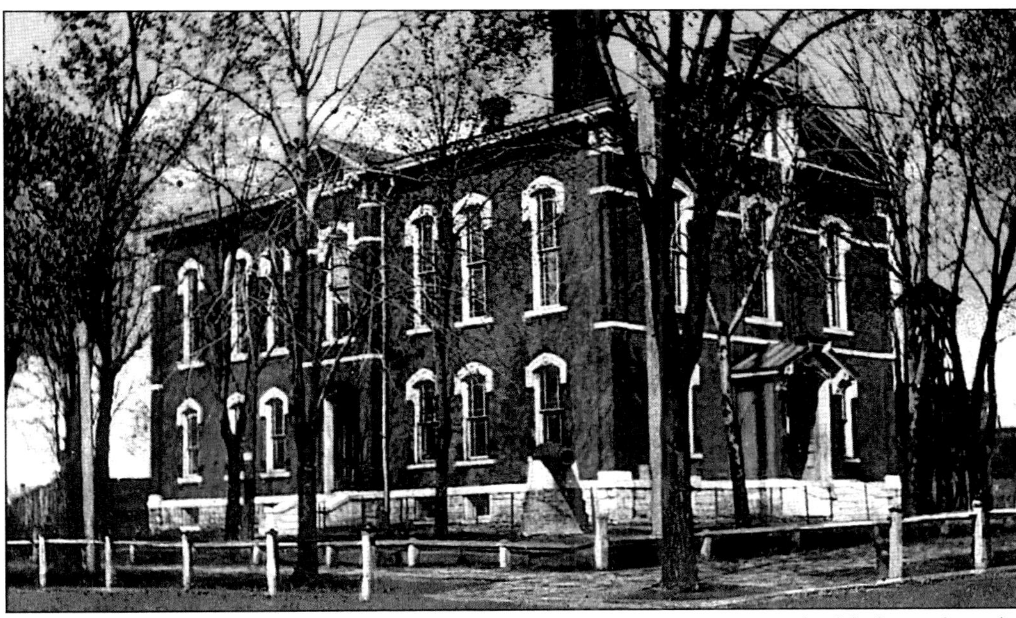

The City Hall, still in use, was built in 1885 on land that at one time had belonged to the Collins family. It features Italianate architecture with hooded window crowns, large overhanging eaves, and decorative brackets. As distinctive as this building is, it played a part in one of the ugliest events in the city's history. On April 5, 1918, Robert Prager, rumored to be a spy during World War I, was hidden in the basement of City Hall. A mob dragged him from the building, marched him through the streets, and eventually hanged him from a hackberry tree at the top of Bluff Hill.

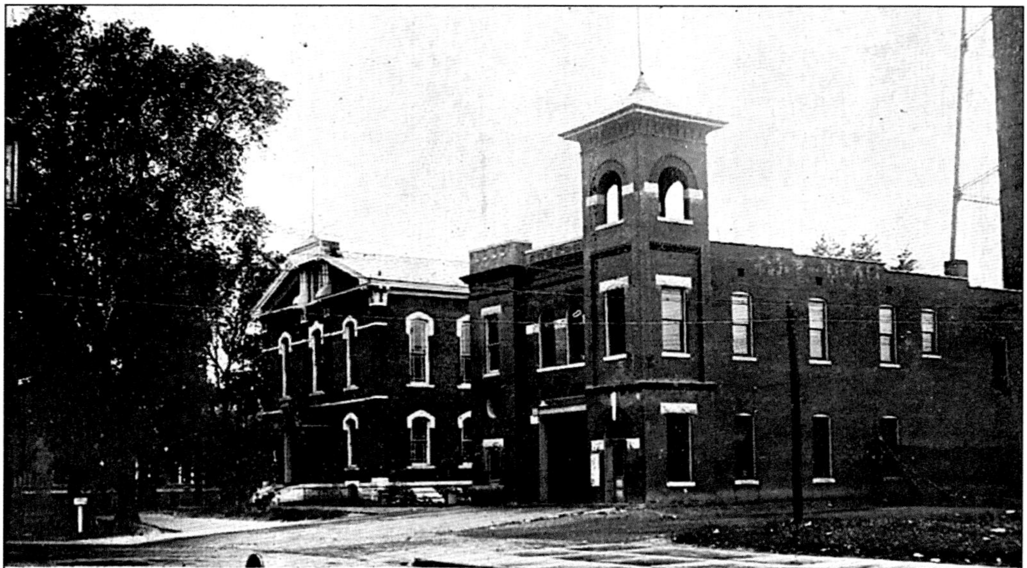

City Hall and Engine House, Collinsville, Ill.

The photo on this postcard was probably taken shortly after the 1911 completion of the fire station. The City Hall and fire station were placed on the National Register of Historic Places in 2002. The station is still in use, has been remodeled and enlarged, but is about to be replaced.

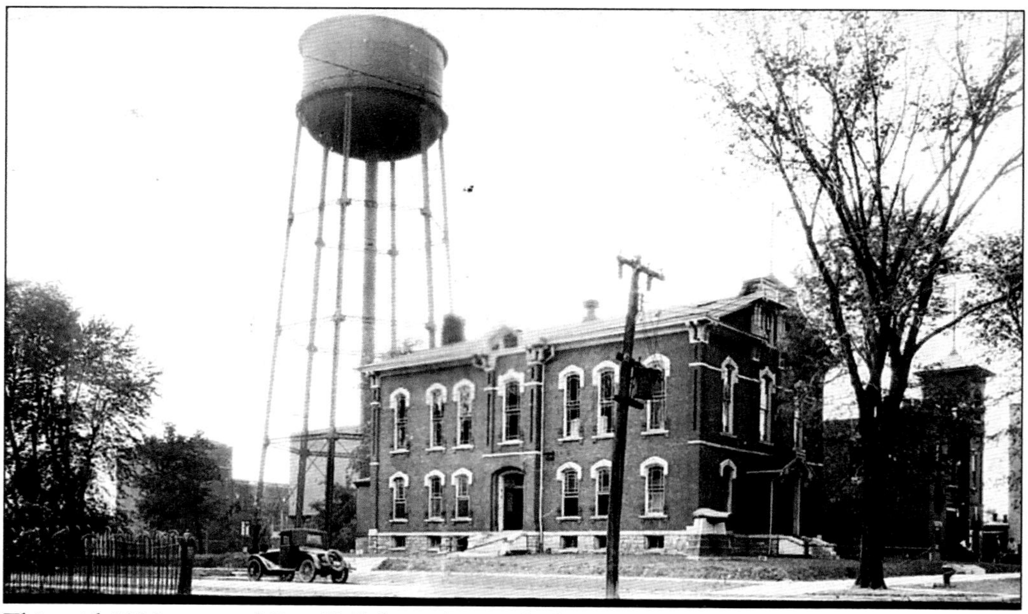

This mid-1920s view of City Hall from the south shows a water tank. Built in 1922-23 by the Chicago Bridge and Iron Works, it held 250,000 gallons of water. It was used until 1996 when a new water tower was constructed a block north and a block west of the one shown. A few years later, a second water tower was added on the north end of town. Bregstone, a respected St. Louis photographer from the early part of the century, is responsible for this image.

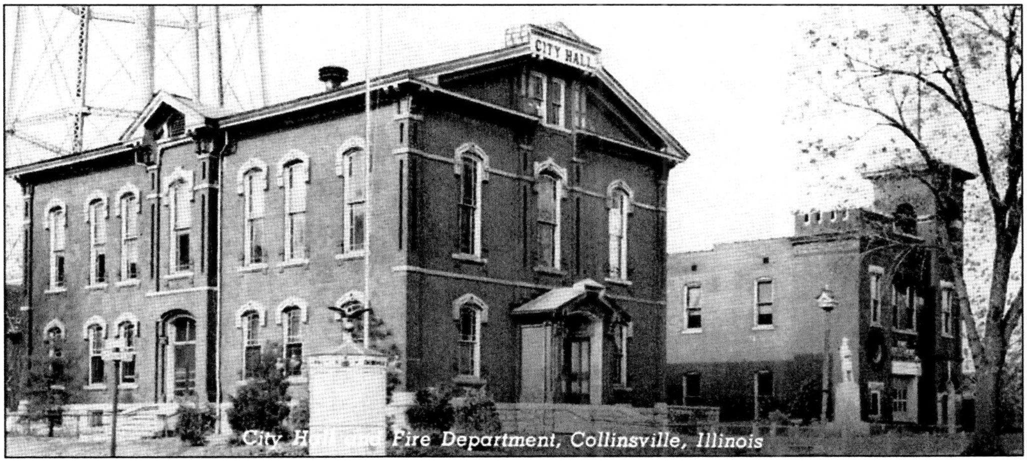

The prominent statue on the east side of the City Hall and fire station is a Grand Army of the Republic memorial to Collinsville veterans of the Civil War. The statue of granite was unveiled on June 14, 1926, at a cost of $1,325. A servicemen's honor roll from World War II was constructed on the northwest corner of Church and Center streets in mid-1946. The honor roll is no longer on display, and the Civil War statue now stands on the southeast grounds of City Hall.

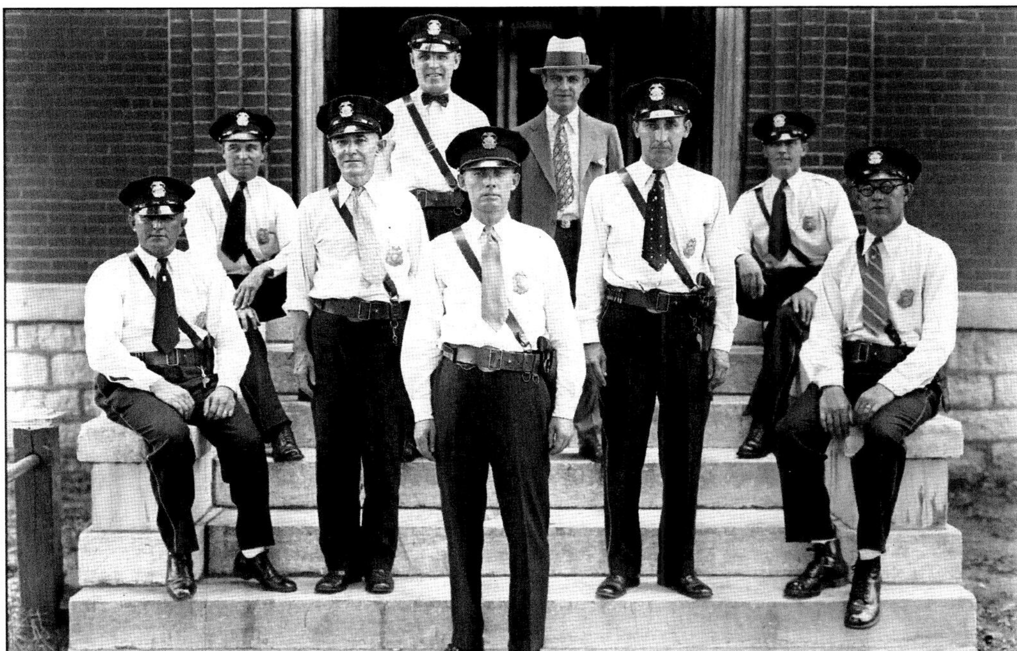

Currently, the Collinsville Police Department is comprised of 38 policemen. The new police station (as of the year 2000) is on the south side of Clay Street between Clinton and Seminary streets. The police department had been located in City Hall until 1975. At that time, it was moved to a new facility at the northeast corner of Church and Clinton. Pictured from left to right are members of the 1932 Police Department: (front) Chief Frank Zamarioni; (second row) Edgar Strong, John Heckle, John Gaizat, and Howard Grafe; (third row) Joe Lee Nichols, Ray Cox, Louis Colone, and Leo Barton.

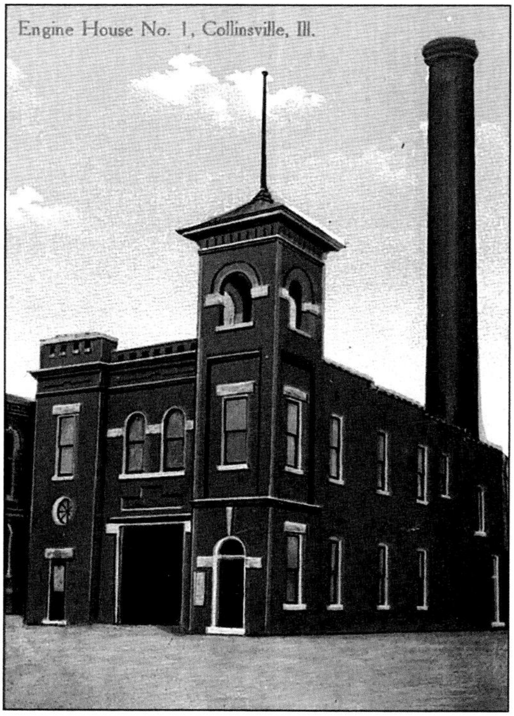

Shown is a closer view of the fire station as it appeared for many years. The bell tower housed the bell that was used to summon volunteer firemen. Engine House No. 1 is still in use and was the only fire station in town until 1966 when the northside station on Belt Line Road was constructed. There are plans to build a new station on the site of the vacant police station at Church and Clinton.

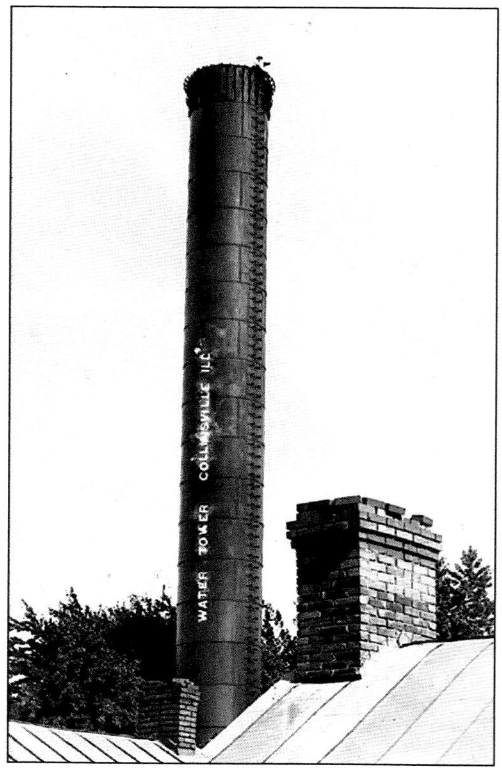

A franchise for a waterworks was ratified in 1889. The construction of the water tower pictured began in 1891. At that time, the supply of water was drawn from wells located in the vicinity of the water tower. The water in Collinsville currently comes from deep artesian wells in the American Bottom. In 1958, a new water treatment plant was constructed; after several upgrades, it is still in use.

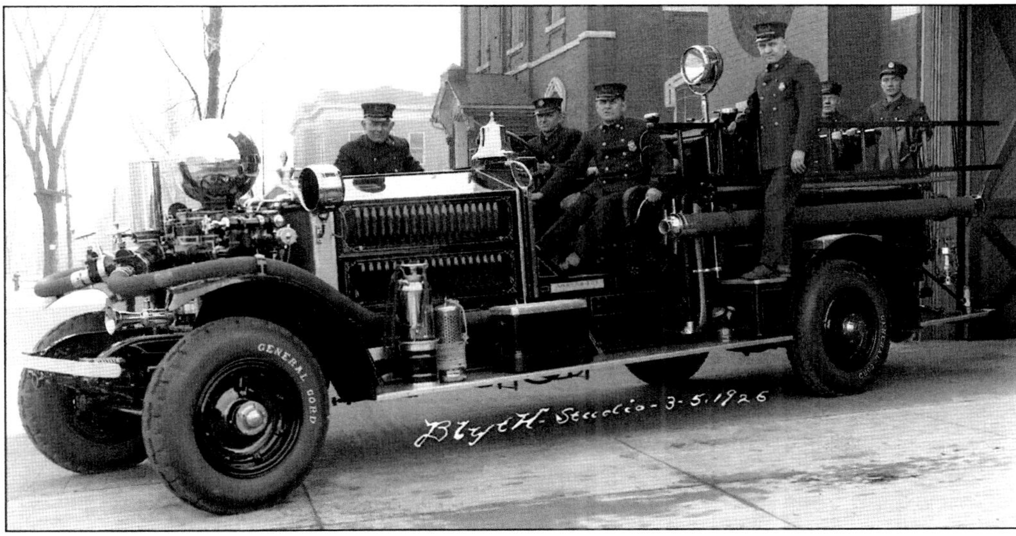

In 1925, this Ahrens Fox 4 cylinder pumper was purchased for $12,450. Fire protection for the city began in 1872 with the organization of the I.C. Moore Enterprise Fire Co. No.1. Mayor Moore donated a hand pumper and helped to organize this volunteer group. As in many towns, the volunteer firemen were civic leaders. By 1888, this unit had organized a reading room with a librarian and established a drama group. In 1880, the cost of running the fire department was $6.05.

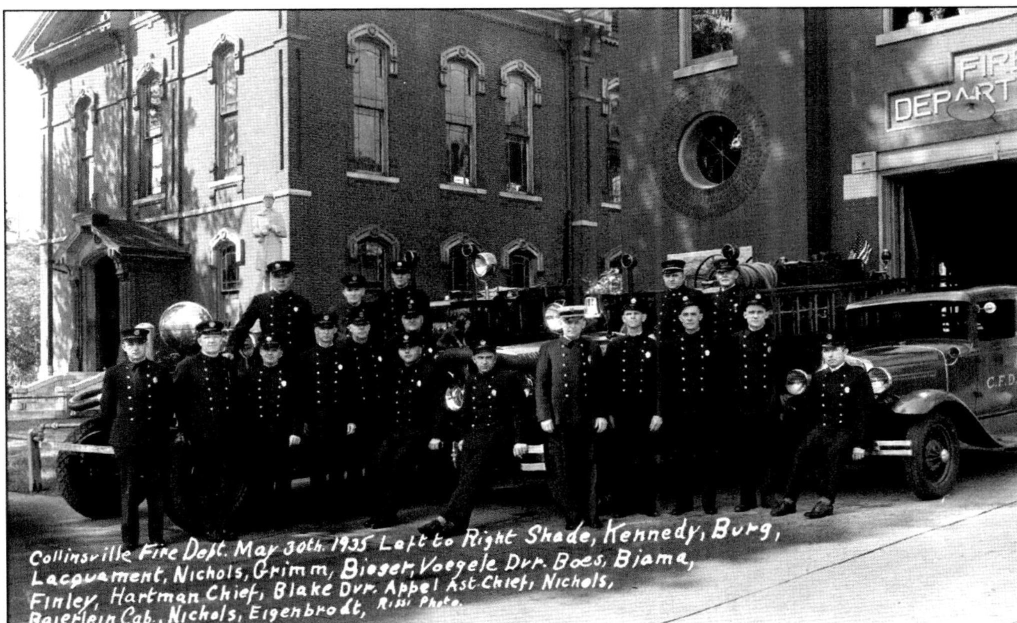

Pictured are members of the Collinsville Fire Department as they appeared in 1935. They include, from left to right: Shade, Kennedy, Burg, Lacquement, Nichols, Grimm, Bieser, Voegle (driver), Boes, Baima, Finley, Hartmann (Chief), Blake (driver), Appel (Assistant Chief), Nichols, Baierlein (Captain), Nichols, and Eigenbrodt. The vehicles are the Ahrens Fox fire truck, an Indiana fire engine, and a fire department auto.

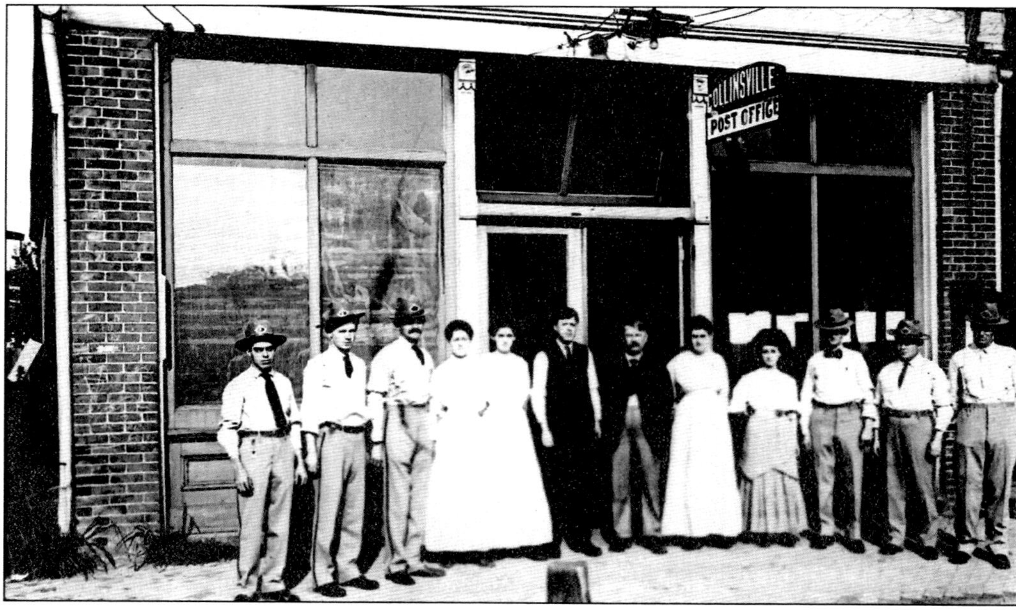

In 1905, the Collinsville Post Office rented this space at 105 South Seminary where the office section of McLanahan Automotive is now located. The post office had been housed in the City Hall. The cornerstone of the 201 West Clay Street facility was laid on May 7, 1915. The land for the post office was purchased from the adjacent Masonic Lodge. (Courtesy Bill and Lois Metzger.)

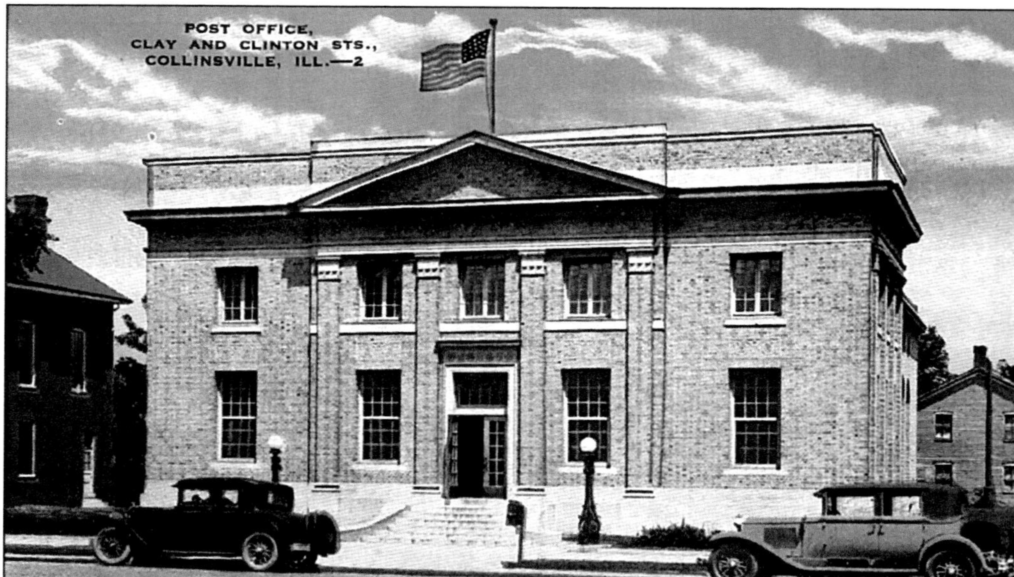

This stately yellow brick building served as Collinsville's post office from 1916 until 1964. It was built in the Jeffersonian architectural style with dentil moldings beneath the eaves and with the simulated columns called pilasters. The Collinsville Unit No. 10 School District has used this building for administrative offices since the post office moved to the northeast corner of Church and Center streets. The post office depot is now located in Eastport on the west side of town.

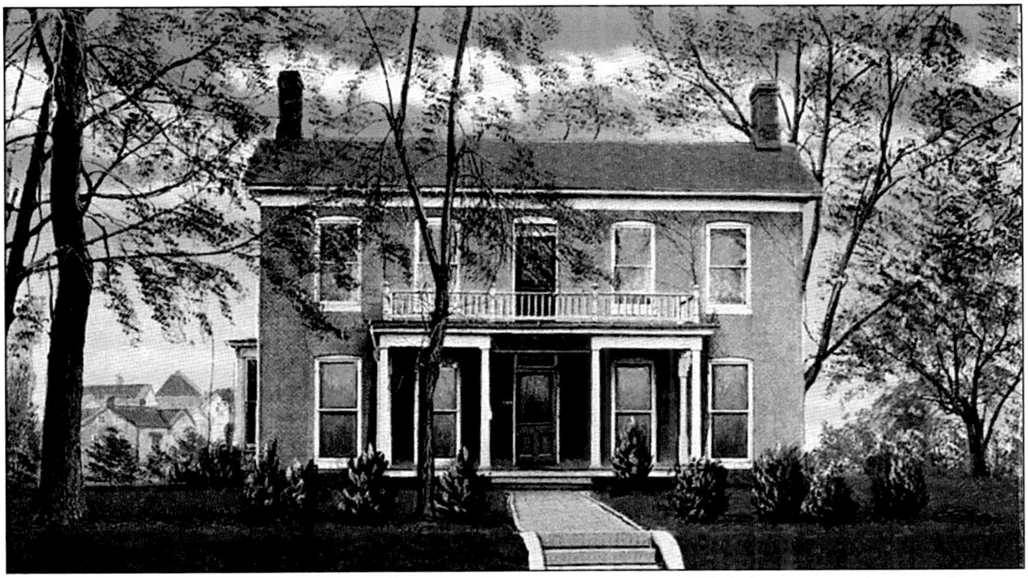

On July 13, 1923, at the request of a community group, city officials approved an ordinance providing a 1.8 mil tax for operating a library. In 1927, the Look-Renfro house at 408 West Main was purchased for $11,300 to be used as a library. The name was changed to the Collinsville Memorial Public Library in recognition of Collinsville's war dead. The contents of the library had been previously housed on the second floor of City Hall, in the Stumpf house on the northeast corner of Church and Clinton and on the second floor of Miners Institute.

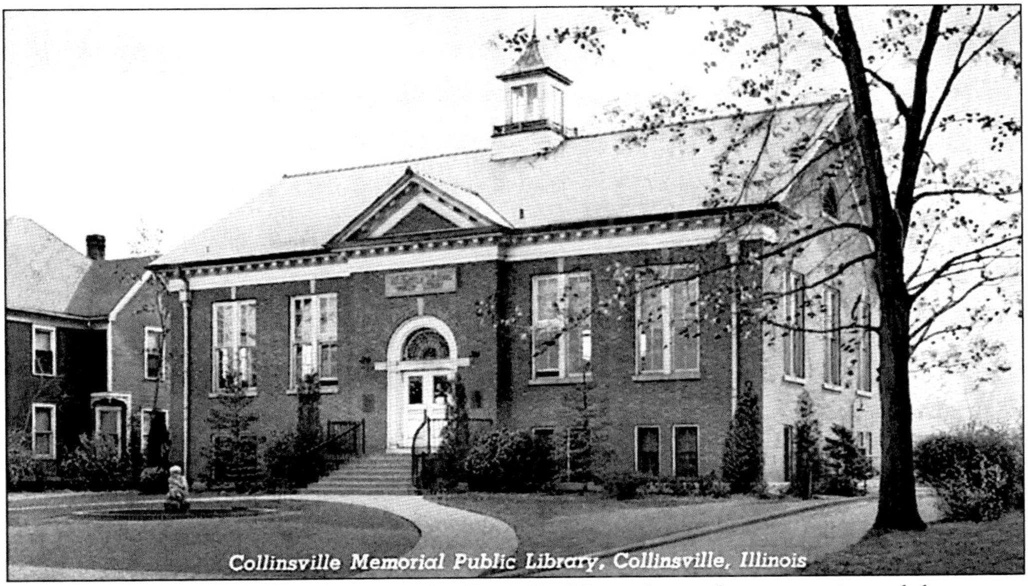

In the same area where the Look-Renfro house had been located, construction of the center portion of the current colonial style library was completed in 1937. A $9,000 Federal Public Works grant expedited the funding of this phase. An east wing was added in 1963 and a west wing in 1967. In 1980, a four-floor addition, constructed behind the center portion, provided much needed additional space and a community room.

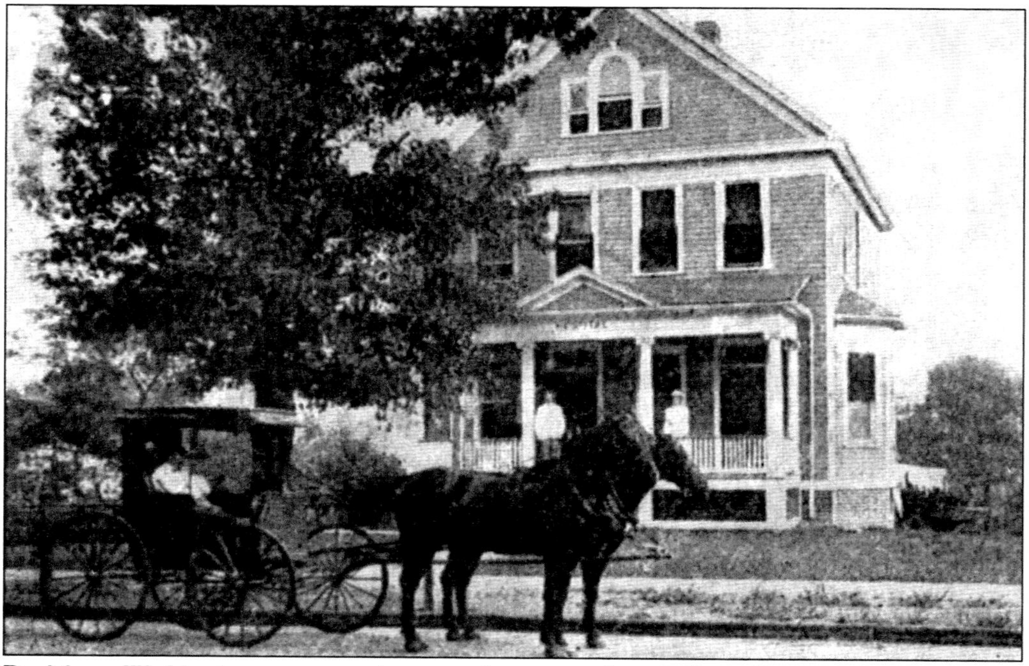

Dr. Moses W. Harrison was a native son who returned to Collinsville to practice medicine. His first office was in a second-floor location on Main Street. The above photo is from a return address on an envelope. It shows Dr. Harrison, Harrison Hospital at Church and Seminary, and his horse and buggy. The hospital was in service from 1910 until 1940, however, Dr. Harrison retained an office there until shortly before his death in 1964. This building still stands. Though it has been remodeled recently, it is currently vacant.

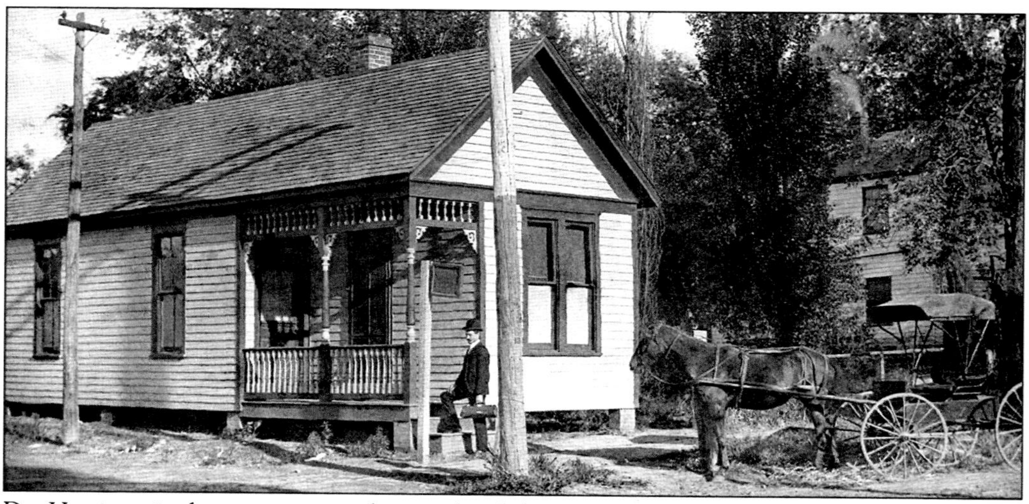

Dr. Harrison is shown entering the porch of the small house at 206 South Seminary. This structure, located directly behind Harrison Hospital, was the hospital for African-Americans. Dr. Harrison resided across the street at 215 West Church Street, the location of the present Methodist Church parking lot. He served as Mayor of Collinsville from 1931-43, during the difficult times of the Great Depression.

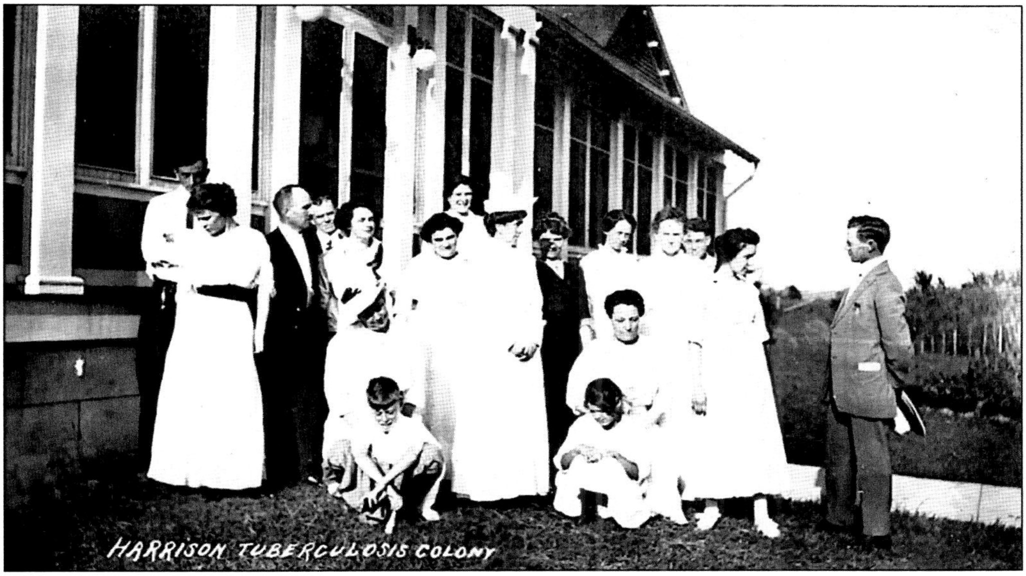

In 1912, Dr. Harrison established a tent city for the treatment of tuberculosis. It was on a 15-acre tract at the end of what is now Western Avenue. A permanent structure was added to provide offices and a lounge for patients.

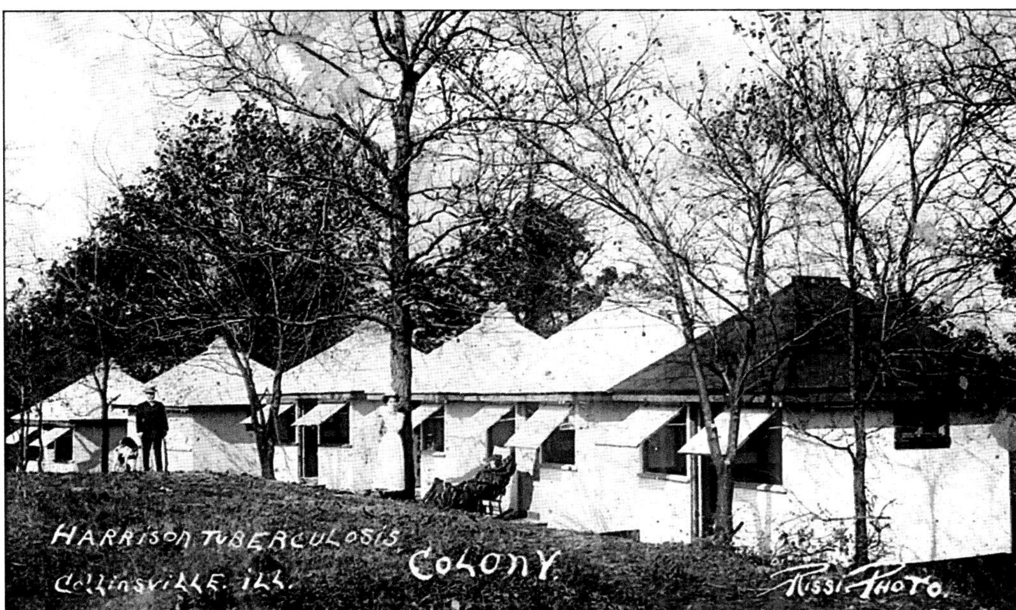

Dr. Harrison was a member of the Episcopal Church and the Modern Woodmen. He was an avowed Republican and avid outdoorsman. He and Professor Albert Arendt, CTHS Principal for many years, developed a purple medicine that was swabbed on sores and burns. During World War I, Dr. Harrison, always the humanitarian, offered his services to the Medical Officers Reserve Corps.

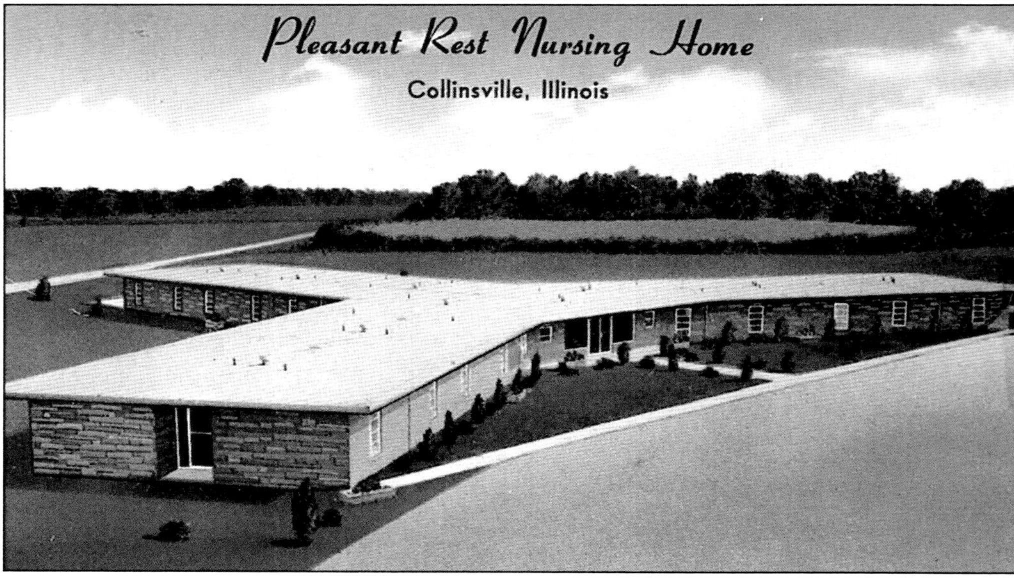

Collinsville Care Center of 615 North Summit was originally named Pleasant Rest Nursing Home. It opened on August 19, 1962. Eunice Keel was the owner and administrator. Later owners were Bill Panell, Dr. Twerski, and Margaret Myler, who was administrator from 1969 to 1982. Additions in 1969 and 1972 increased the number of beds from 68 to 122. Before the nursing home was constructed, this property was occupied by Quonset huts as temporary government housing.

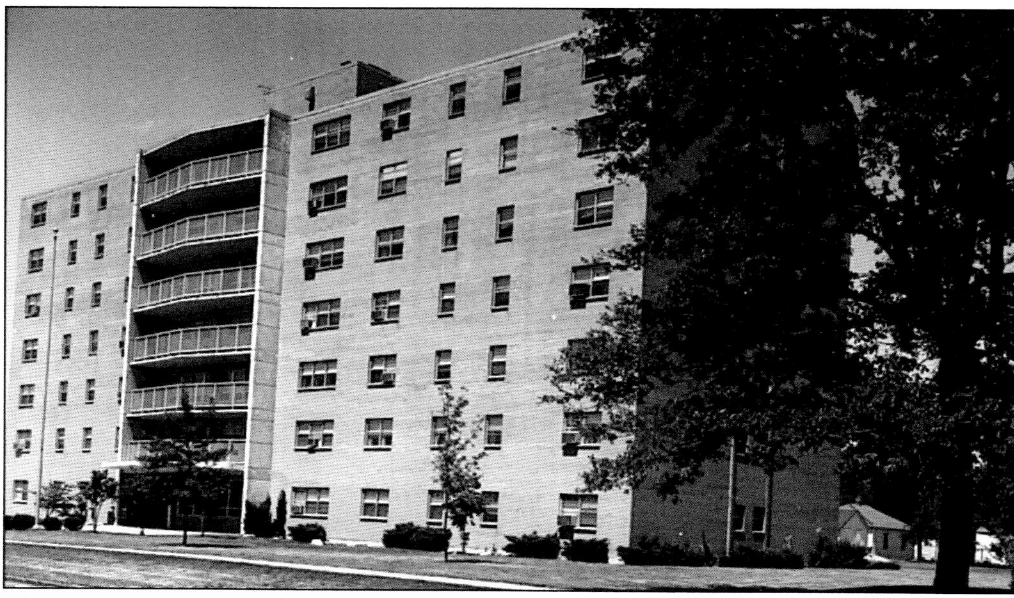

The Braner Home, a seven-story government housing complex stands on East Main and South Aurora and was opened in 1963 under the administration of the Madison County Housing Authority. The structure was named for local resident Dute Braner, a director of MCHA. This was previously the site of Fred Jobusch's Collinsville Lumber Co. with the Wing house located on the Church Street side.

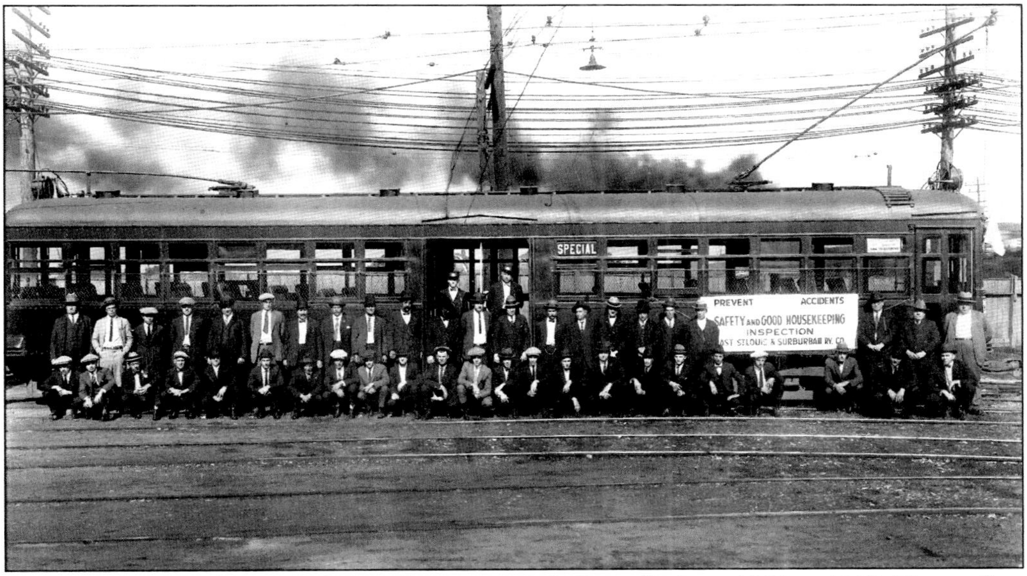

This is a photo of the type of train that serviced Collinsville from 1900 to 1930. The trolley, streetcar, yellow hammer or interurban, by whatever name, was widely used in its heyday. In 1905, the East St. Louis and Suburban Railway Co. opened an office at 308 East Clay and permission was granted to lay rails in the middle of the street or wherever needed. Earlier lines were managed by the Mississippi Valley Electric Railway Company.

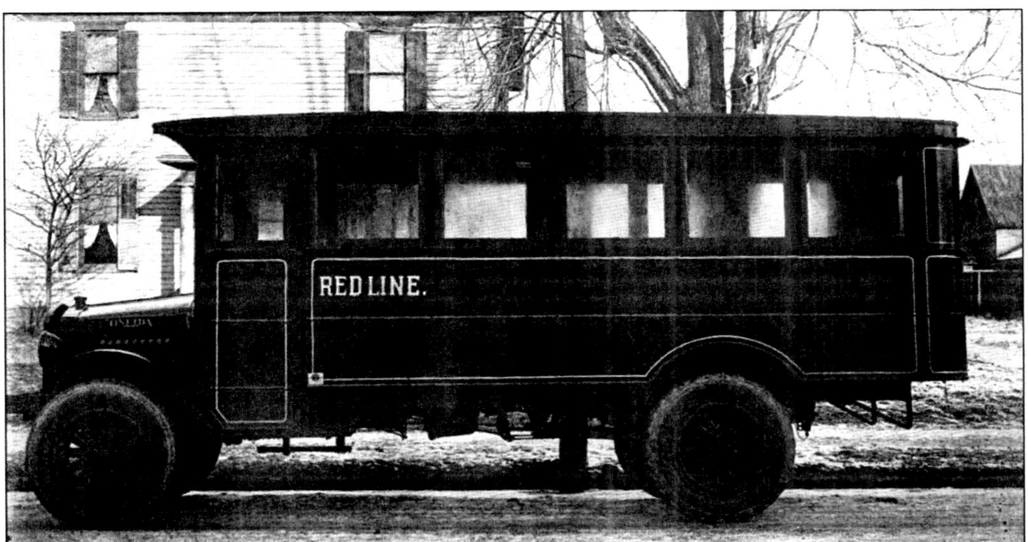

The Vandalia Bus Line (an earlier bus is pictured) was an integral part of local transportation from 1925 to 1960. In the 1950s, the orange buses with black and white trim ran a regular route from Collinsville to East St. Louis and on to St. Louis and back. Some routes went as far east as Vandalia, Ill. The buses were used for going to work and school and to shop. The local bus station was at Schmacker Confectionary at the southwest corner of Main and Seminary, and the bus garage was on the east side of the 100 block of St. Louis Road. The bus could stop for passengers at nearly every corner along St. Louis Road, Main and Vandalia streets.

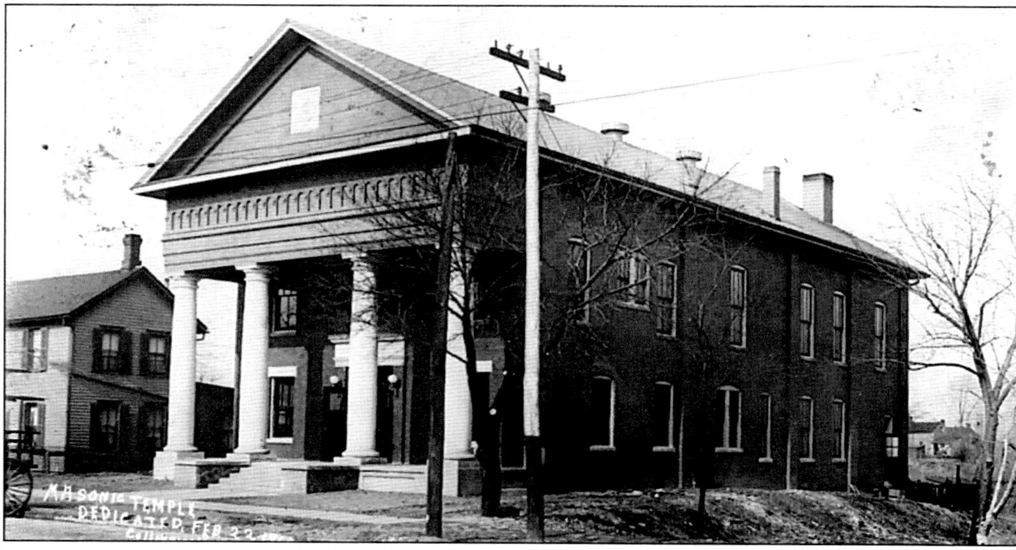

The Masonic Temple at 213 West Clay Street was built in 1912 at a cost of $15,000. The bricks in the structure were made in Collinsville by the Illinois Hydraulic Press Co. The unique facade is Greek Revival. Among the early events held in this edifice were the funerals of prominent citizens Dr. J. Morgan Sims and Leighton Evatt, the first local veteran to die in World War I. The local chapter of the American Legion is named after Leighton Evatt.

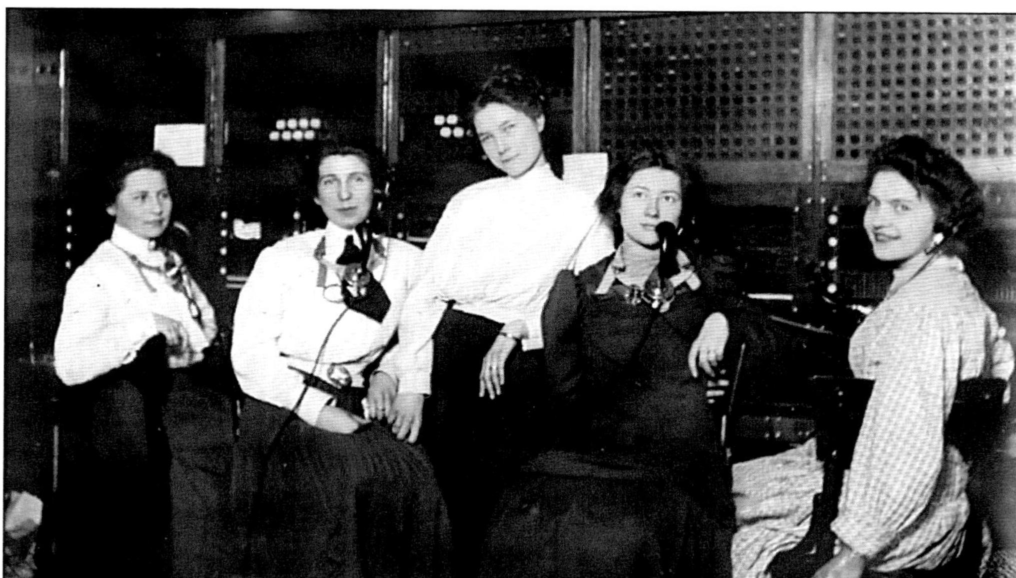

The Central Union Telephone Co. appears to have provided the original phone service in Collinsville followed in 1900 by the Kinloch Telephone Company. Both companies had their offices and switchboards on the second floor of the original State Bank building at the northeast corner of Main and Center. On March 20, 1933, a first floor furniture store fire gutted the building. No equipment was saved but within nine days of the fire, service was again available for the 1,300 subscribers. The above picture is the Kinloch Phone Co., c. 1907.

Two

Churches and Schools

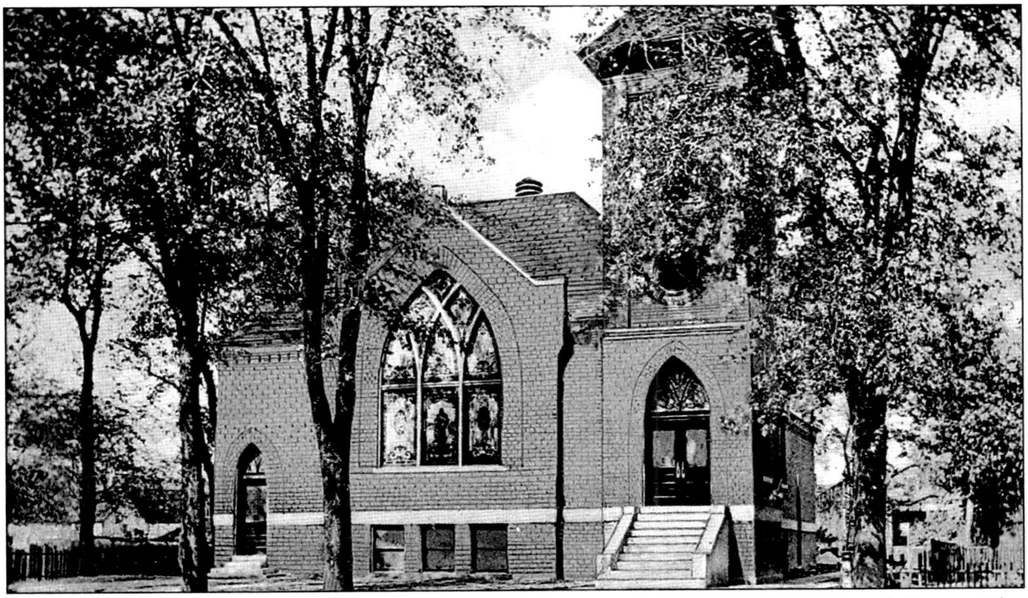

For many years, the Methodist Church has been at the same location on West Church Street. The first church building was moved there from Pleasant Ridge. The cornerstone of the present church was laid in 1907. Henry Eberhardt was the general contractor, and the bricks were made locally by Illinois Hydraulic Press Brick Co. Members of the First United Methodist Church recently assembled an informative booklet of church history as part of its 160th-year observance.

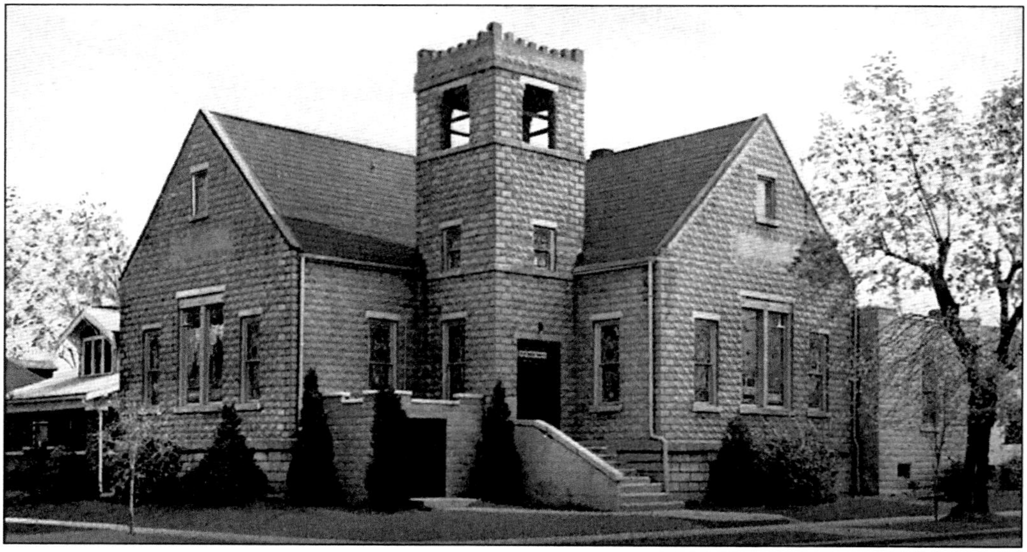

Constructed from 1908 to 1912, this building on the southeast corner of West Clay and Hesperia was the First Baptist Church for many years. Reverend Colbert, with some assistance from his two sons, was largely responsible for assembling the church of decorative concrete blocks. An expanding congregation made it necessary to move to a new facility. The vacated church changed owners a few times before the Jaycees purchased it. The structure was recently destroyed by fire and subsequently razed in 2004.

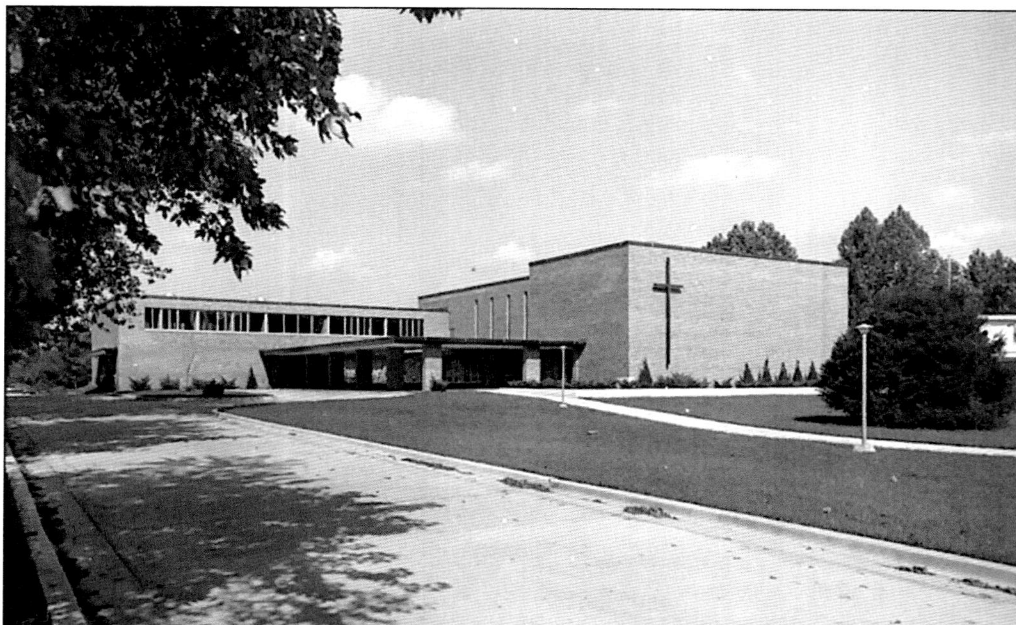

The current First Baptist Church is located at 723 St. Louis Road. The cornerstone of the edifice was laid in 1957. The spacious facility houses a pre-school and accommodations for social activities as the result of recent building expansions. At one time, the West End Market that became Gaskill's Market and Ed Morlence's Esquire Cleaners were located on this property.

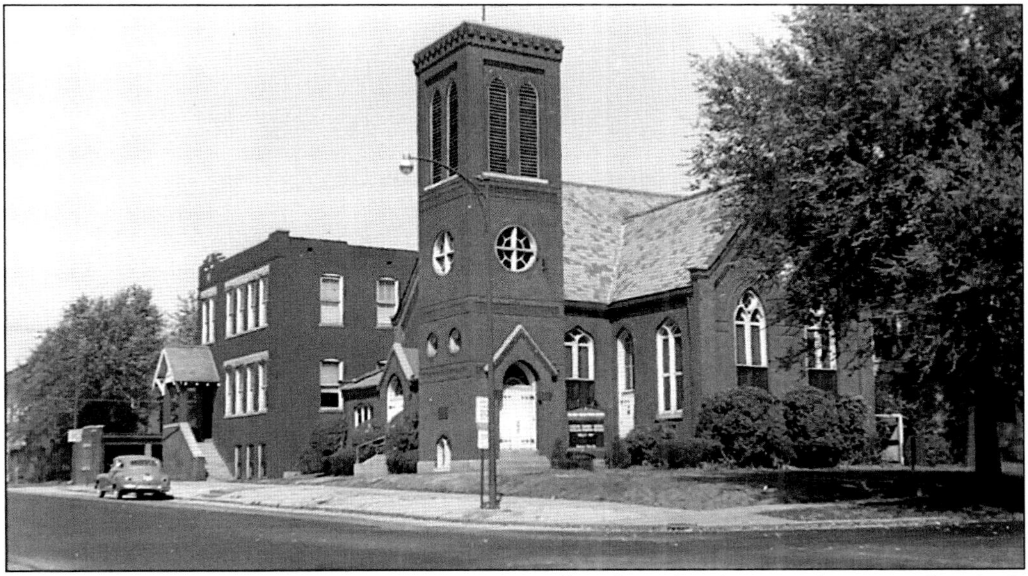

A small building was erected in 1843 as Collinsville's first church, a Presbyterian church. It was one of the first churches in the state and the oldest in Madison County. This structure was destroyed by a storm in 1879. Some of Collinsville's patriarchs belonged to this church: members of the Collins family, O.C. Look, J.W. Peers, Dr. J.L. Wadsworth, and J.H. Wickliffe. Located at 201 East Church Street, the brick church was built in 1884. The second building on the left in the photo is Baraca Hall, which was added in 1913-14.

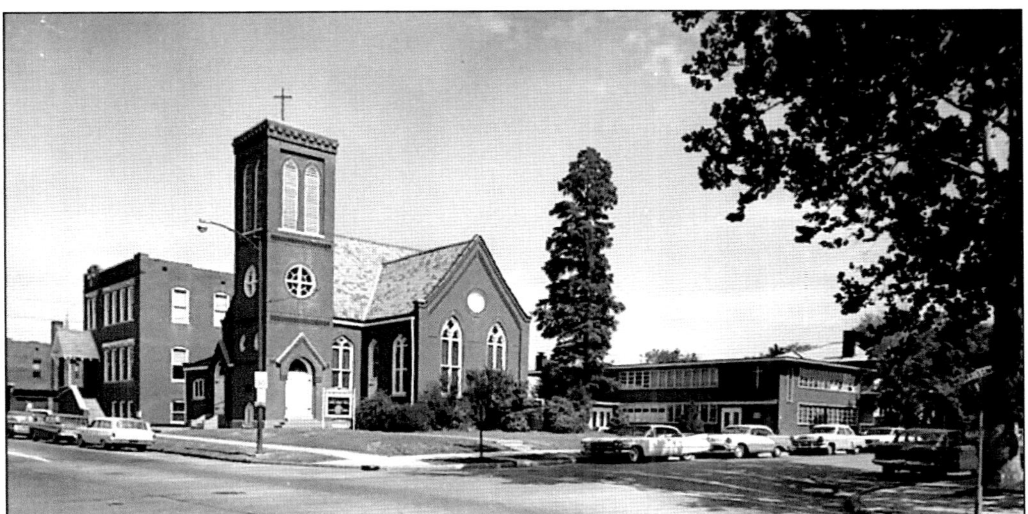

Baraca Hall, also shown on the left of this postcard, was dedicated to young people's activities. The hall contained a gym and reading room. Baraca means happy or blessed, and the group that helped raise funds for building the hall adopted "We do things" as the class motto. Sunday school, recitals, and plays were presented here. Young women were permitted to use the hall one night per week in the early years. Baraca Hall was removed when the new church was constructed in 1976. This postcard shows the 1959 addition, Westminster Hall and the education wing.

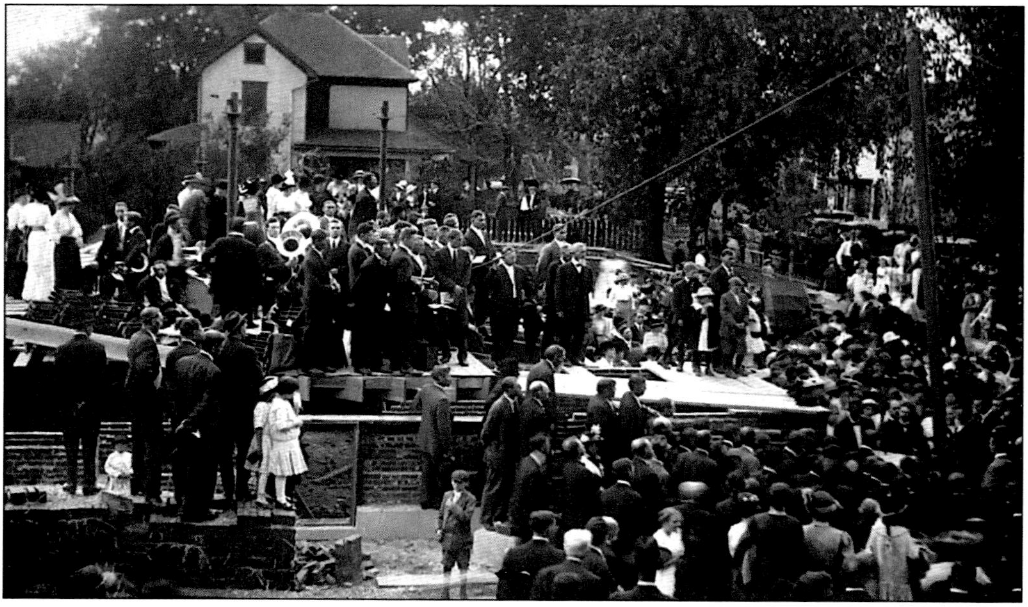

This postcard captures the early stages of the construction of Holy Cross Lutheran Church at 304 South Street. The people appear to be at a church service or perhaps a dedication of the new building. It was dedicated June 13, 1915. Church member John Schroeppel donated half of the bricks that were used in the building.

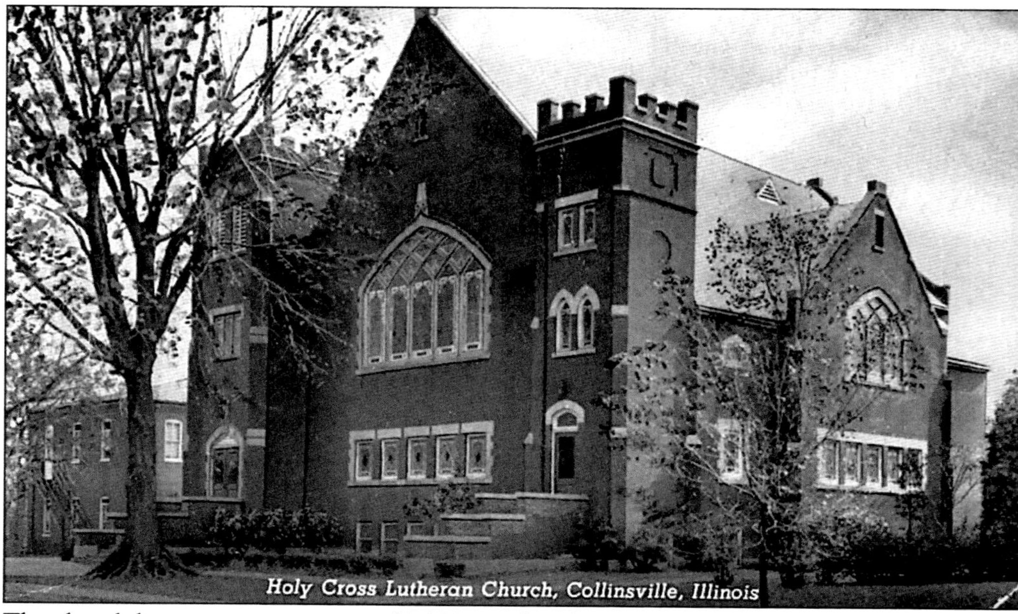

The church has a seating capacity of 1,000 people. The pipe organ was installed by Wicks Pipe Organ of Highland, Ill. Before World War I, services were held in German, but the church school was taught in English. German services were gradually phased out and discontinued by 1950. In 1958, Good Shepherd Lutheran Church was organized and purchased land on Belt Line Road (Route 40) for the construction of a church and school.

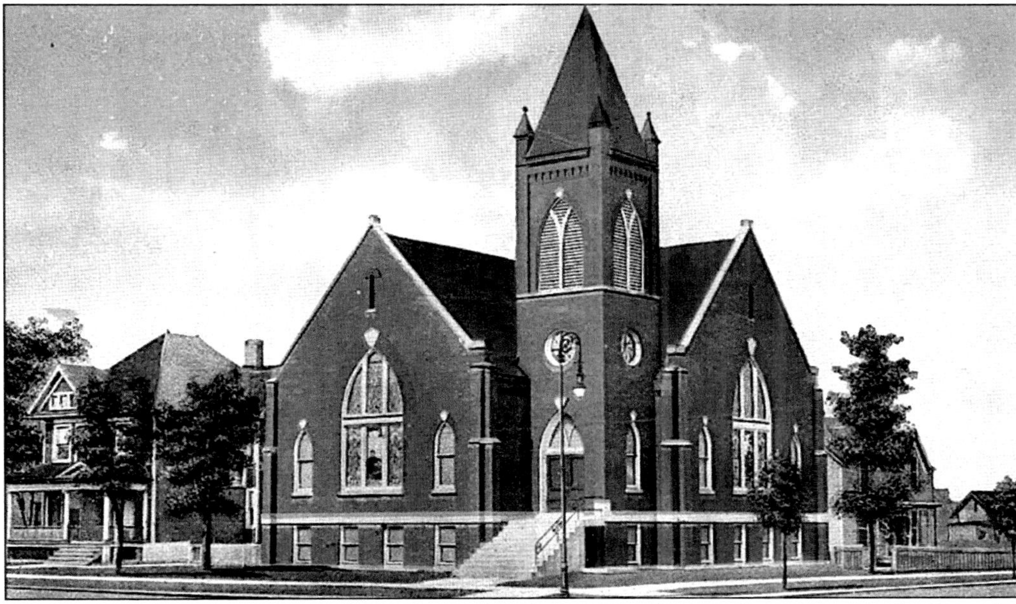

The original German Evangelical St. John's Church was a small white frame structure built on this site in 1895 and later sold and moved across the street for another purpose. The pictured church at 307 West Clay Street was constructed in 1908 at a cost of $12,000. German speaking people were among the organizers and some services were conducted in German until the early 1930s. In 1928-29, the church was remodeled and St. John Hall was added. It seated 800 people, contained a stage, and was the center of many family activities and church presentations.

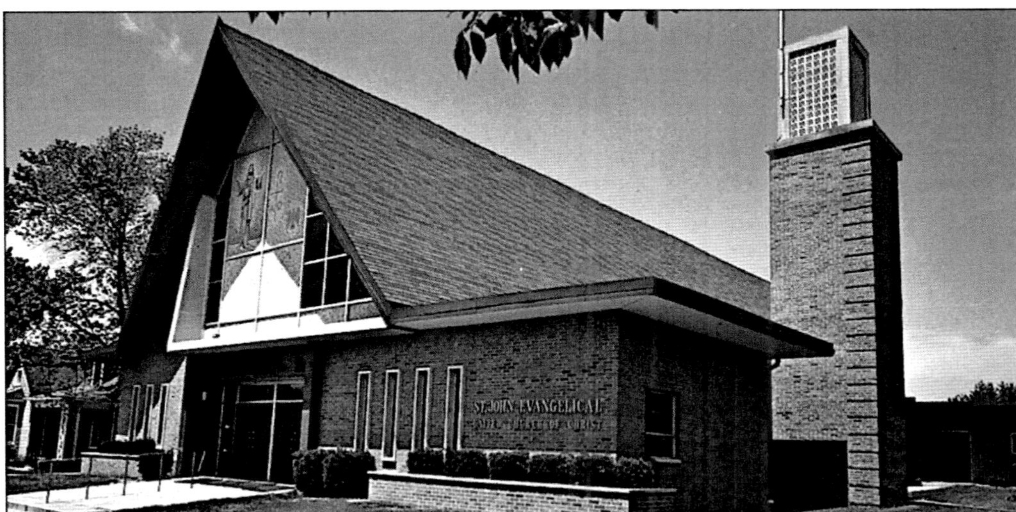

The current St. John's Evangelical United Church of Christ was constructed in 1963 on the site where the parsonage stood. The education wing stands on the site of the previous church. Recent additions include the Centennial Addition that connects the education building to the church. It also provides a reception area and offices. A Home and Community Building is located on the back of the property at 222 Goethe Street and Faith Hall is currently under construction. It will be a family intergenerational center including a gym and stage.

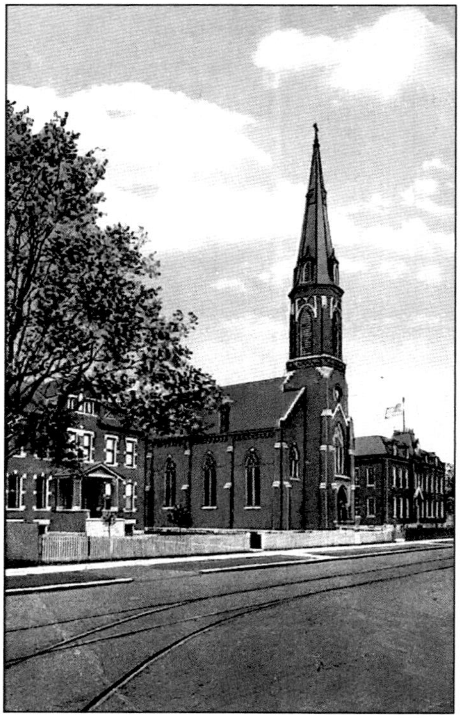

S.S. Peter and Paul parish had its beginning when Collinsville was still a village. A small group of parishioners headed by Dr. Octavius Lumaghi began plans for a church on the current site. In 1856, a small frame building was constructed. In 1860, D.D. Collins built a home next to the church. Some years later, it became the church rectory. In 1880, the Gothic style church shown was completed.

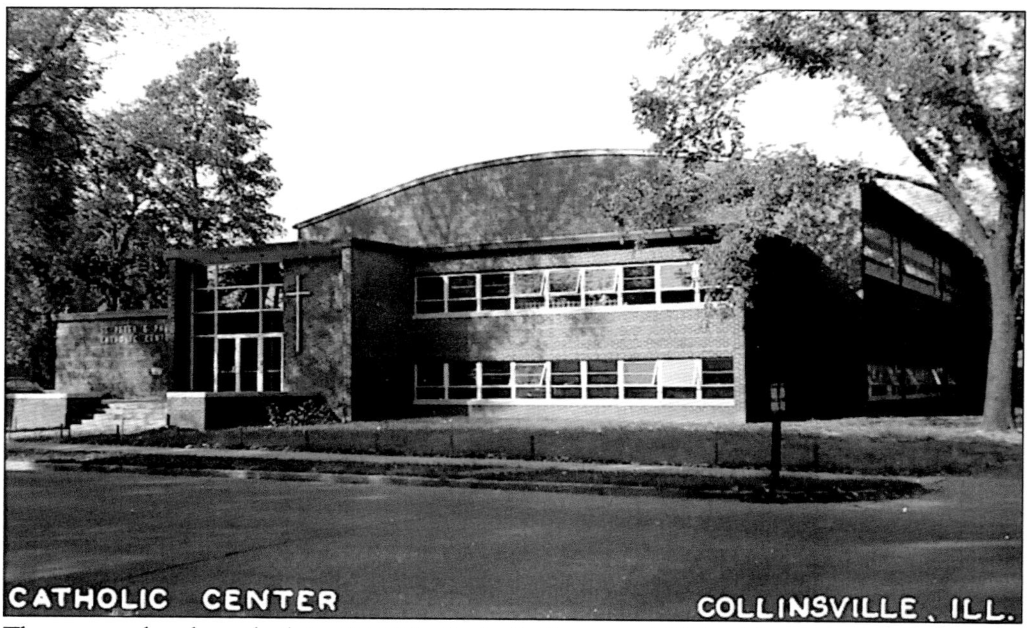

The present church was built in 1966. The Catholic Center at 303 Vandalia was completed in 1953 and contains both a gymnasium and a cafeteria. The new hall of the Knights of Columbus, just off Bluff Road at 1 Columbus Place, is the home of fried fish, bingo games, and other activities.

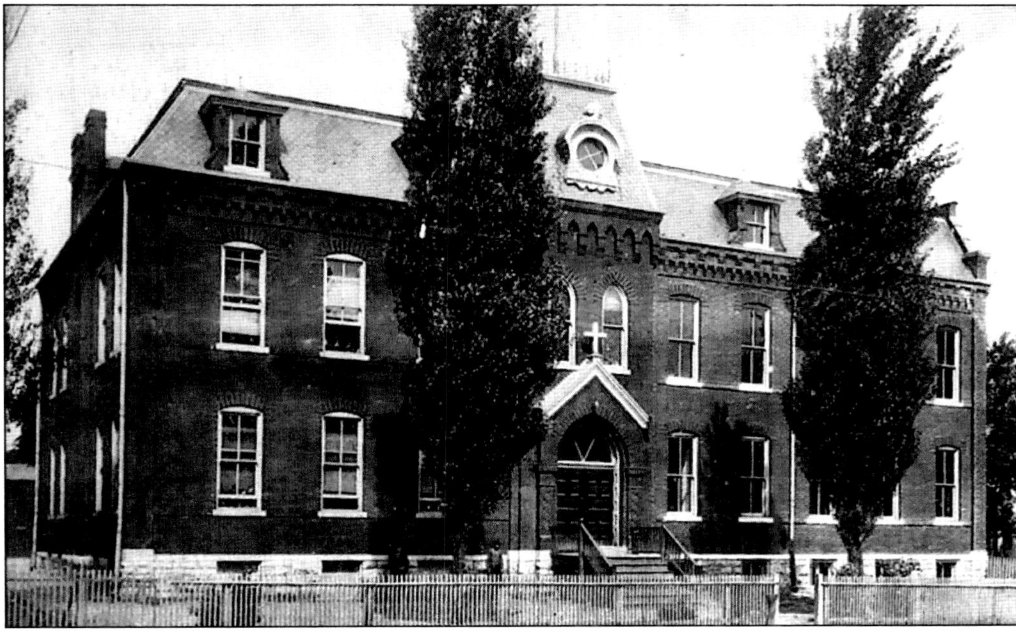

The S.S. Peter and Paul Catholic School was built in 1895. It was on the southeast corner of Vandalia and Johnson streets next to the church. Originally, the Ursuline Nuns of the Daughters of St. Angela Merici taught at the school.

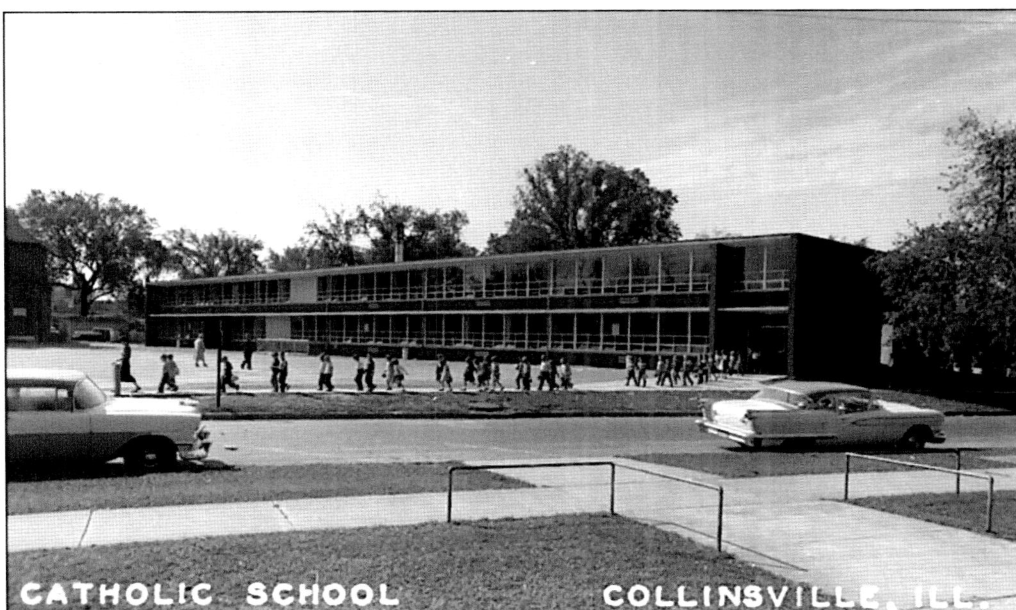

The current Catholic School, located behind the church, was built in 1960 at 210 North Morrison and contains 18 rooms. A one-block section of Johnson Street is closed during the school day so that students can move safely to the cafeteria in the center. Manning Hall, the school library, is at 239 North Morrison; Morris Hall, a hospitality and youth center, is at 300 North Morrison.

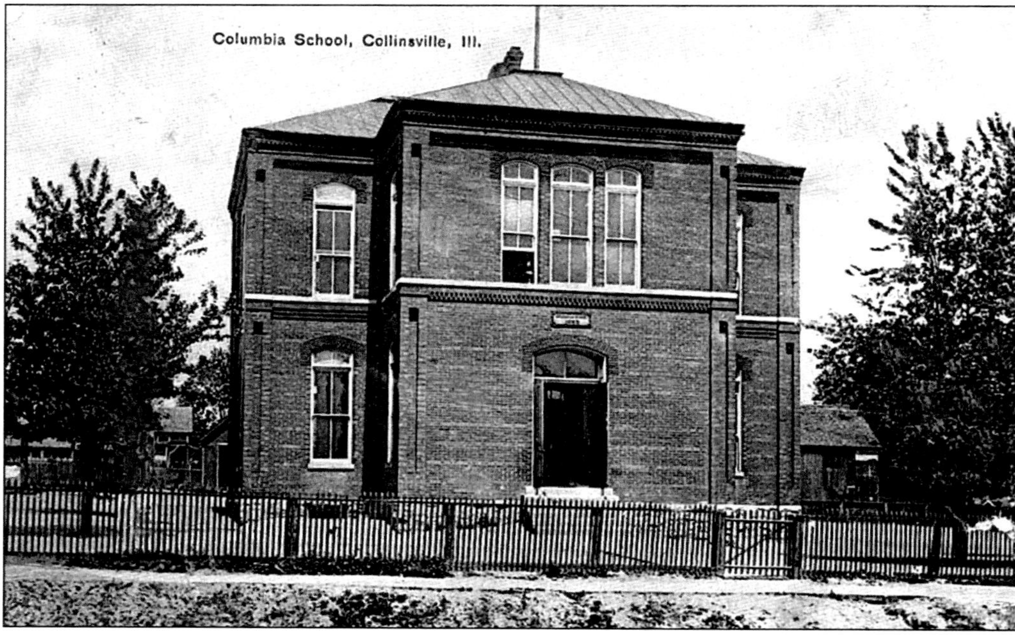

Contrary to the title on these postcards the correct name of the school was Columbian. The four-room school at 803 West Main Street was built in the mid-1890s by Milan Cochran at a cost of $5,075. Part of the early curriculum was a boys' drum and bugle corps.

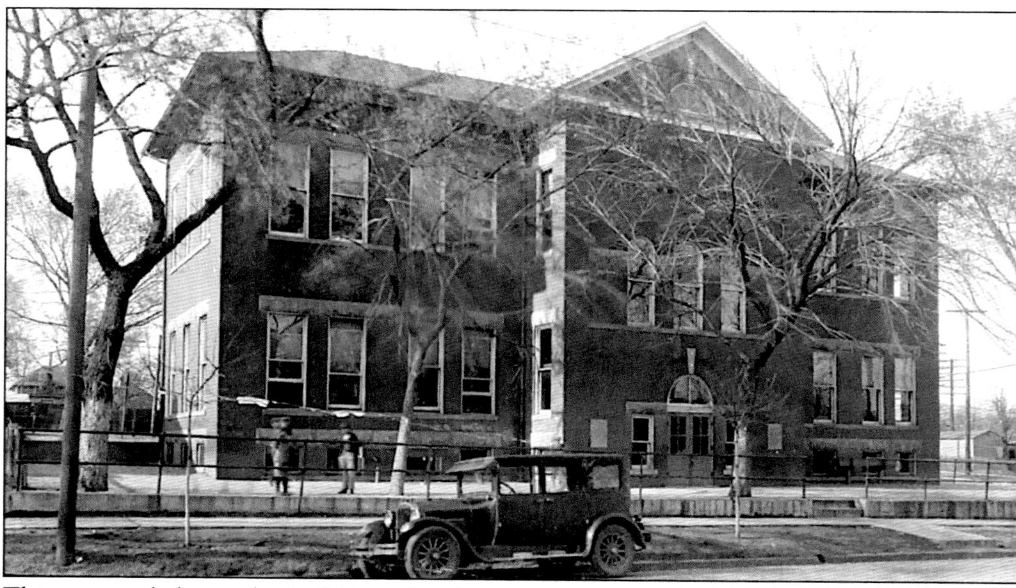

This postcard shows the building after four rooms were added in 1910. Henry Eberhardt, the contractor, was paid $9,300 for the work, excluding heating and plumbing. Its limited facilities, small playground and closeness to traffic hindered the use of this site as a school. Columbian was closed by the district in the mid-1960s and sold for $65,000 in 1974. It is currently an office building.

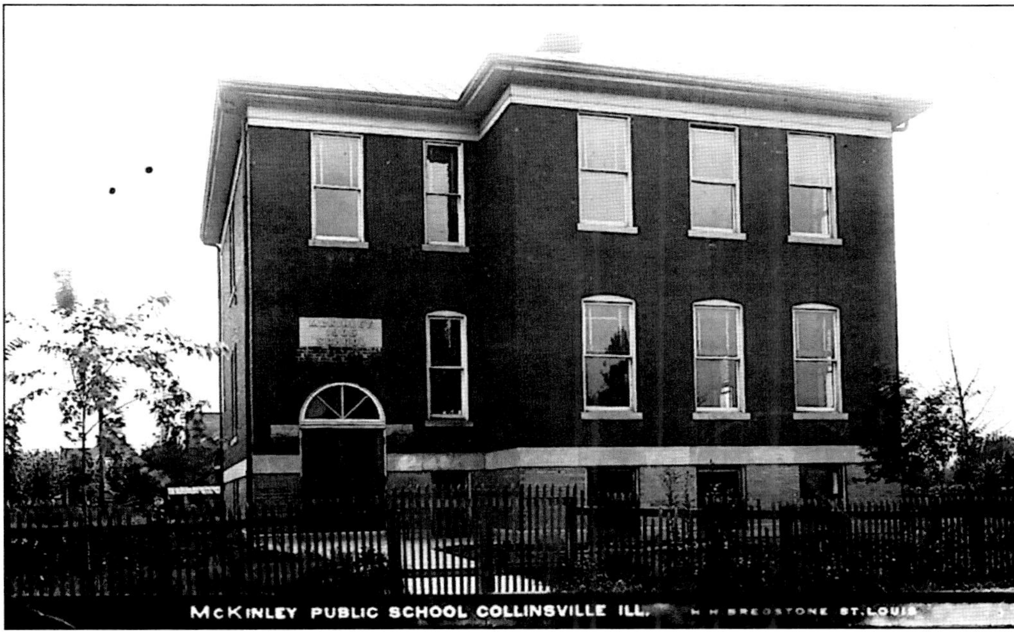

McKinley School's doors were opened in 1905. The four-room school was located on the southeast corner of Wadsworth and Constance, one block off Vandalia Street. Contractor Henry Eberhardt was paid $8,170, excluding heating and plumbing, to build the structure. The school was closed in the mid-1970s, but stands today as an apartment building.

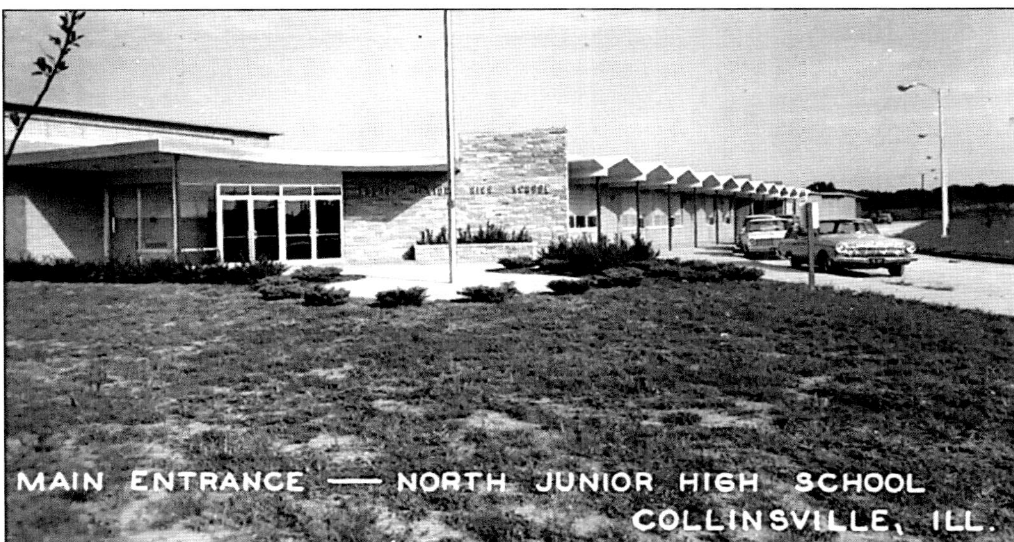

North Jr. High School opened in 1962 for grades 7, 8 and 9. However, after 1970, it was attended predominantly by 7th and 8th graders. In a peak year in the 1960s, it held 1200 students. After an eight-room addition in 2003, the remainder of the building was extensively renovated in the summer of 2004. It now houses all of the district's 5th and 6th grade students and is renamed the Collinsville Intermediate School. All of the 7th and 8th grade students now attend a new facility on the west side of town, the Collinsville Middle School.

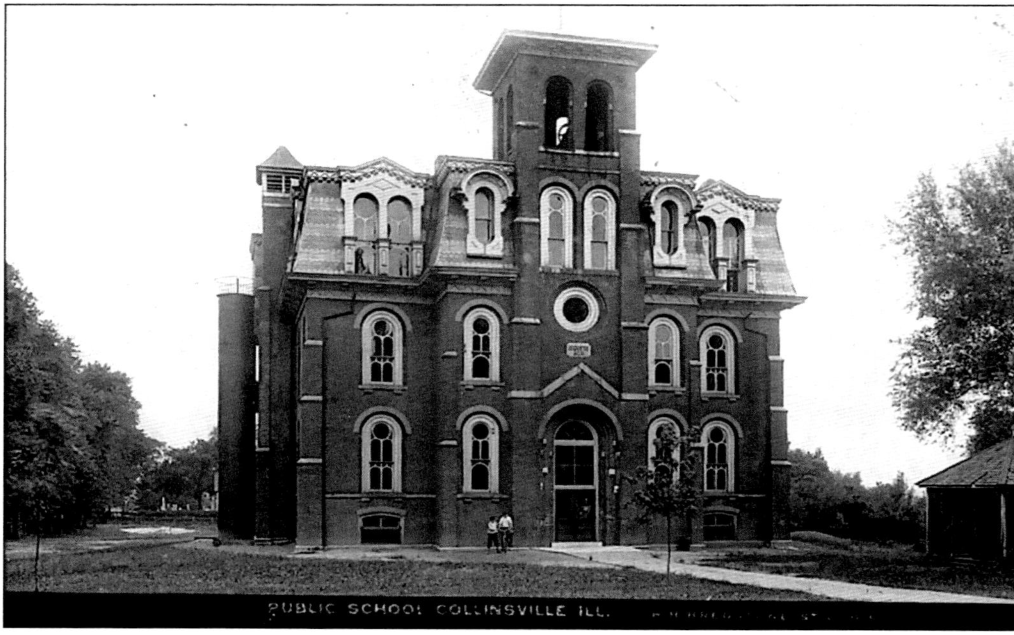

The original Webster School was destroyed by fire in 1872 and replaced a year later for $25,000. This structure was severely damaged by a tornado in 1879 and was repaired to look as it does in this picture. It stood 100 feet south of Church Street midway between Center and Clinton streets.

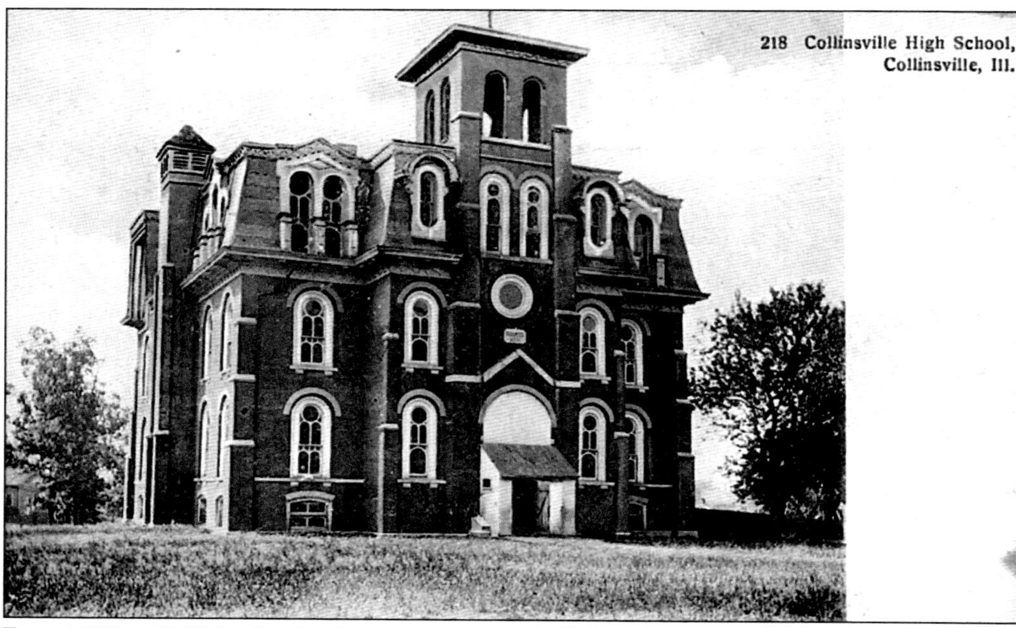

From 1882 to 1908, high school students attended Webster School as there was no high school building or district for them. The high school classes were on the third floor. Graduation was held in Temperance Hall which was located on South Center Street directly across the street from the current City Hall entrance.

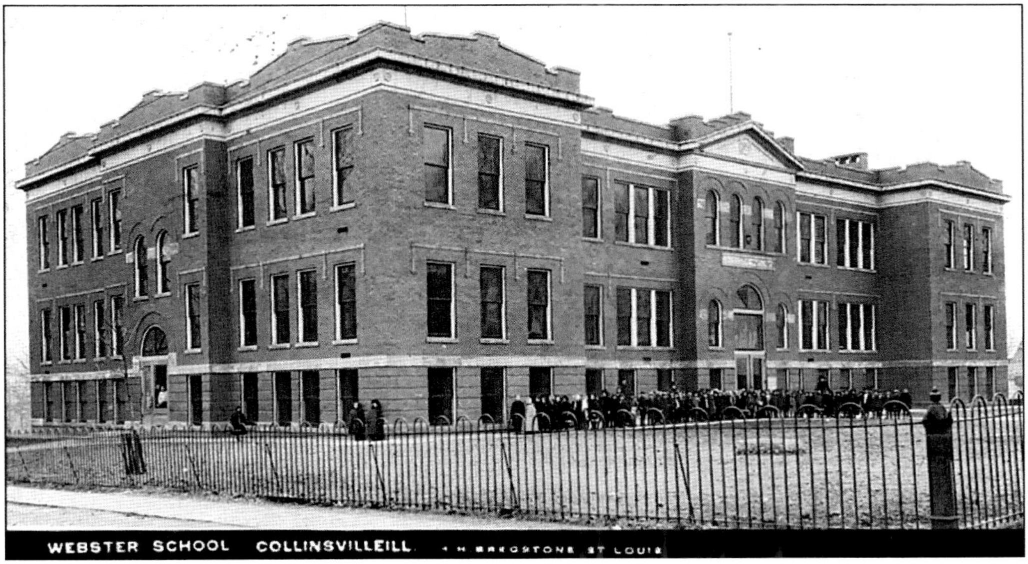

In 1914, this building at 108 West Church Street was constructed by Henry Eberhardt for $37,447. J. Wm. Kennedy was the architect and Peter Johnson was the heating and plumbing contractor. The building was placed directly in front of the older Webster School. A third level bridge or walkway connected a fire escape between the two buildings. The school contained a small gym with a rather low ceiling. The building was razed in 2002. A new K-4 wing adjoining the 1953 structure has recently been completed.

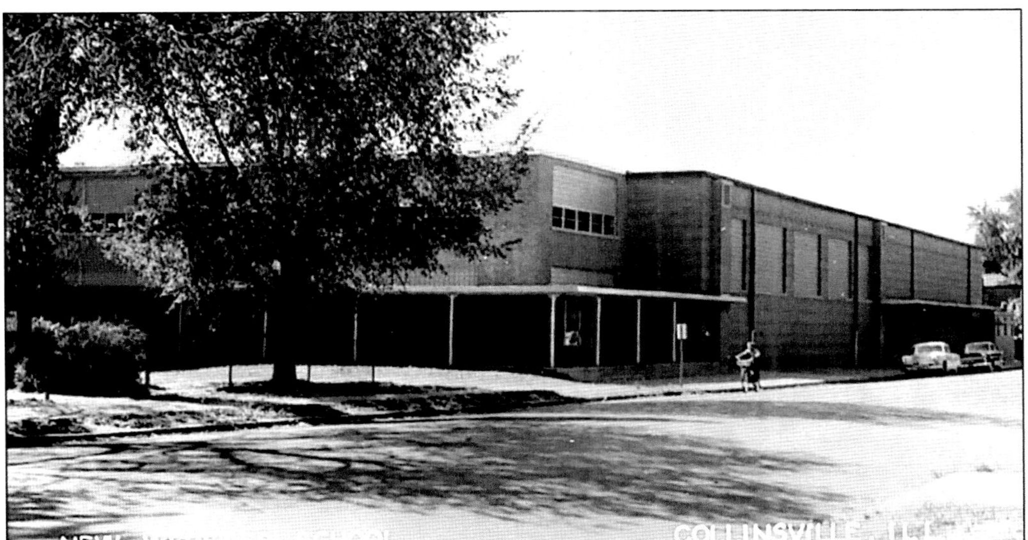

In 1953, a major addition was connected to Webster School. This facility includes a gymnasium, library, and the Franklin C. Kreider Auditorium. In the mid-1950s, 1200 people packed the auditorium to hear the renowned trumpet player Raphael Mendez accompanied by the CHS Band. In 1962, due to overcrowding at the high school, 9th graders attended the junior high at Webster. By the mid-1970s, all of the 7th and 8th graders attended North Jr. High School, and the 9th graders attended the high school.

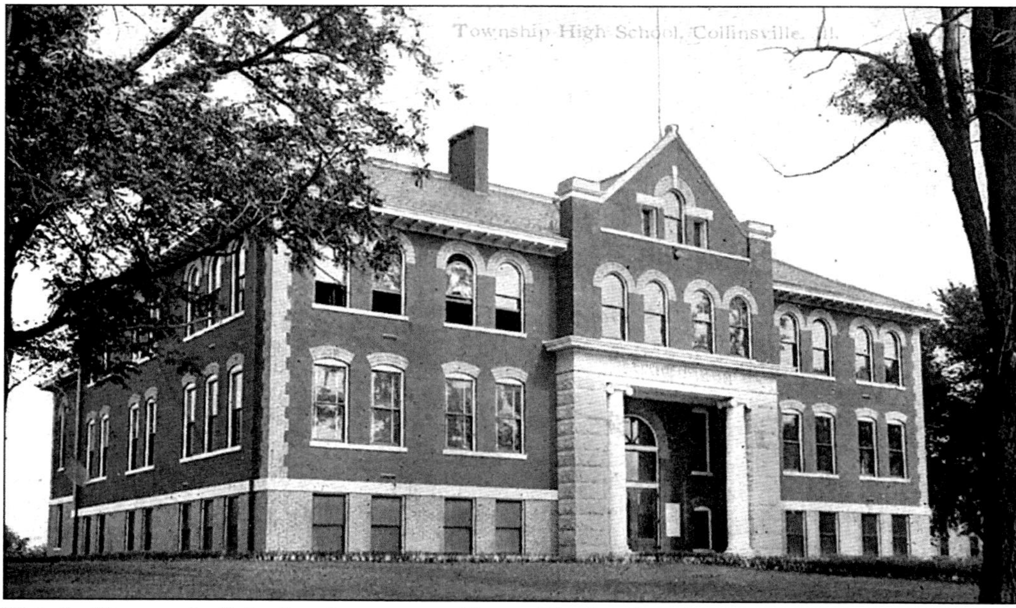

This facility was built by local contractor Henry Eberhardt to house 250 students at a cost of $50,000. Collinsville Township High School at 1203 Vandalia Street opened in October of 1908. In attendance, were 116 high school students and ten special students with a faculty of eight including an administrator. Because space permitted, 76 eighth grade students also attended the high school.

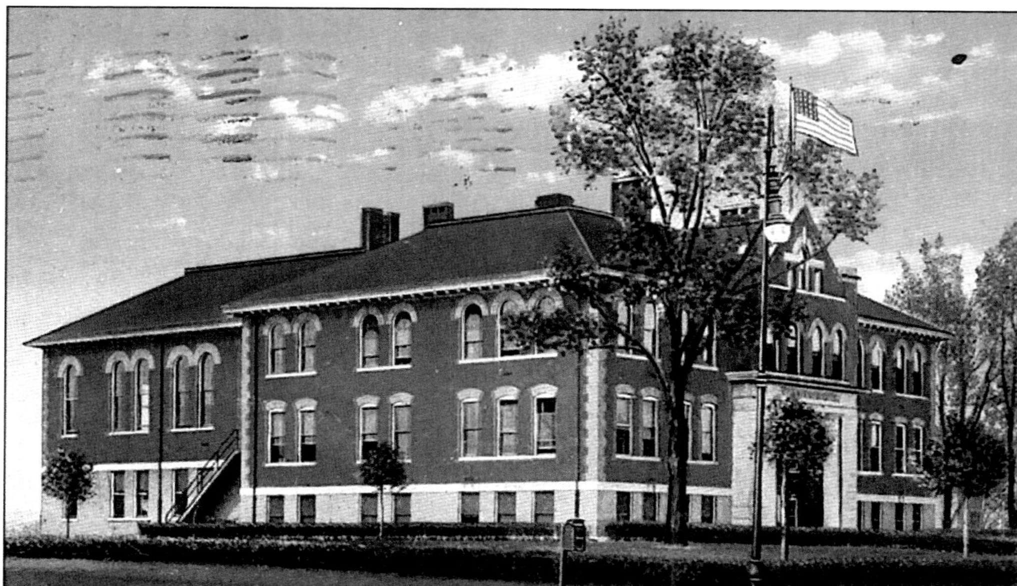

This postcard provides a side view of the 1908 building. The gym was located on the lower level of the west wing. The building had three levels. This high school, with additions and alterations, served the community until a new school was constructed at a different site in the early 1970s.

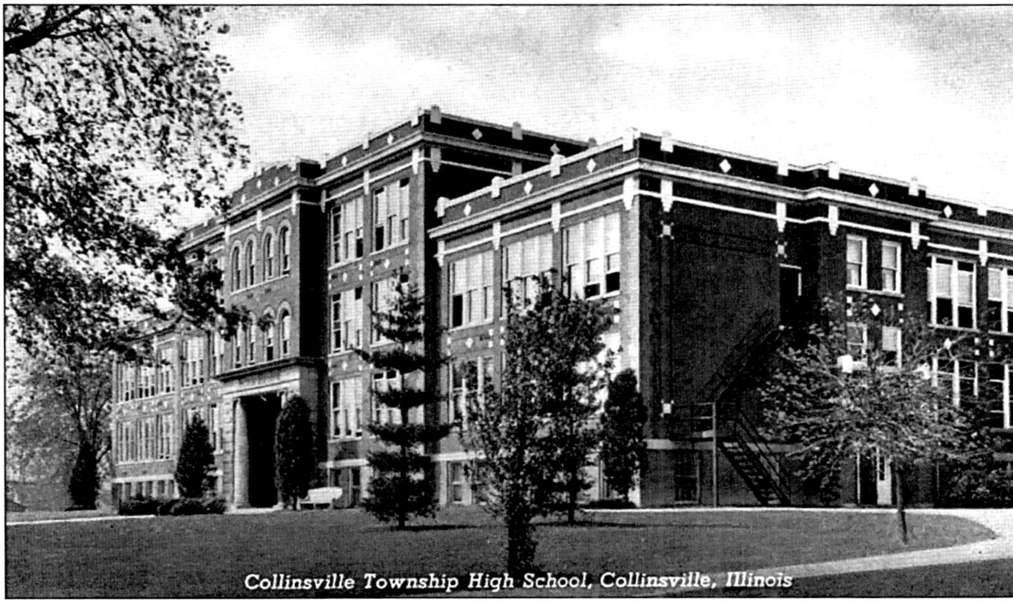

Collinsville Township High School, Collinsville, Illinois

In 1922, CTHS was remodeled and enlarged. As a result, the center portion of the building now has four floors and a wing on each of the north and south ends. In 1929, space for industrial arts classes was added. In 1940, the building was again remodeled, and the old gym became a cafeteria on the lower level. The upper levels contained a library and classrooms. In 1940, the school had 25 teachers and 925 students, with a graduating class of 180.

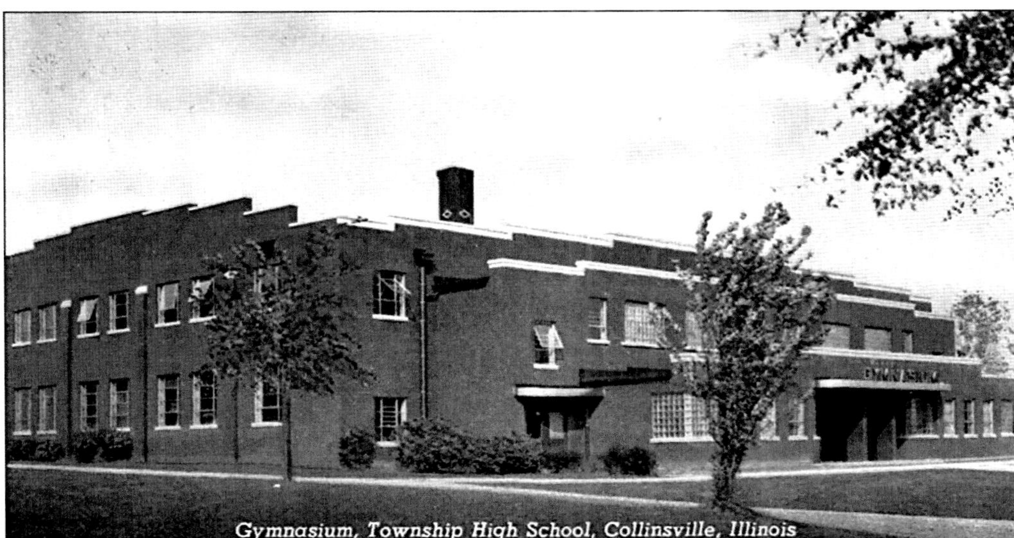

Gymnasium, Township High School, Collinsville, Illinois

In 1940–41, a large gymnasium was constructed by local contractor Norman Dieu at a cost of $100,000. The edifice measured 120 feet by 150 feet. The bleachers seated 1800, and with chairs on the gym floor for stage productions, it held 3000 people. In 1983, Son Life Church purchased most of the Collinsville High School property on the west side of Vandalia Street for $450,000. A portion of the classroom building is now being used by the Collinsville Christian Academy for a K-12 school. The gym was remodeled and is currently the Son Life Fellowship Temple.

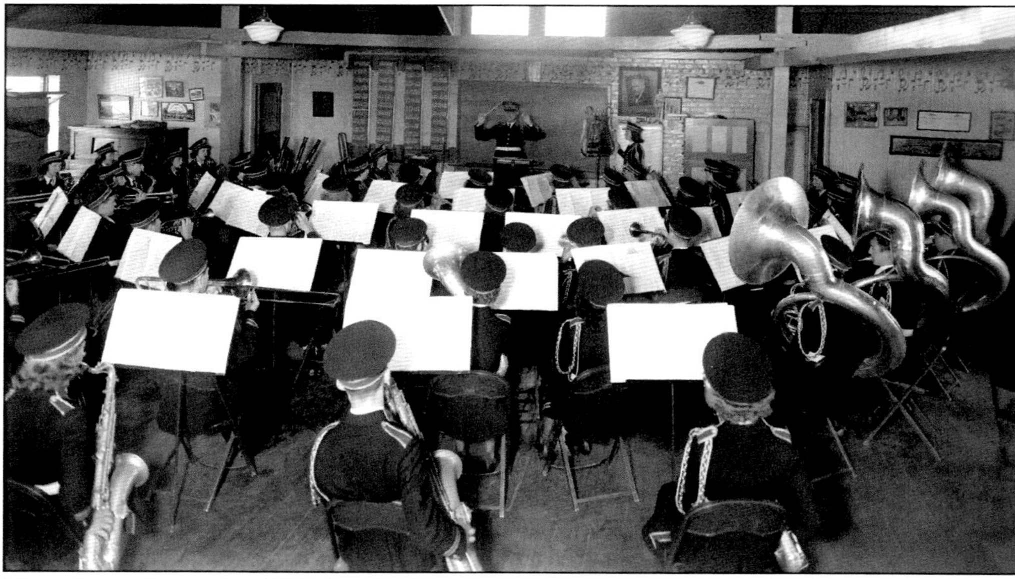

This photo shows the CHS Band rehearsing in the band building that was located across Vandalia Street adjacent to the VFW Home. The building was originally a livery stable for the D.D. Collins' home. The band used this facility from 1940 to 1957 when a new band room was built adjoining the gym. At that time, a major classroom wing was added on the south end of the building along High School Avenue.

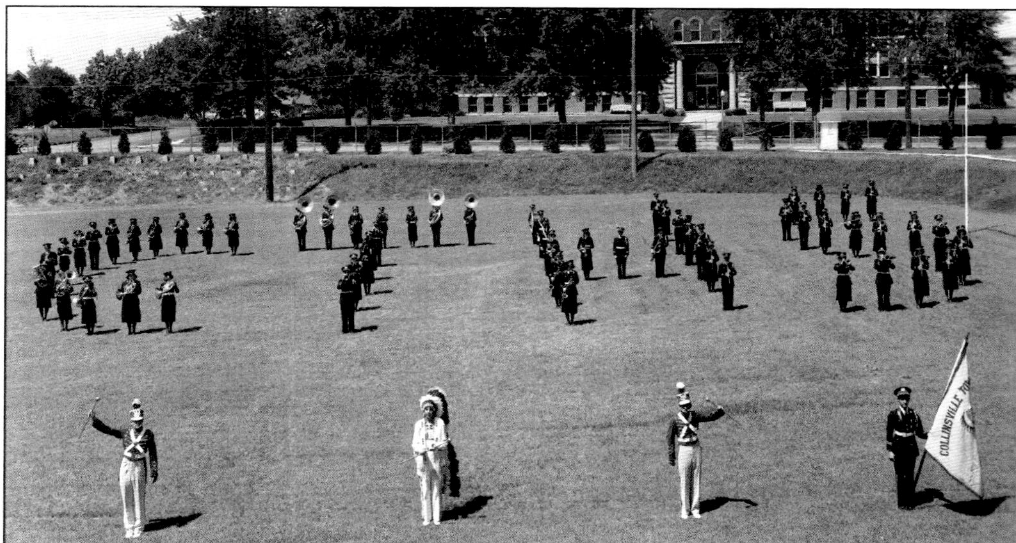

A 1940s photograph shows the band practicing in the WPA-built football bowl. The twenty-acre tract also included a track, a baseball field, and Dorris Elementary School. In the 1970s and 1980s, the vocational school at the new high school (2201 South Morrison) constructed and sold several houses on the west side of the original campus. The land on the east side of Vandalia Street, once a part of the CHS campus, is now an Osborn Co. development that includes 65 new homes and an Automatic Teller Machine. The Baudino Mortuary is in the planning stages.

Three

STREET SCENES

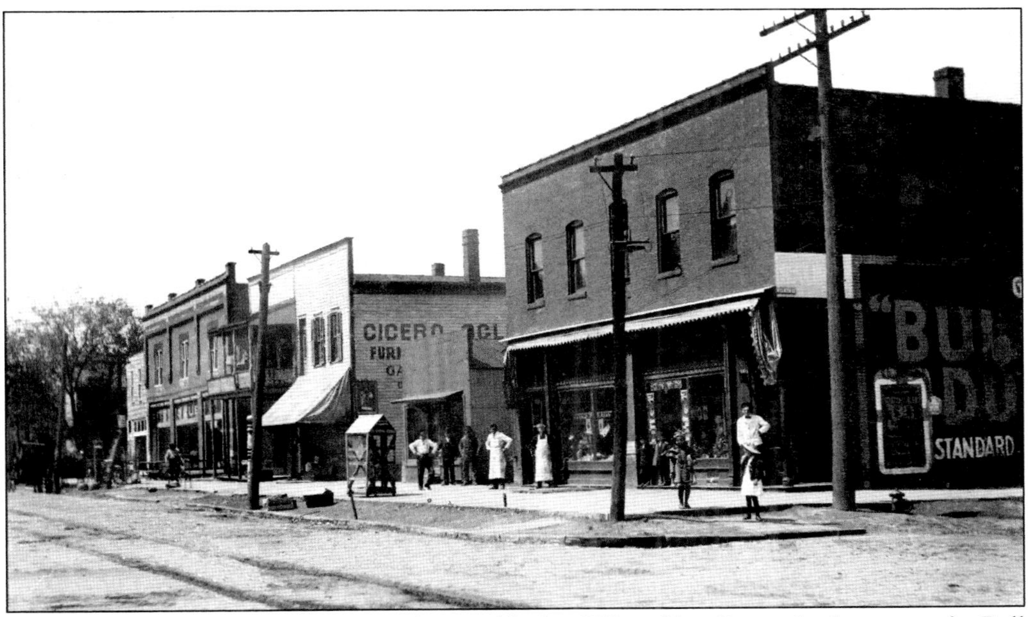

A c. 1910 view of the north side of the 100 block of West Clay Street displays part of a Bull Durham mural and part of Cicero Ogle's sign. The corner building, 101 West Clay, is the Benjamin Jokerst Grocery Store that by 1913 had become Peck's Market. Down the street is the Ogle building that became Ogle-Hiken Furniture and then Hiken Brothers a few years later. Ogle also sold real estate and insurance. (Courtesy Bill and Lois Metzger.)

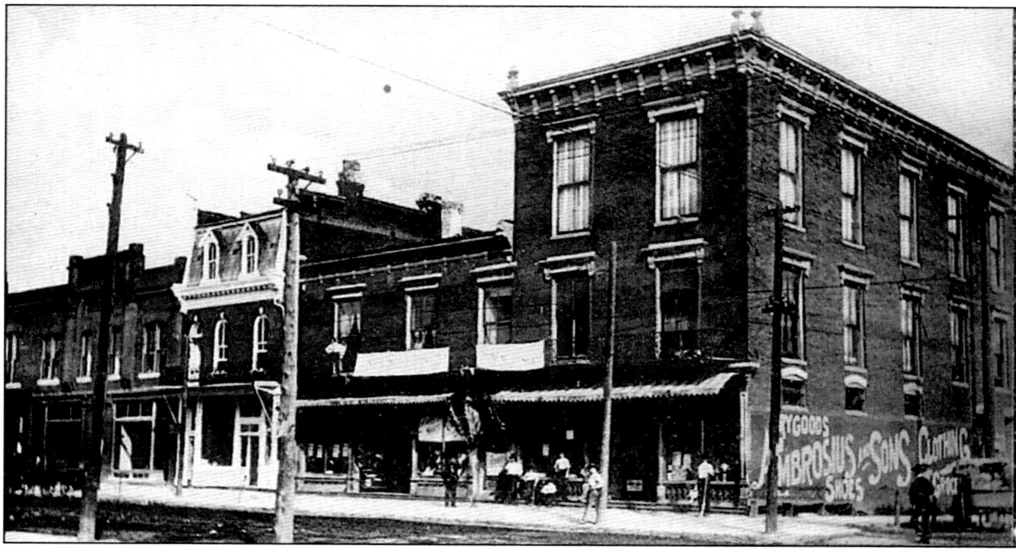

The Ambrosius and Sons store of 1891 became Yates-Ambrosius Mercantile Co. in 1907, and by 1916, it was Yates Company. It offered dry goods, groceries, shoes, and furnishings. The store was located on the northwest corner of Main and Morrison streets. For a few years, the second floor became the second location of the *Collinsville Herald*. One door west was the First National Bank.

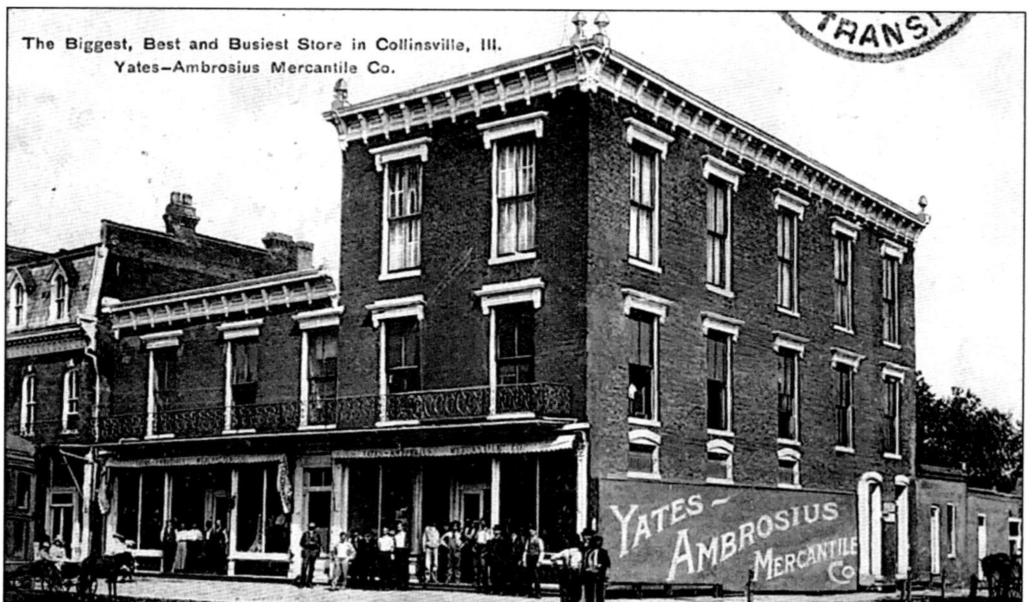

Shown is a later view of the Yates-Ambrosius Mercantile Company. About 1912, neighboring businesses at this intersection were Charlie Salel's Ye Old Corner Bar on the northeast corner, the Merchants Hotel on the southeast corner and the Nicholas Welzbacher Saloon on the southwest corner. Poletti Grocery in the mid-1920s, Schwartz Furniture in the early 1930s, and Home Furniture Co. since 1936 are other businesses that have occupied the northwest corner of this prominent intersection.

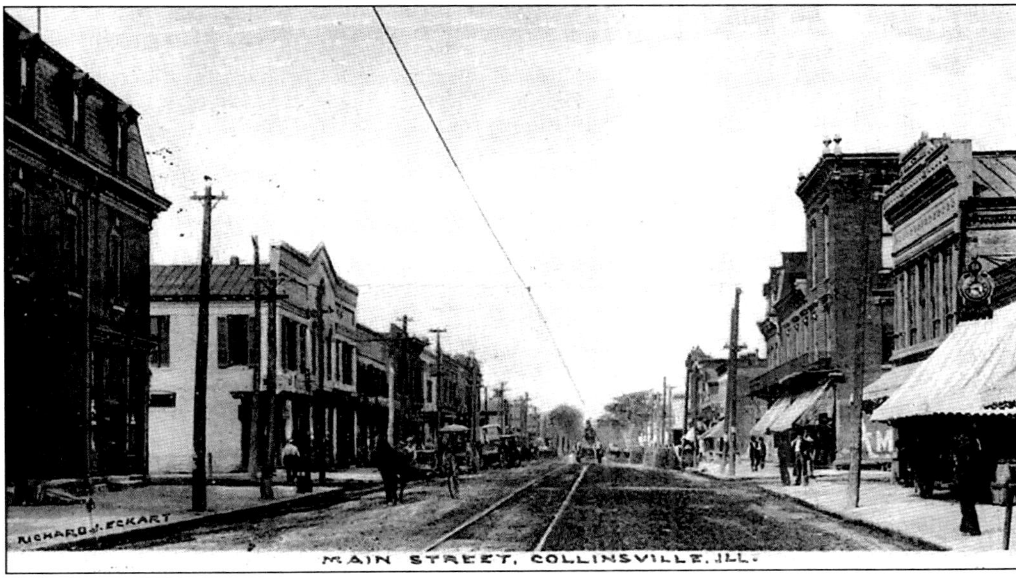

This scene from about 1905 is of East Main Street facing west at the Main and Morrison intersection. This postcard, one of a series, was produced for Richard J. Eckart probably for resale at his drug store. Main Street was unpaved and included interurban tracks. In 1907, the streets were paved with bricks as pictured in the photo below.

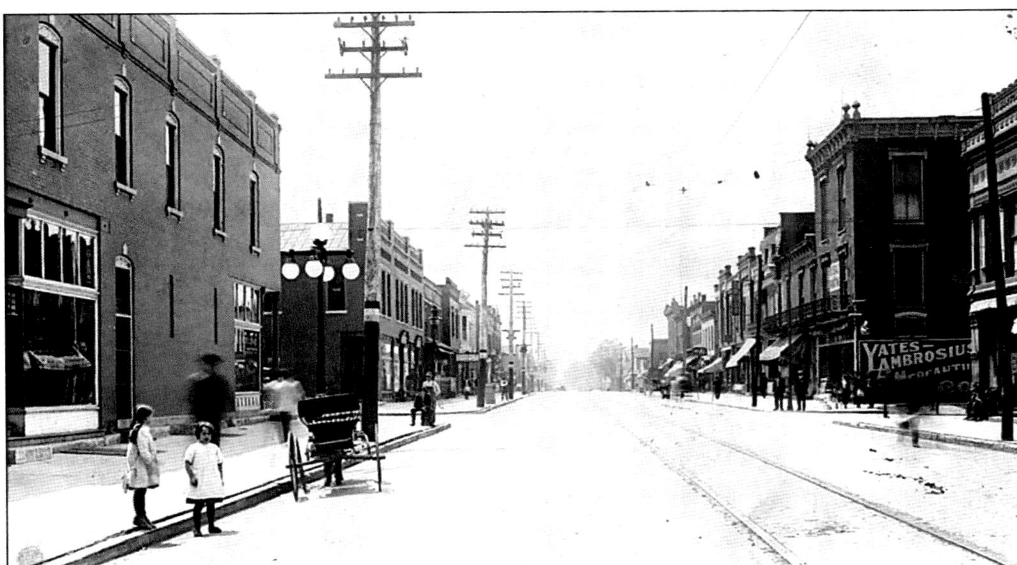

This is eight or ten years later, but virtually the same view as the one above. In 1912, a fire did a great deal of damage to the Merchants Hotel. It was extensively remodeled and then reopened as the Commercial Hotel. An ornate light pole is visible at the corner of the building. The main entrance to the hotel is on the Morrison Street side. Businesses on the north side of the 200 block of East Main were Rachun and Galinat Grocery Store, Arth Jewelry, Musical Instruments, Locksmith and Guns, and Krafft and Co. General Merchandise.

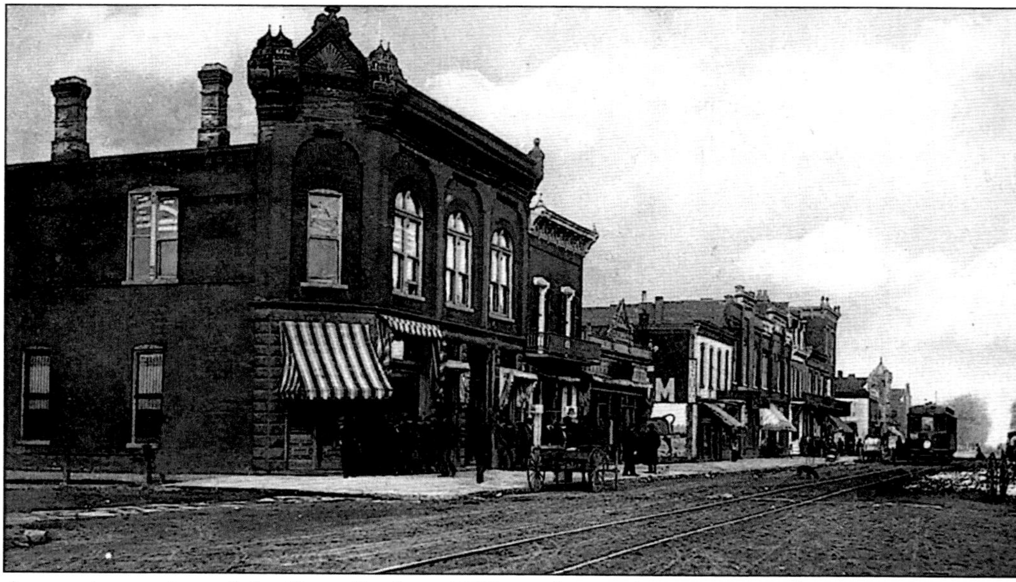

A prominent view of the State Bank *c.* 1905 on the northeast corner of Main and Center is shown. Please note the unpaved streets and the interurban car. Part of the Bull Durham mural is also visible. Next to the State Bank is Union Clothing, followed by Schoettle Bros. Pharmacy, the Airdome, Schroeppel Furniture and Undertaking, Wittenfeld Jewelers and Optical, and Cravens Saloon.

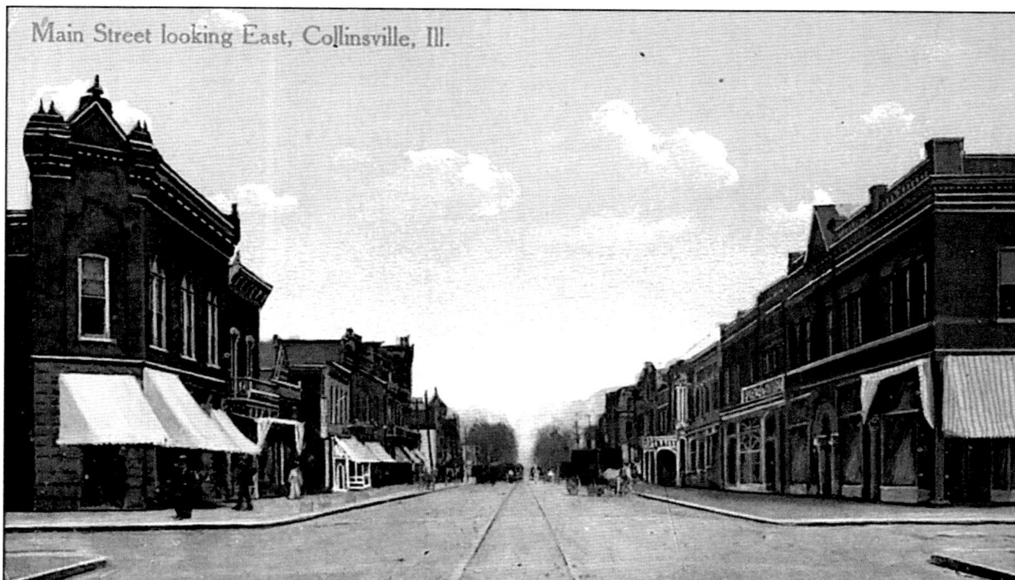

On the right side of the photo looking east, or the south side of the 100 block of East Main Street, are Seebode & Co. Saloon, then Blake & Warner Grocery, Rosenberg's Grand Leader, Bertino Saloon, Kluge & Fischer Shoe Store, Albrecht Meat Market, Saladin & Hughes Saloon, the Moore Barber Shop, Alxszhtts Saloon, and Glass & Cohn's the Famous. The Socialist Reading Room was at 102 1/2 East Main Street.

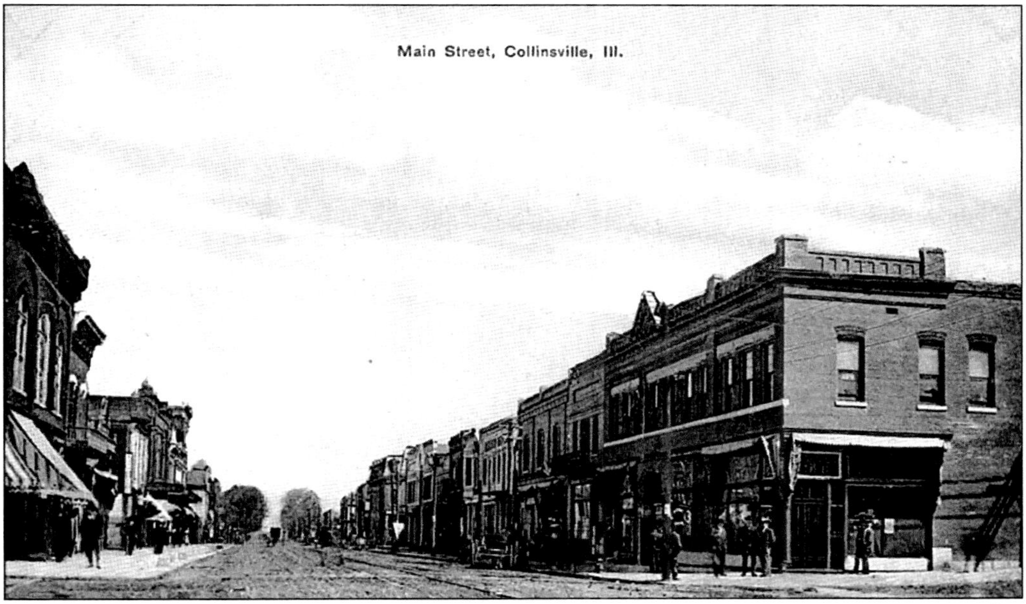

This is a scene from the mid-1920s at Main and Center streets. To the east, past the Mueller Drug Store on the corner, were the Bowker Gift, Paint & Wallpaper Shop, Grand Leader, Thomas Riggin Grocery Store, Sam Deutsch Clothing, Home Bakery featuring Golden Crust Bread, "Coffee Joe" Holten Coffee Store, Moore Barber Shop, Popolsky Clothing, Katz's Ladies Clothing, Glass's The Famous, Vigna and Rodgers Hardware, and the A & P Tea Company.

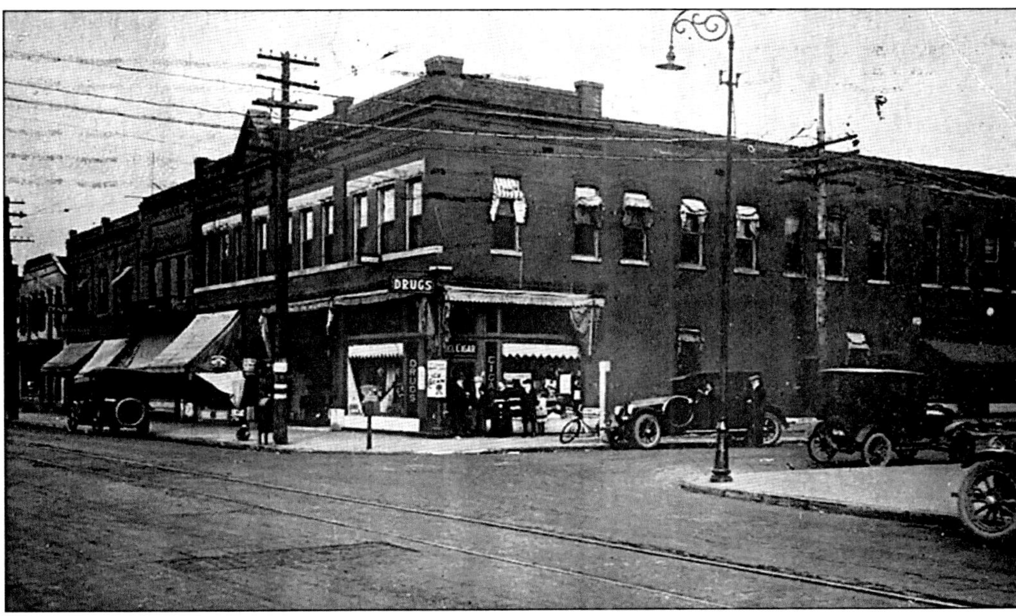

This postcard shows the Curt Mueller Drug Store at the prominent intersection of Main and Center, 100 East Main Street. Mueller was in business for many years and was previously located at 206 Main and then at 300 West Main Street. The streetlights of today seem to be modeled after the one shown in this late 1920s photograph.

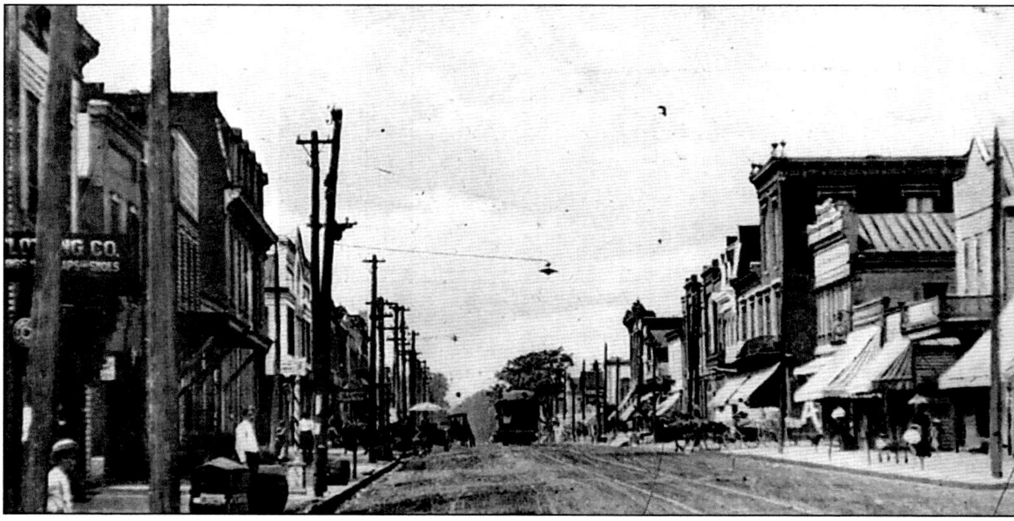

This is the 100 block of West Main Street c. 1905 looking east. A streetcar is pictured on the unpaved street. Beginning on the west end of the block on the south side of Main Street was the Opera House, which also housed a barber shop and bar, The Palace, Silverblooms, Fletcher and Whittiker Restaurant, Tesky Shoes, Holten Tea and Coffee, Simon Jewelers, T. Riggin Grocery, and Laura Krite Millinery. The State Bank at 100 West Main had not yet been constructed.

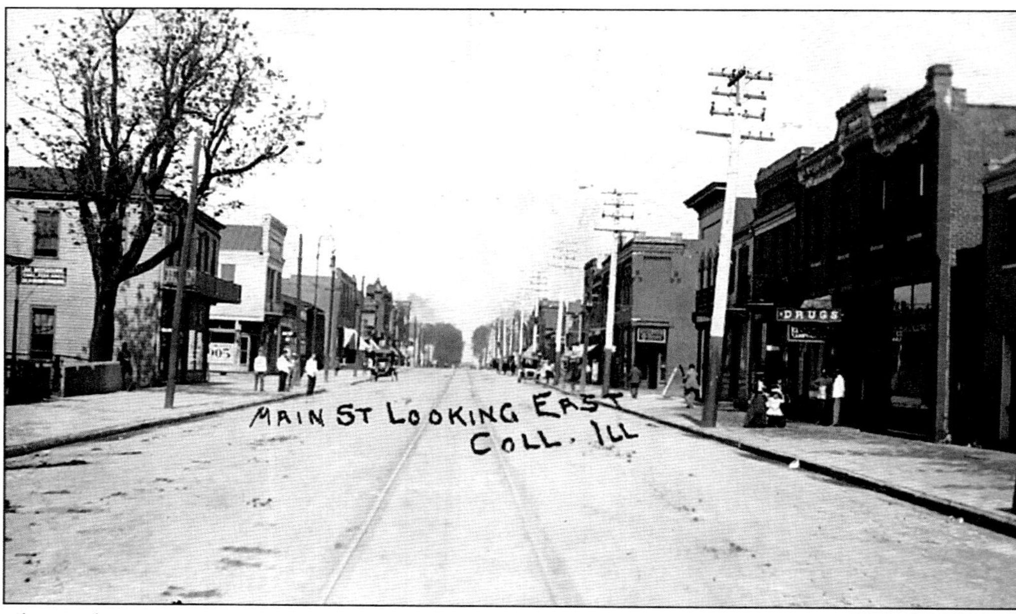

This is the 200 block of West Main around 1912 looking east. On the near right side are the Collinsville Electric Company, Chris Mueller's first drug store, L.W. Riggin Grocery, a Highland Brewing Co. office, and Styszynski Saloon. At the time of this photo, the Opera House stood at 126-128 West Main across the street from the future site of Miners Theatre. In 1918, Miners Theatre was constructed at 200-202 West Main.

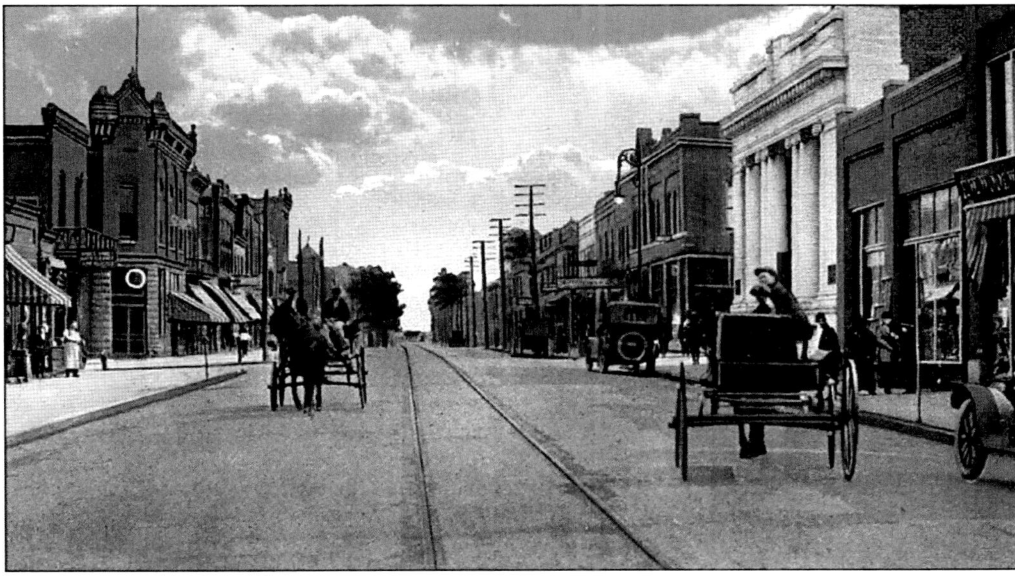

The 100 block of West Main looking east reveals an early 1920s scene of brick streets, interurban tracks, early automobiles, horses and buggies, and the new State Bank at the Center Street intersection. Moving west from the bank are Laura Krite Millinery, Krite Hardware, Woolworths, B & E Shoes, Silverblooms, Union Clothing, Sam Hiken Furniture, and Plattner's Shoe Store. The Hiken and Plattner stores are in the Opera House building.

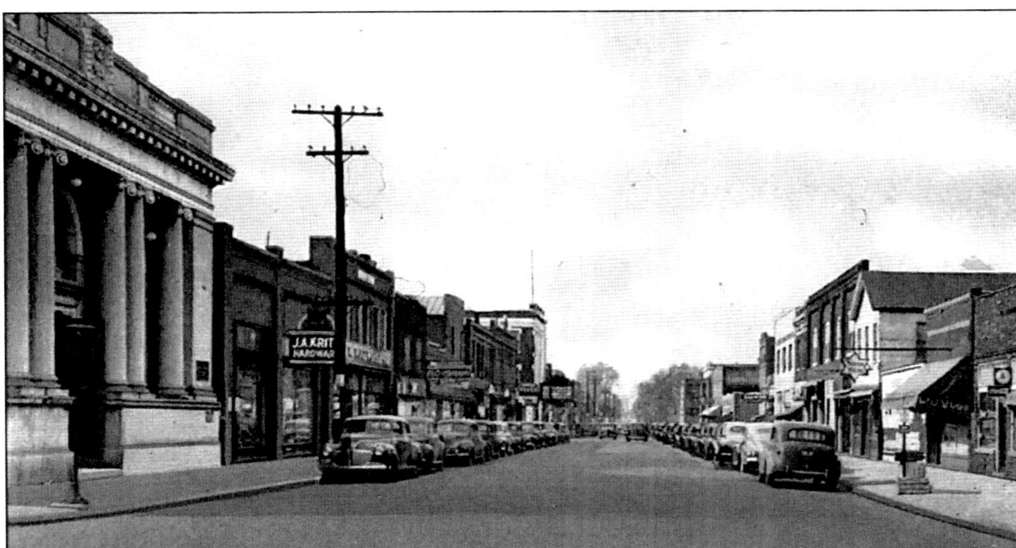

This is a mid-1930s photo of the 100 block of West Main Street looking west after the streetcar tracks have been removed. The businesses on the north side of the street beginning at Center Street are Tri-City Grocery, Vogue Boot Shop, United Cigar, O'Farrel Insurance, Collinsville Ice and Fuel, Edwards' Lunch Room, Francis Shoe Repair, LaSur's Paint Shop, Kluge Bros. Hardware, Union Clothing, Paris Style Shop, Collinsville Candy Company, Chamber of Commerce Office, Collinsville Building & Loan, and Lerner Ladies' Clothing.

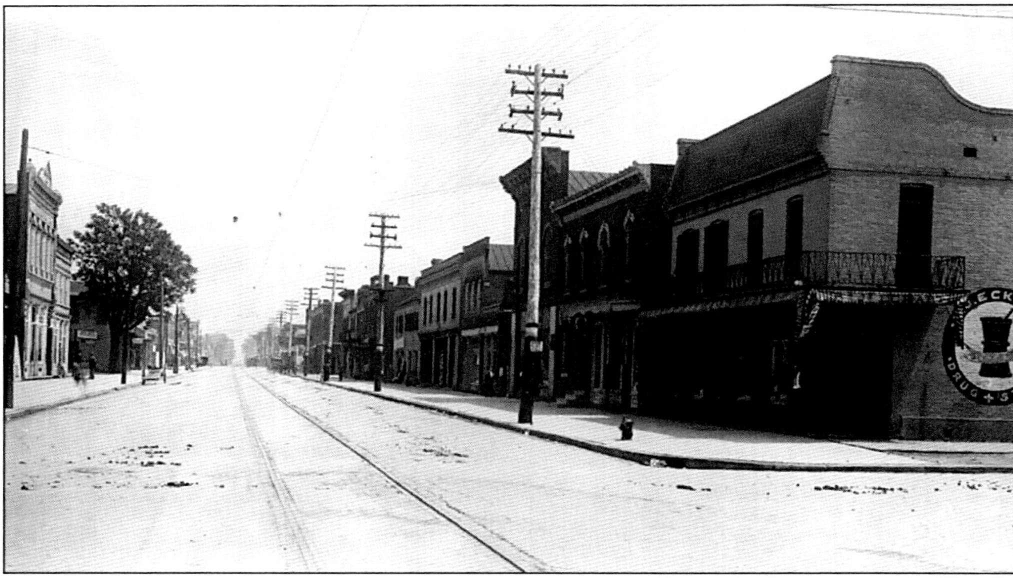

A pharmacy, the oldest continuous business in Collinsville, has been on the southeast corner of Main and Seminary for over 100 years. In 1880, Herman G. Grosse began a pharmacy at this location. Upon his death in 1899, R.J. Eckart operated the drug store. After Eckart died in 1930, Melvin Ostle and Robert Campbell ran the store. They also bought out two other local drug stores. In 1940, the partnership was dissolved, and Melvin Ostle and later his son Jim tended the original store. Today Jim's daughter, Judy Weiss, operates the business, and Jim works for her.

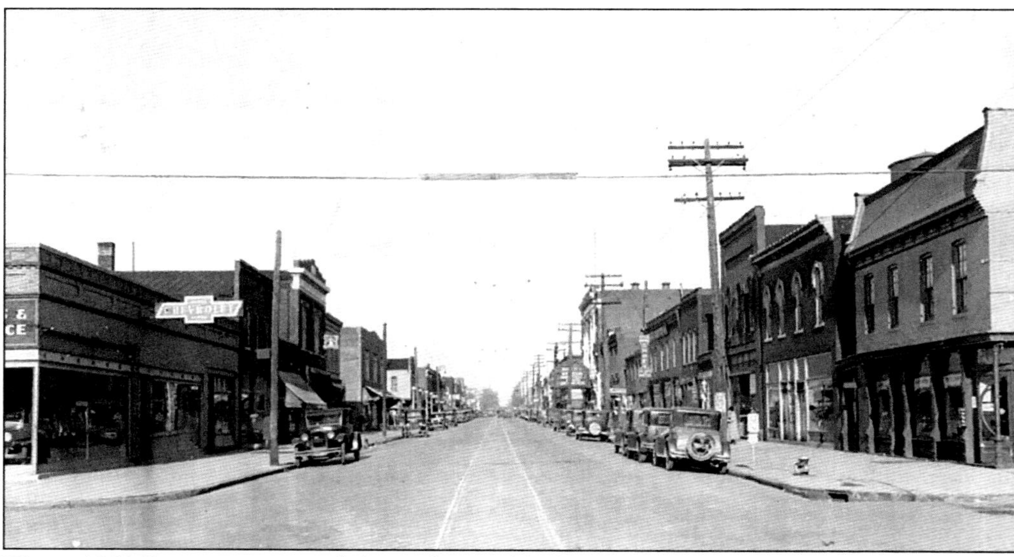

This *c.* 1928 Bregstone postcard shows the 200 block of West Main Street looking east. On the left or north side of the street are Eichman-Laythrop Chevrolet, Walter Fischer's Collinsville Heating and Plumbing, Kroger Grocery Company, Shilling Millinery and Collinsville Packing Company. On the right side or south side of Main Street are Ostle-Campbell Drug Store, Schultze Market, Hecker Barber Shop, Bert Gray Cigar Store, Star Cleaners and Abe Mann Shoe Store. The Ostle building as shown has been altered and no longer has a balcony.

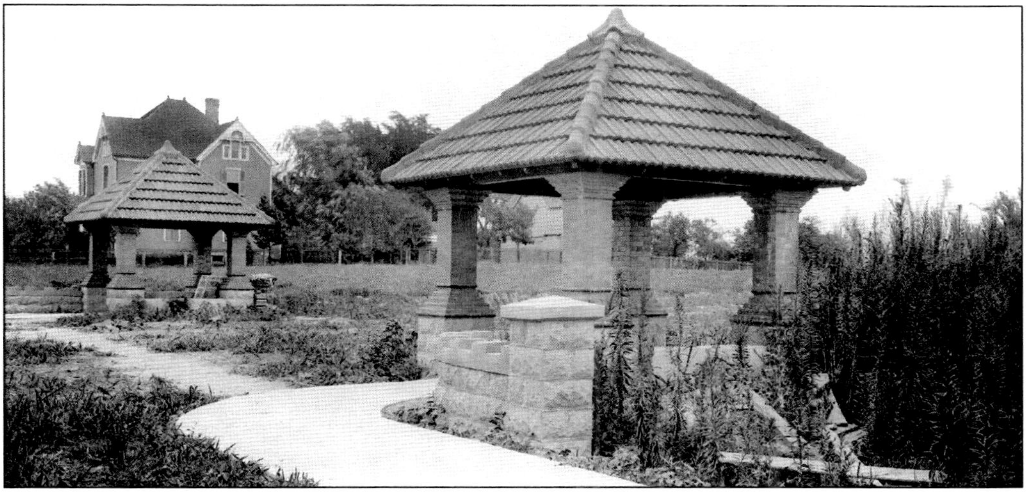

The unique belvederes at the entrance to Courtland Place at 600 St. Louis Road are displayed on this Bregstone postcard. The belvederes, which were constructed in about 1912, featured a decorative block wall and four brick columns supporting a roof of slate with red clay tile trim. They stand today with some modifications including concrete benches and a roof of soft cedar shakes. Courtland Place is in the Kreela Addition that was platted in 1910 by Louis Kreela, C.A. and Nettie Hartmann. C.A. Hartmann, vice-president of the State Bank, lived in the house in the background of this scene from 1911 to 1936. The house became Joe's Barbershop in 1949 and is now named The Barbershop. (Courtesy of Bill and Lois Metzger.)

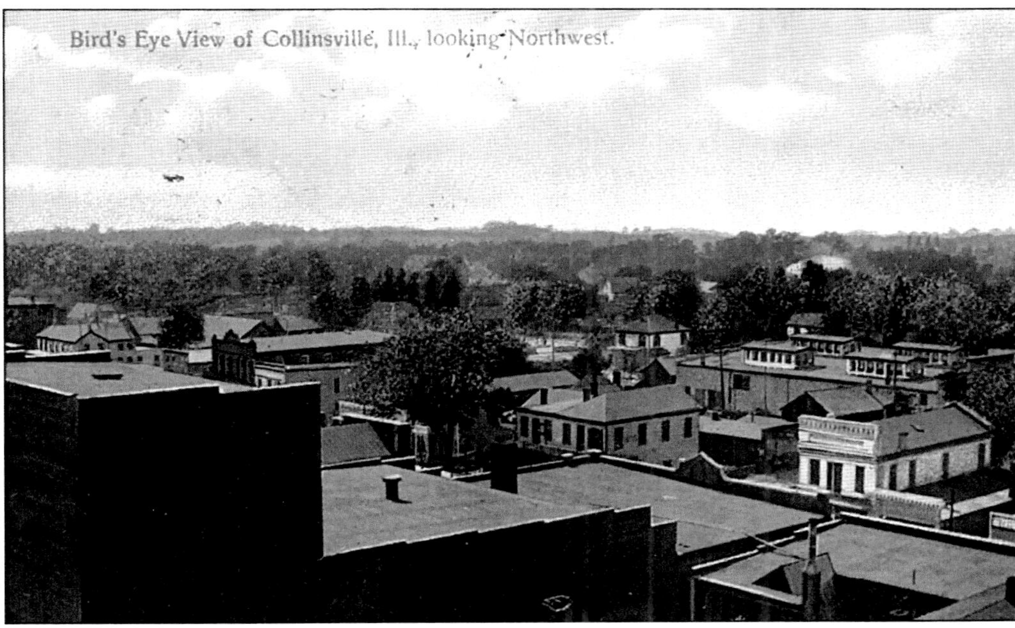

This c. 1923 birds-eye view of downtown Collinsville was likely taken from the water tower shortly after it was built. The view overlooks the Opera House that stood at 128 West Main Street. In the distance on the right side of the picture postcard are four windowed box-like structures that appear to be vents or skylights on the roof of Ardison Hall.

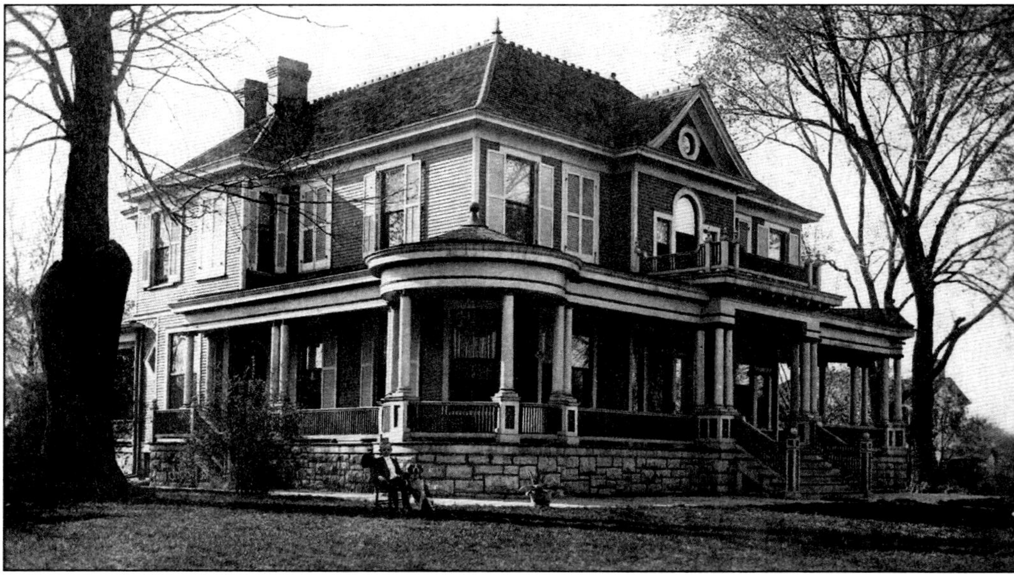

Early owners of the property where this house stands at 429 Vandalia Street were Jonathon Berkey, Henry F. Mayer, Jackson M. Johnson, H.H. Keebler, and James Wickliffe. The structure housed the Cottage Sanatorium for a few years beginning in 1889. W.D. Parr, Ike Schwartz, and Ferd Keller were other owners of this 14-room house. The current owners and residents of the house are Dan and Caryl McClaskey. They had the house extensively renovated in 1995. Dan is the grandson of Ferd and Anna Keller. The photo postcard is by Ritchie Bros. of Centralia, Ill., a prominent commercial postcard photographer of the 1905-1930 era. (Courtesy of Bill and Lois Metzger.)

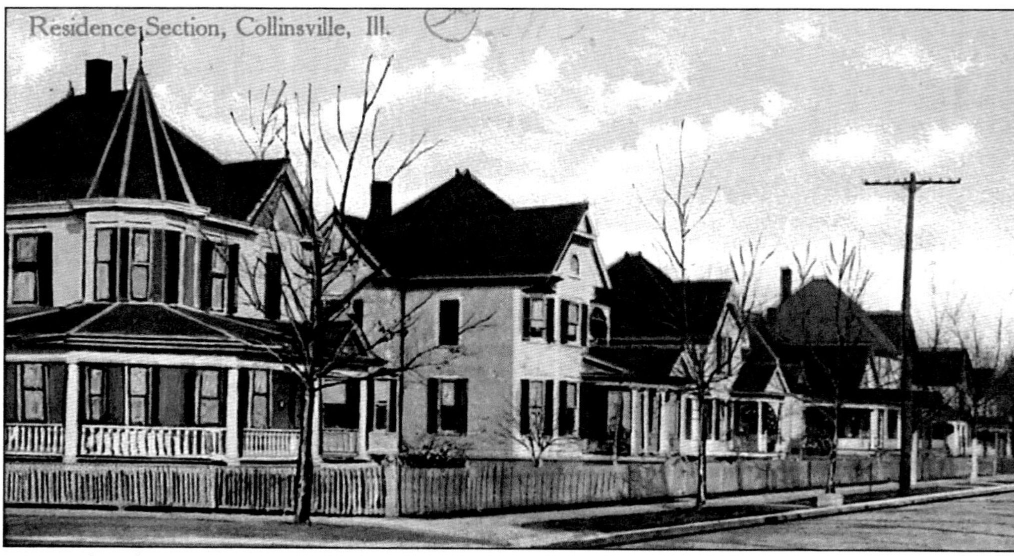

Pictured is the north side of the 500 block of East Clay Street looking east. Taken a few years later than the picture on the next page, this is a photo of the same group of houses. Residents of the homes shown in the 1916-26 era were from left to right Thomas Sauer and a bit later Louis Bertram at 503 E. Clay, A.C. Gauen at 509, Emma Pinkel at 515, Ed Sauer and later John Bertram Jr. at 519 and H.E. Gillaspy at 521. These homes stand today in an altered state.

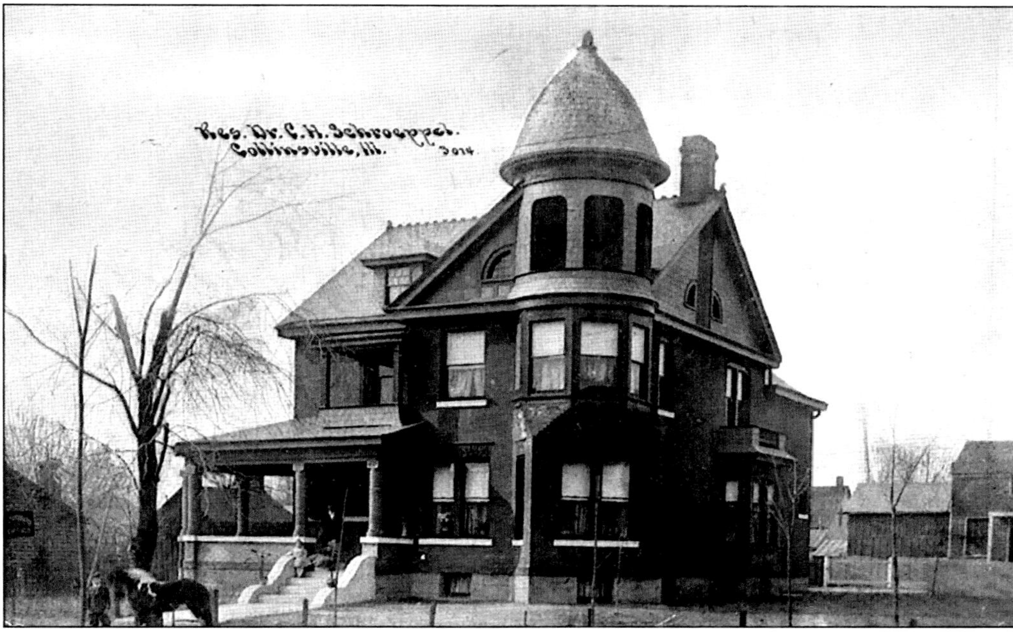

Complete with a turret and bay windows the Schroeppel house stands at 317 West Main Street. This Queen Anne style house was constructed around 1908 for Dr. G.H.R. Schroeppel. After Schroeppel's death, Dr. Wendell W. Brown purchased the home and attended patients in his residence. He had an elevator installed. On the second floor, he and his wife raised orchids in a greenhouse. The Flower Basket, a florist, has occupied the house for several years. From 1993-98, the Lavender Rose Tearoom was also located in this structure.

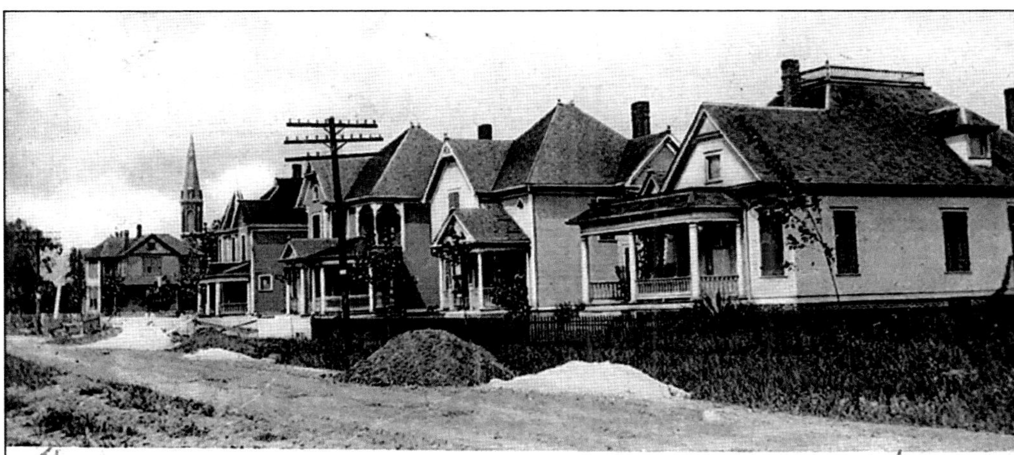

This scene of the same group of houses as the picture across the page shows the 500 block of East Clay looking west. At this time, the area was known as North Lawn. On the left in the distance is the steeple of the S.S. Peter and Paul Church. This postcard picture was taken c. 1914.

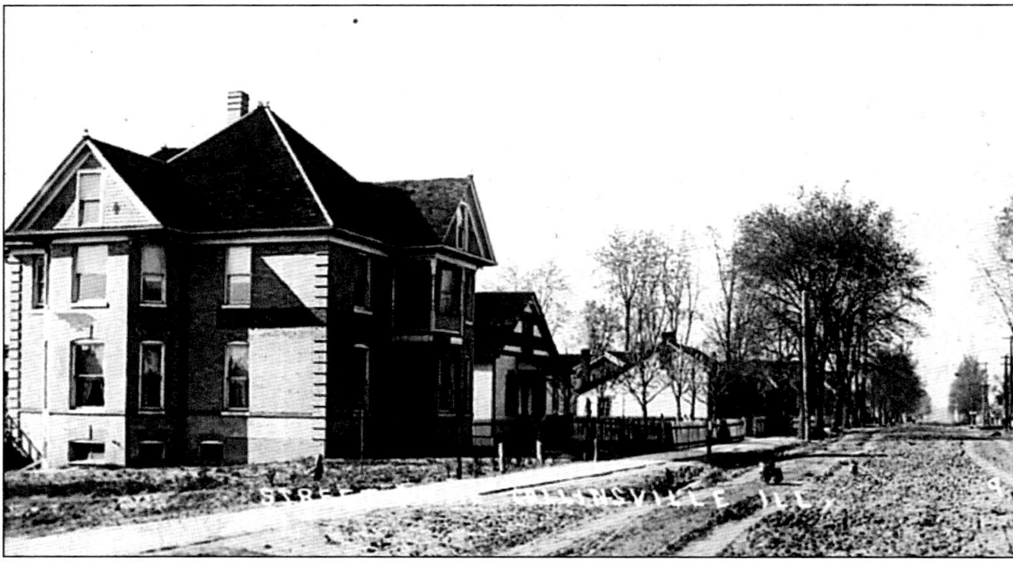

This Victorian brick house, on the northwest corner of Morrison and Johnson, was constructed in the mid-1850s. The outer walls of the first floor are twelve inches of solid brick. Note on this circa 1910 picture the absence of the wrap-around porch that is so prominent today. Among the owners of the past were Ladimil Mashek, a clerk for Donk Mine, and his wife Sadie who lived here from 1929 to 1969. The current owners purchased the house in 1994; their extensive restoration has included finishing the third floor.

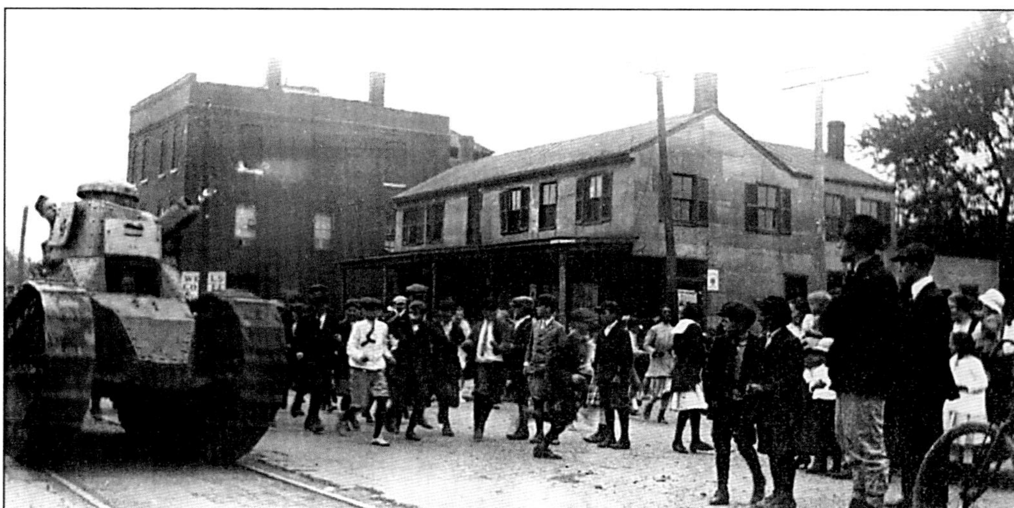

World War I changed people's lives in Collinsville in many ways. 725 servicemen from Collinsville participated in this conflict. Liberty bond campaigns were conducted. The National Defense League was formed and patriotic songs were sung in churches and schools. Because of the anti-German sentiment, German was no longer taught in the schools, and fewer services were held in German in the churches. People looked down on "slackers" and were encouraged to look for spies. In 1919, after the war, this tank visited Collinsville and neighboring towns as part of patriotic events.

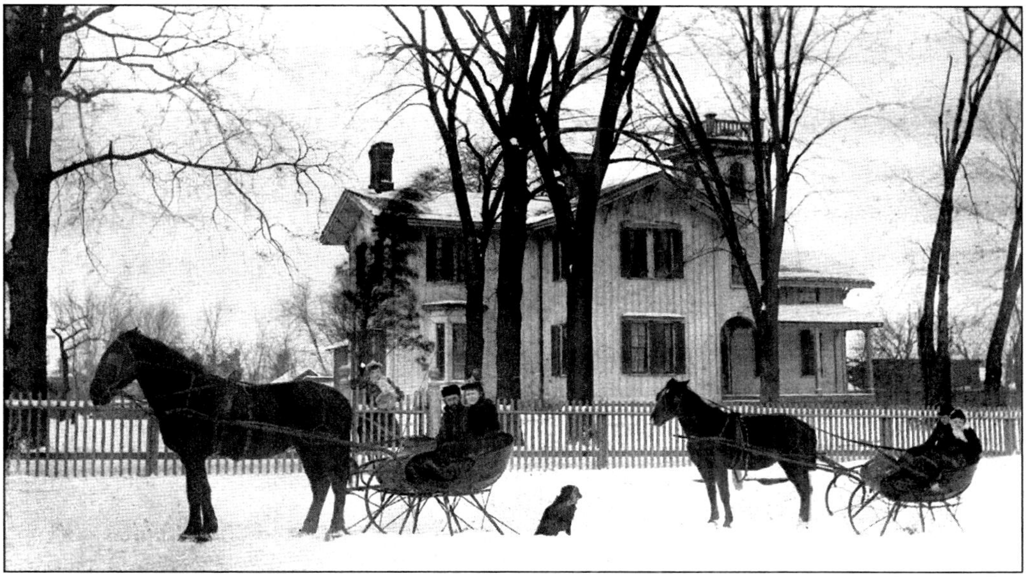

The home designed for Dr. Henry Wing in 1865 was Italianate in style and stood at 506 East Church Street on the south end of the current Braner Building lot. This picture from about 1890 shows Florence Look Seaman at the gate. Horace Look and his sister Emma Look Combs are in the front sleigh. Belle Wadsworth and Florence Harkelroad, friends of the Look family, are in the second sleigh as Coalie, the dog, watches.

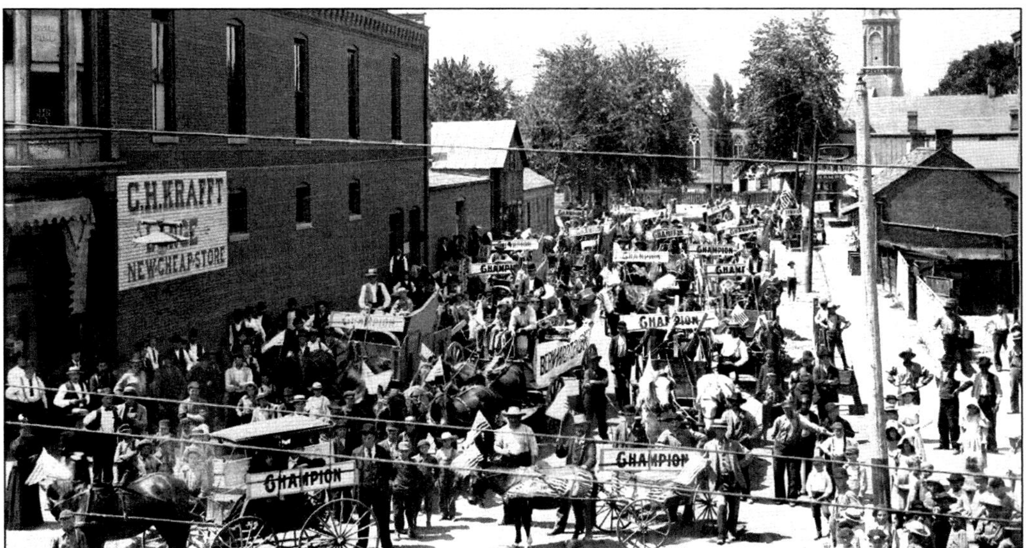

Champion Day took place in the 100 block of Vandalia Street between Main and Clay streets on June 2, 1898. The activity was sponsored by Champion Farm Implements. The prominent building on the left is C.H. Krafft Co., a general merchandise store. In the distance on the right side of the image is the steeple of the S.S. Peter and Paul Church. Situated in the middle of the block on the right or east side of the street is Bernhardt-Niehaus Co., a wagon maker, blacksmith and farm machinery dealer who later sold automobiles. William F. Niehaus was elected mayor in 1927.

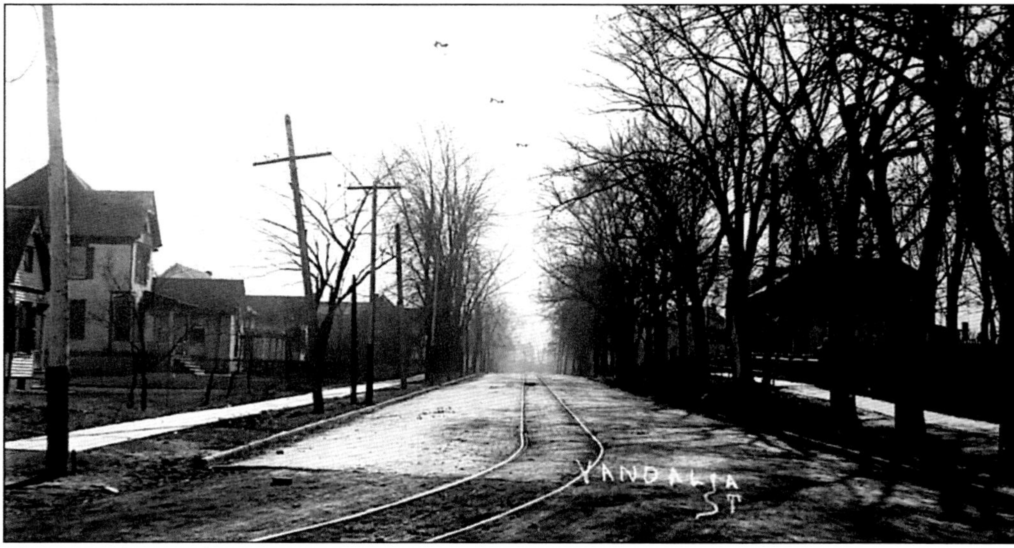

This is a photo taken at Vandalia and Wickliffe streets facing south. Notice the interurban tracks and the curve at Wickliffe. The interurban station was four blocks south at 308 East Clay before moving across the street to 303 East Clay. Henry Dervalis, C.D. Kneedler, Isaac Schwartz, and J.D. Cravens lived on the west side of the 400 block of Vandalia Street in 1915. The Mier Grocery Store was on the corner at 445 Vandalia. Dr. Lay Burroughs, Joe Vacca, Ben Raymond, Dr. L.H. Kraft, and August Schiller lived on the east side of this block.

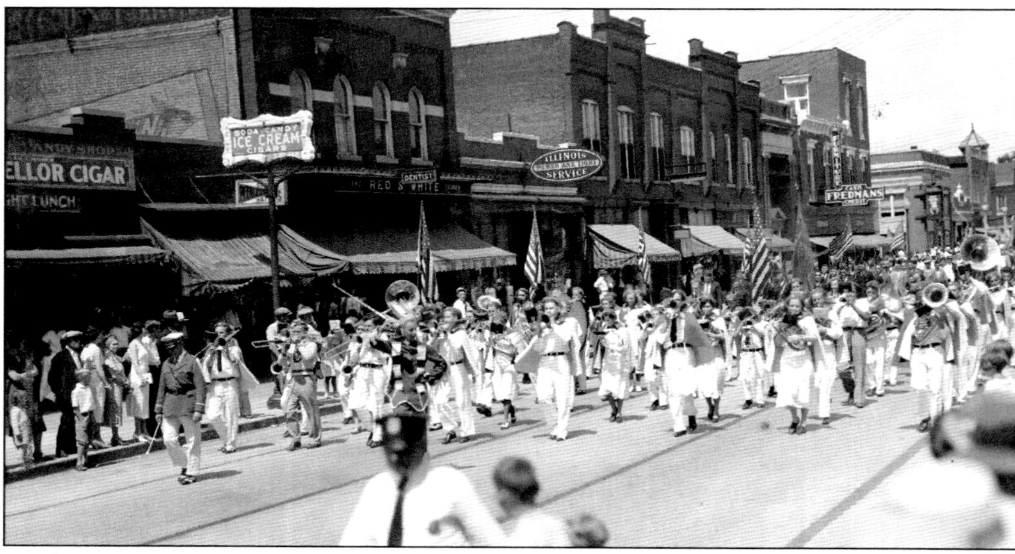

Band Director Franklin C. Kreider and the Collinsville Township High School Band march in a westerly direction in the 100 block of East Main Street in this mid-1930s photo. On the left at the ice cream sign is the popular confectionary, Paradise Candy Shop, affectionately known as "The Greeks" operated by Tom, Peter, Frank, and John Prineas. Continuing down the street are Ideal Market, Illinois Power Co., Rissi-Salel Saloon & Billiards, Bachman Jewelry, Gerding Drug Store, Home Building & Loan, and Fredman Brothers Furniture. The building with the turret in the distance is Ostle-Campbell Drug Store at 209 East Main Street.

Four

Business and Industry

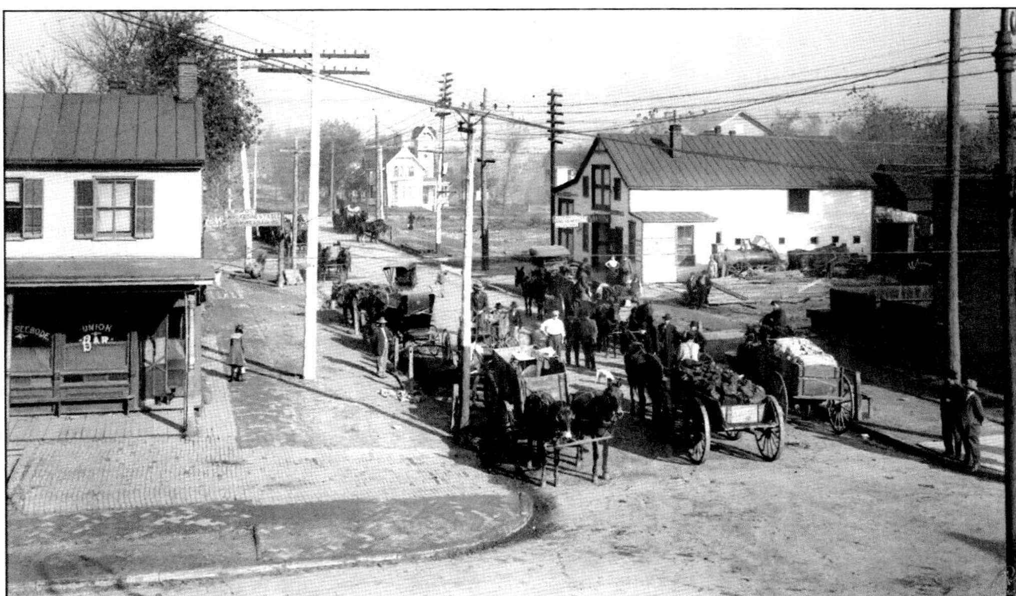

This scene of the potato market was on North Seminary between Main and Clay streets on October 25, 1913. As Lucille Stehman pointed out in her book on Collinsville, there are four modes of transportation shown: horses with buggies and wagons, a steam tractor, a Model T, and a streetcar. In the left foreground is the Seebode Union Bar. The building on the right is the J.C. McLanahan Livery Stable. In the center background is the Rosevear home on the northeast corner of Clay and Seminary. Over the top of the McLanahan building part of the Masonic Temple can be seen.

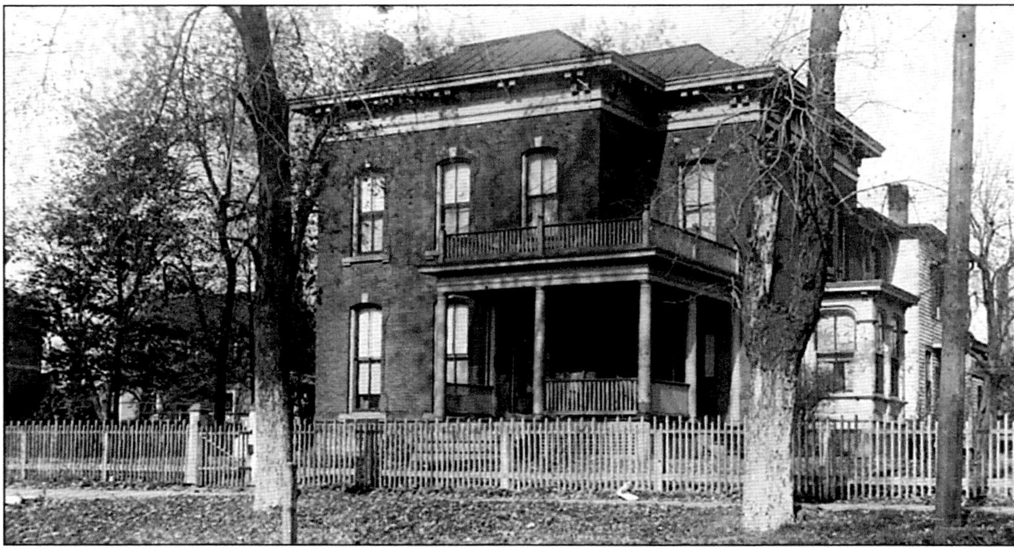

The Beidler Hotel was built in 1879 as the second home of Frederick and Angeline Penney Beidler. Its location at 315 East Church Street is significant because it was at the top of Depot Hill (Reed Avenue) and was likely the closest place for train travelers to buy a meal and rent a room. Mrs. Beidler continued to operate the hotel after her husband's death in 1904. Her 25 cents all-you-can-eat fried chicken dinner and orange cake were well known. The house, which still stands, includes a two-story addition that was attached around the turn of the century.

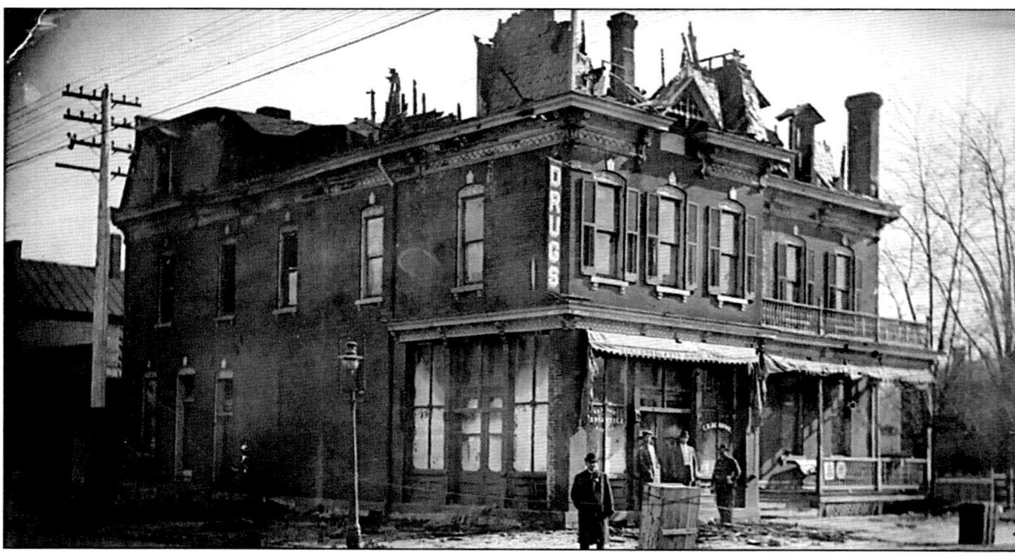

The 32-room, three-story Merchants Hotel was built around 1870 and was owned by John Mersinger. Containing a drug store and bar, the hotel on the southeast corner of Main and Morrison, was the scene of a spectacular fire on January 2, 1912. There were 25 occupants of the building at the time; two people were seriously injured. The building stands today. As a result of the fire, it has no third floor. Attorney William H. Wille, who resided there for many years, allegedly originated the national custom of placing one's hand over his or her heart during the Pledge of Allegiance.

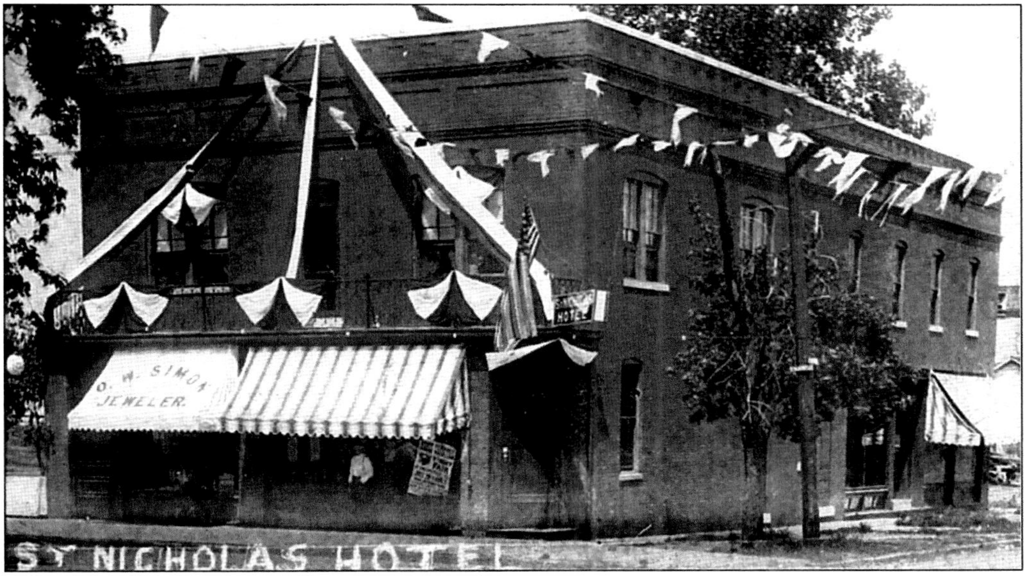

The St. Nicholas Hotel was located at 107 North Chestnut Street just off Main. It was originally the residence of Mr. and Mrs. Bartholomew Vujtech and housed a tailor business and a saloon. Their daughter, Lottie Bullock, had the structure remodeled into a hotel by her brother Joseph. The hotel was on the streetcar line and about six blocks from the railroad depot. It was ready for business in 1913 and was named after the leaseholder Nicholas Welzbacher. After closing as a hotel in the mid-1930s, it became the township tax collector's office, Walter Lauth's Red & White Food Store, and for many years the Fraternal Order of Eagles Hall. The Township Office's parking lot is now situated where the hotel stood.

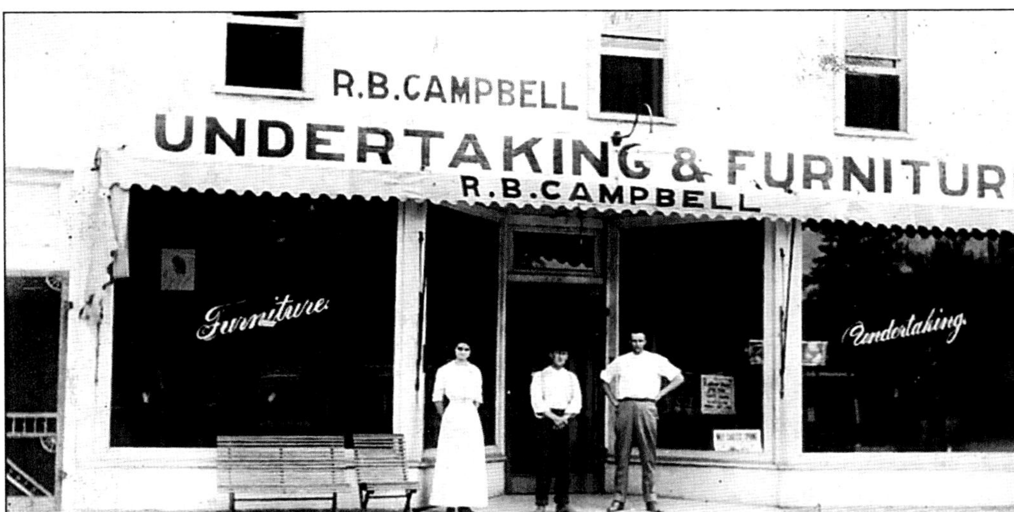

The R.B. Campbell Undertaking and Furniture business was at 118 North Morrison Street. Campbell was the successor of John E. Schroeppel in December of 1912. They advertised having an embalmer, a funeral director, and a lady assistant. The Campbell establishment sold rugs, linoleum, window sashes, matting rugs, parlor furniture, kitchen cabinets, lawn goods, lawn settees, and porch swings.

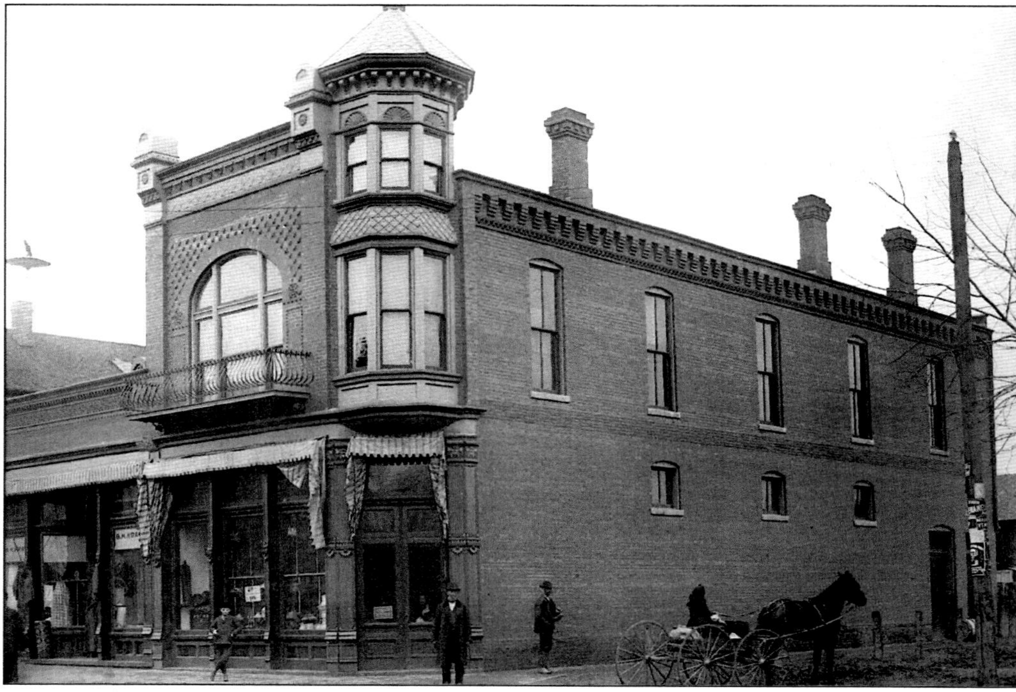

In 1894, the C.H. Krafft Co., a general merchandise store, opened at the northwest corner of Main and Vandalia streets. W.B. Resplica, postmaster and businessman from Glen Carbon, IL, bought out Krafft in 1910. At some point, the turret was removed from the building. In the mid-1930s, this was the site of Ostle-Campbell Drugs and later Campbell Drug store. About 1965, it then became Ashmann's Prescription Pharmacy. Currently Leonard and Sandy Locust own and operate the business.

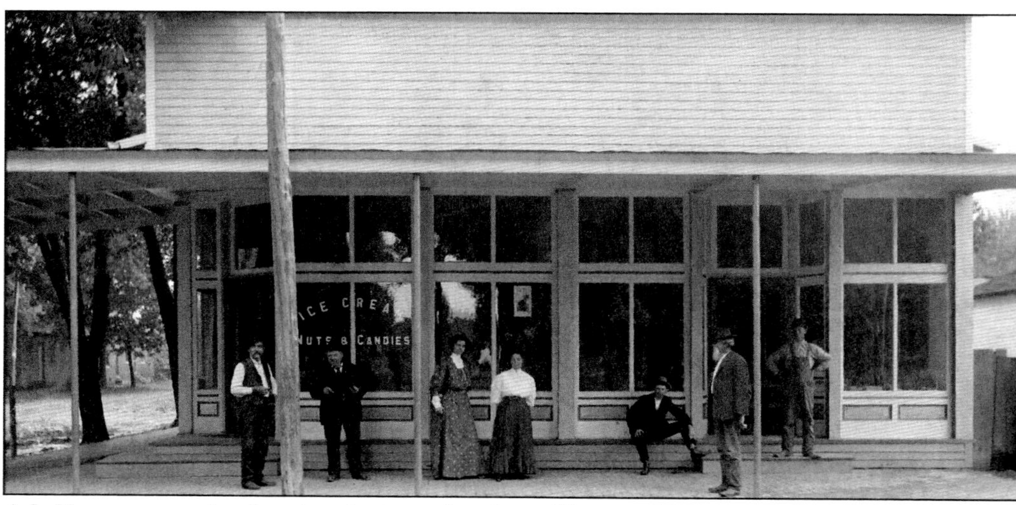

A.J. Hartman was in the cigar business for about 50 years. His store is pictured at 103 West Main where he sold imported and domestic cigars, tobacco, and smoker's supplies. From around 1920 to the mid-1950s, Hartman's cigar store was located in the northeast corner of the Miners Institute building.

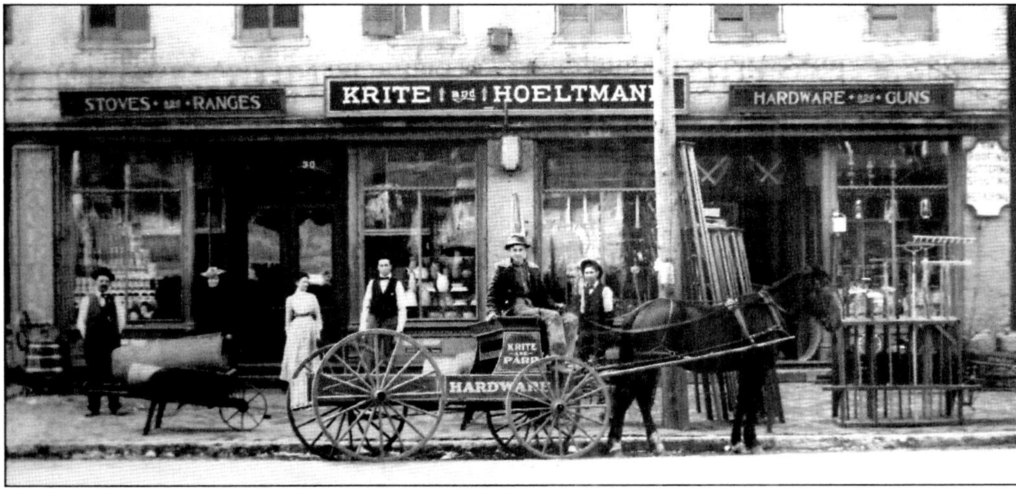

John A. Krite was the founder of Krite & Kirschbaum in 1885. John worked for Witte Hardware in St. Louis before he opened his own store. According to H. J. Marshall, the Mersinger building housed Krite & Kirschbaum as well as Hadley & Smith at 124-128 East Main in 1886. In the next several years, the name changed to Krite & Parr, then to Krite & Hoeltmann, and then to J.A. Krite by 1904. The hardware store was located at 106 West Main from the early part of the 20th century to the mid-1970s. George and William, sons of John, ran the business for many years.

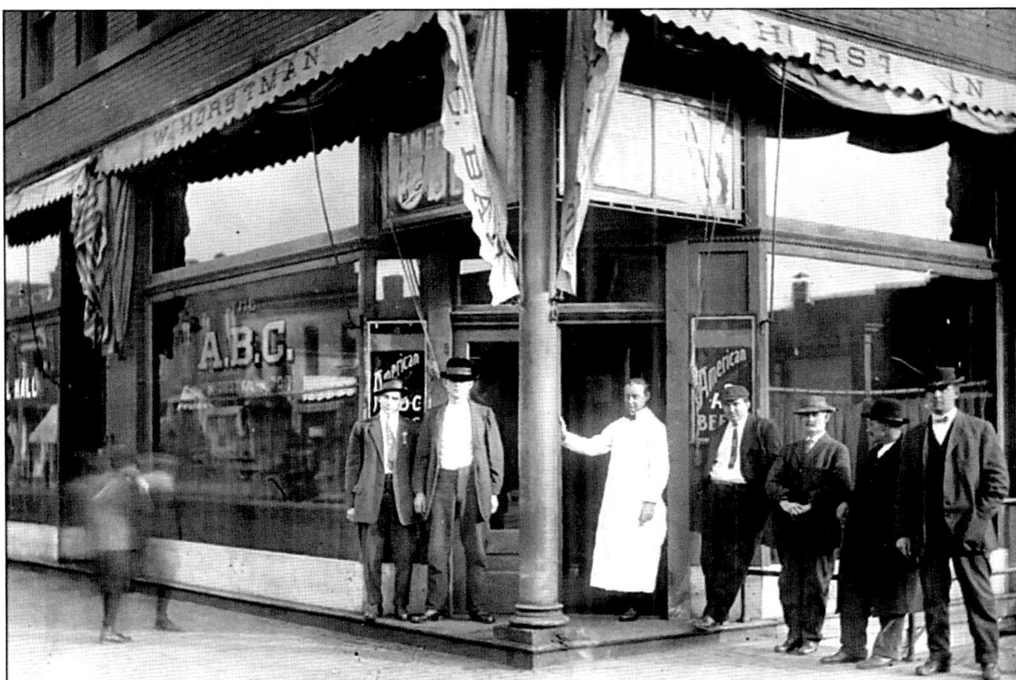

In 1911 the ABC Bar, operated by William "Fifty" Horstman, was located at 100 East Main Street. Beginning in the 1920s, this was the site of the Curt Mueller Drug Store and Soda Fountain. Another prominent occupant was the Mary Ann Shop, a ladies' apparel store. Through the years, the building was known as the ABC, Kneedler, and currently, Apex building.

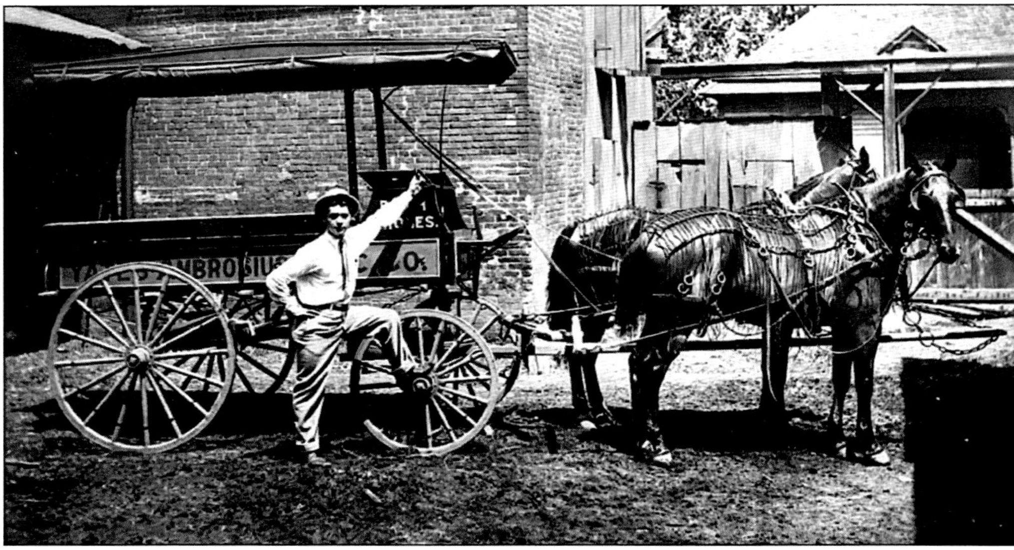

A *c.* 1913 postcard shows the delivery wagon of Yates-Ambrosius Mercantile, which was located on the northwest corner of Main and Morrison streets. It was known as Ambrosius and Son from 1891 to 1907, and by 1912 was Yates and Co. Their slogan was "the big store with the little prices." Bargains in 1911 on sale days were 10 cents for a dozen fresh eggs, 10 cents for a pound of assorted candies, 15 cents for two cans of corn, 25 cents for eleven bars of Busy Bee soap, and 10 cents for a lady's summer vest.

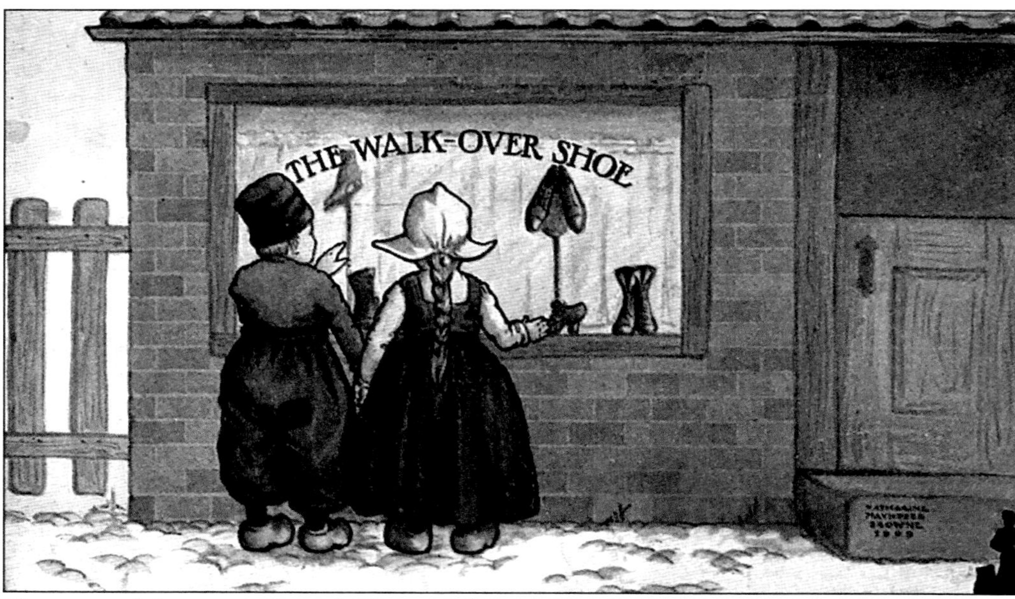

The postcard shown is a Yates-Ambrosius advertisement for Walk-Over shoes. Statements made on the back of the card are "in the forefront of fashion—Walk-Over shoes" and "biggest, best and busiest store in town." One of the newspaper ads of the day mentioned "Hummer Days." It further explains that each child accompanied by a parent will be given a FREE hummer, an interesting toy that will bring a child lots of pleasure.

These advertising postcards were done by Richard Felton Outcault, cartoonist for *Life*, *Judge*, *Truth*, and *New York World*. They are part of a 1906 set of calendar postcards complete with cartoon, verse and slogan personalized for Ambrosius and Son. The characters shown are Buster Brown in the middle, flanked by his sister Mary Jane and Tige.

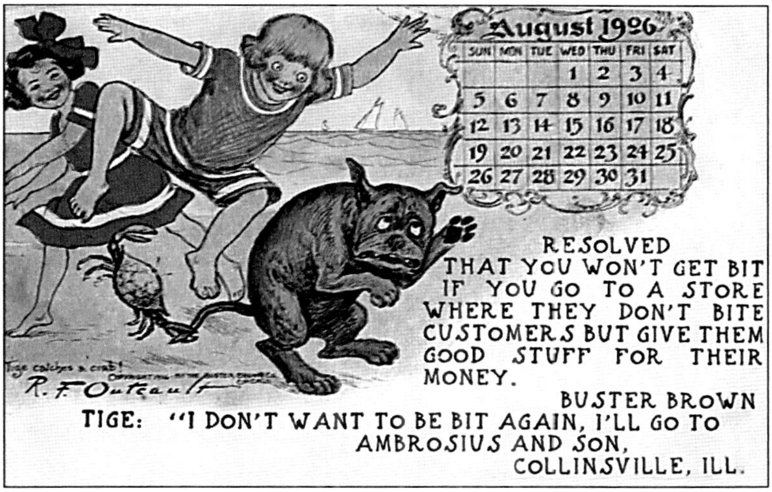

Outcault created Buster Brown in 1902 and used his two children as models for Buster and Mary Jane. The cartoon Buster Brown appeared in newspapers, books, and advertising premiums.

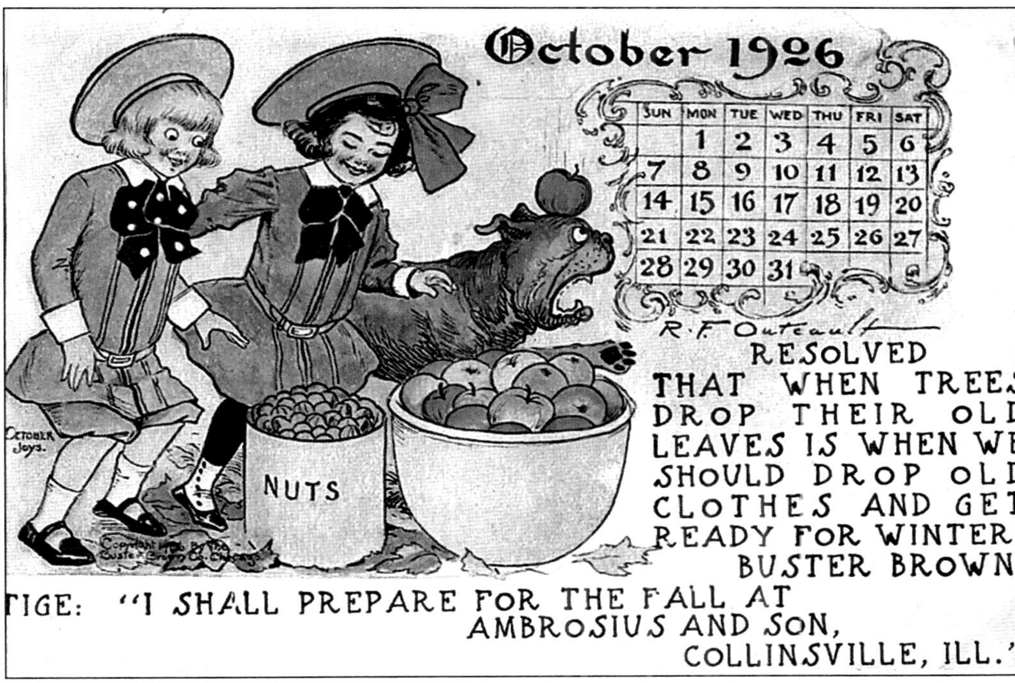

Outcault lived from 1863 to 1928 and was hailed as "father of the modern newspaper supplement." Newspaper tycoon Randolph Hearst hired Outcault away from the magazine companies. As a Hearst employee, Outcault created the series, *Hogan's Alley*. It was the first cartoon printed in color. The series featured a small bald child in a yellow nightshirt. The combination of Hearst's sensational journalism and the flashy Yellow Kid led to the term "yellow journalism." Hearst's Sunday newspapers issued sheets of postcards that readers cut apart and used or collected.

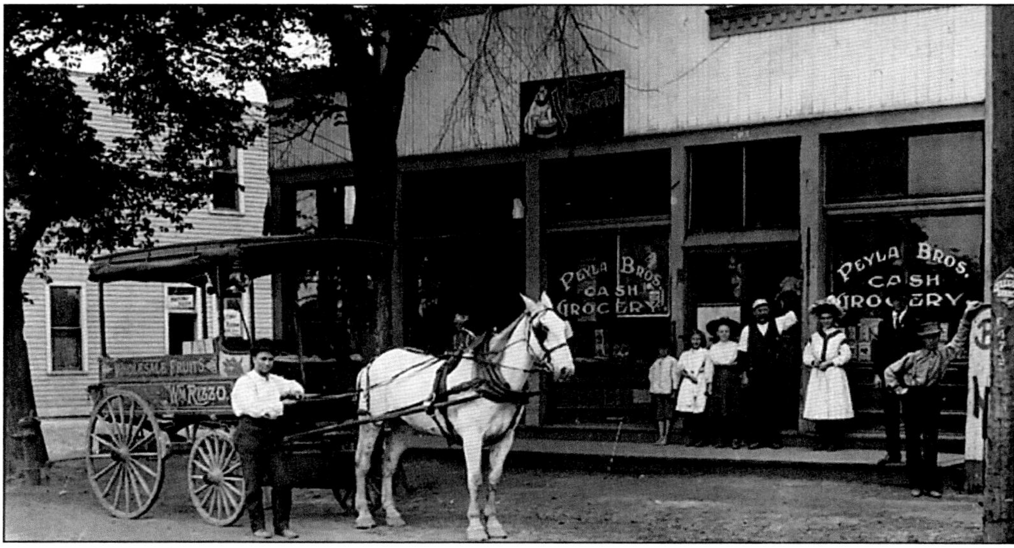

The Peyla Brothers Cash Grocery is shown at 703 Vandalia Street. From a coal mining family, Frank and Dominick ran this business around 1910. The grocery was the second door of the building on the northwest corner of Vandalia and Park streets. By 1916, the Peyla store had become a Star Meat Market branch operated by Henry Dervalis. The wagon in the picture carries the name of Wm. Rizzo, wholesale fruits. The 701 business was a saloon for most of the century; early keepers were Dominick Vercellino in 1911 and Peter Prenitors in 1916.

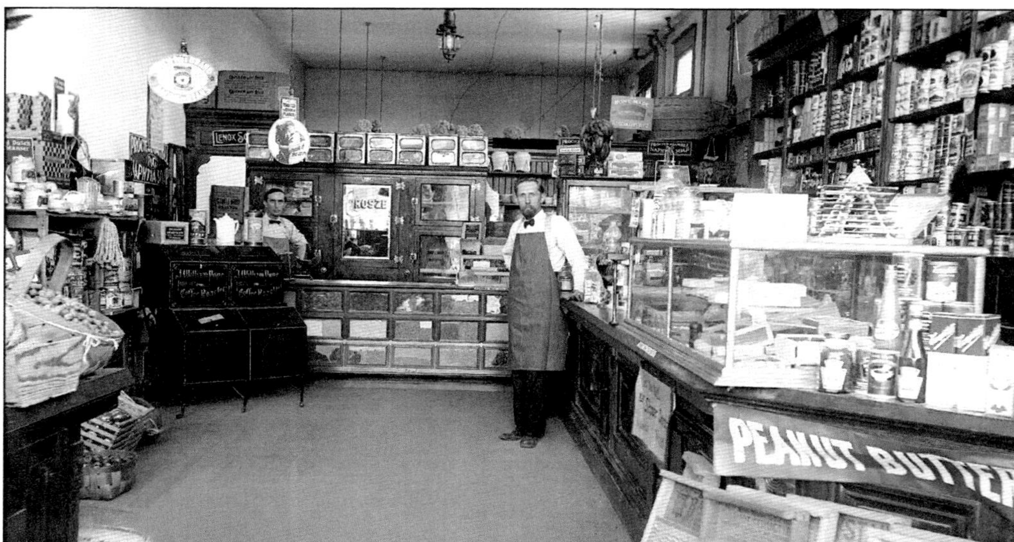

Grosze Bros. Co., self-described as "dealers in fancy and staple groceries," was located at 304 West Main Street. The brothers Martin and Fred were in business from about 1905 to 1915. They advertised their location as being close to the post office which was just around the corner at 105 South Seminary. Signs on the front of the store were "Grosze Bros. Quality Shop, we sell everything good to eat and gasoline for autos." Visible products on the store shelves are National washboards, Lenox soap, Old Dutch cleanser, and Campbell's soup.

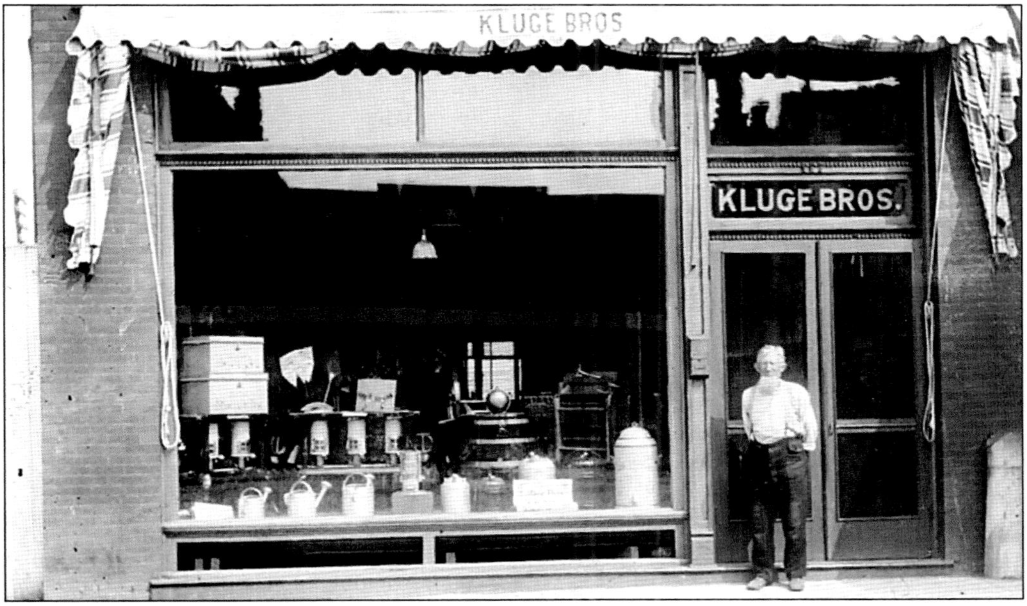

John G. Kluge, one of the pioneers of Collinsville, moved here in 1850. He worked as a coal miner, blacksmith, and carpenter. His sons, Henry and John A., opened Kluge Bros. Hardware Store in 1892. The business was housed at 117 West Main Street for over half a century. They sold hardware, tools, cutlery, stoves, furnaces, tin roofing, guttering, and spouting.

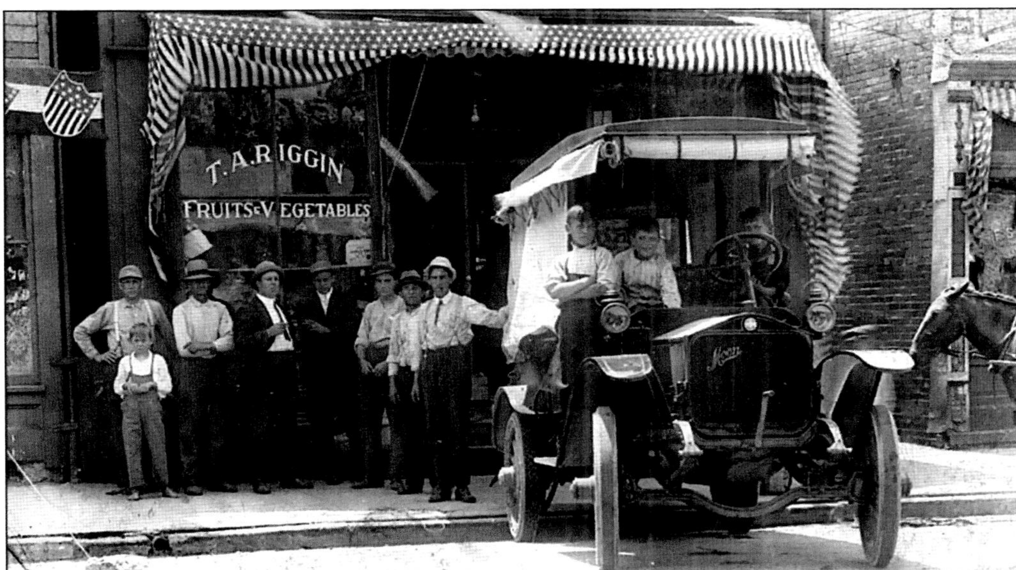

From shortly after the turn of the century until 1938, Thomas A. Riggin ran a grocery store in Collinsville. After two earlier locations, Riggin settled at the 106 East Main spot by 1915. The c. 1912 real photo postcard captures the Moon truck backed up to the door of Riggin's Grocery Store at 102 West Main Street. At this time, the Fred Simon Jewelry Store was one door west, and next to Simon was the J.A. Krite Hardware Store. Lawrence Riggin had a grocery store from 1915 or before until 1936 at 222 West Main.

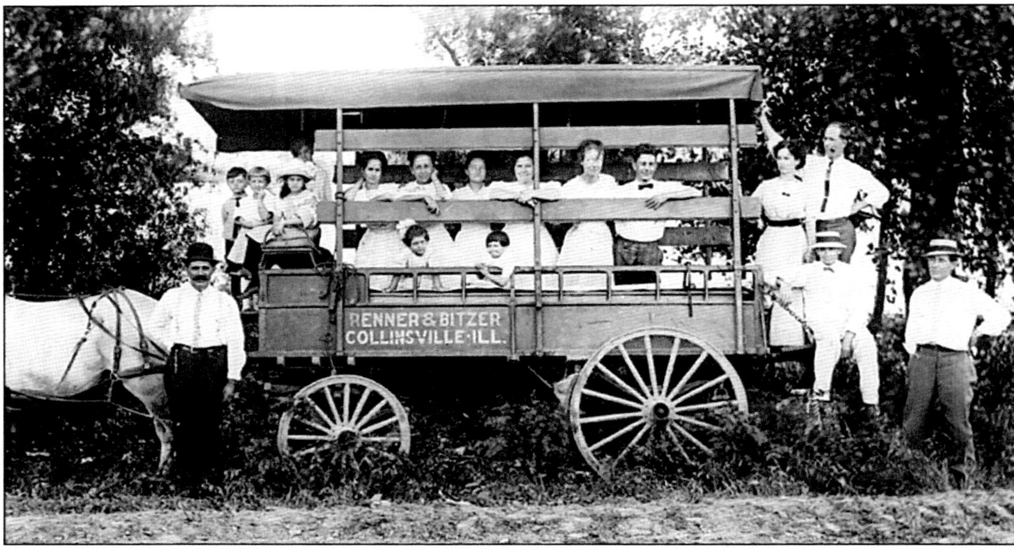

In 1905, Peter Renner and Walter Bitzer left farms near Lebanon, Ill., to start a business in Collinsville. By 1911, they had a livery, feed, and moving business at 118 West Clay. In 1914, the establishment was named Bitzer & Co., and in 1917, they claimed a Dodge franchise. A new brick building was constructed on the southeast corner of Clay and Clinton in 1926. By 1972, the business was named Bitzer-Croft, and by 1980, the dealership, now Dave Croft Motors, Inc., was moved to the present location on Route 157.

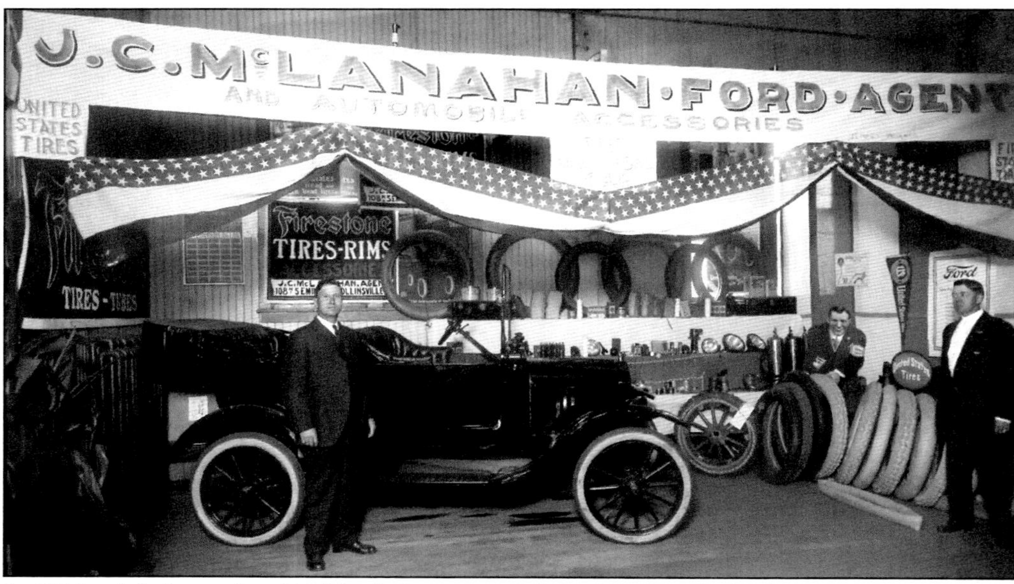

In 1911, while located at 108 North Seminary, J.C. McLanahan had a livery, moving, and coal business. J.C. also moved houses. This photograph of the McLanahan Ford Agency showroom was taken about 1915. In the mid-1920s, McLanahan also sold Fordsons (Ford tractors) at 306 West Main. At one time, there were 70 people working in the business. In the 1950s, Bob, son of J.C., had a Studebaker franchise. Jeff Stehman, grandson of J.C., now owns an automotive and towing business at 105 South Seminary.

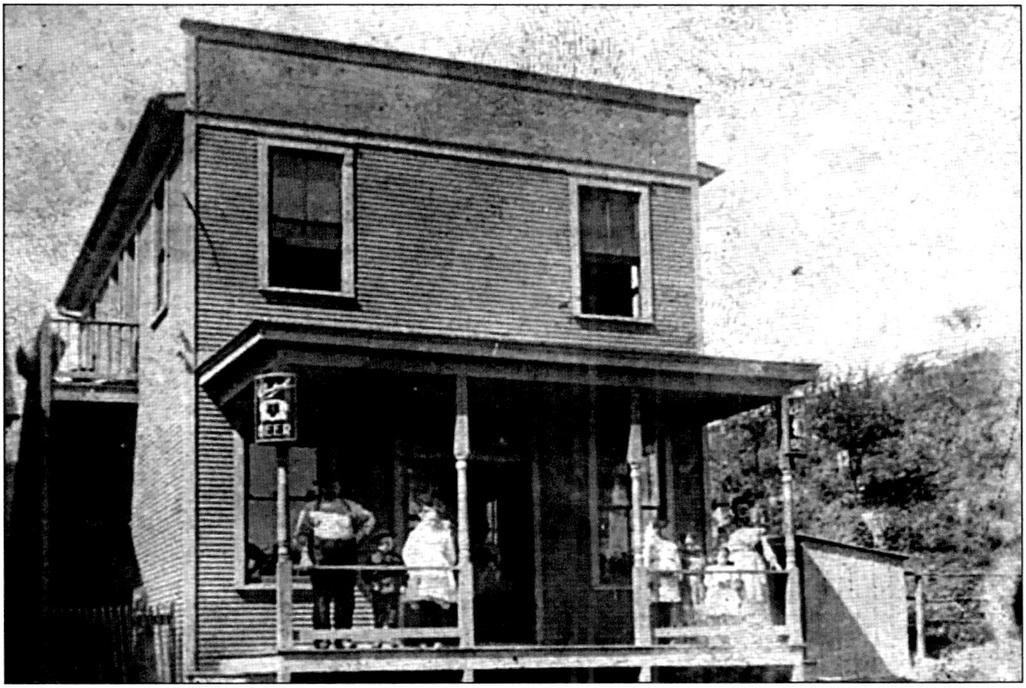

This tavern was owned and operated by Richard Froehrich from about 1905 to 1912. It was located on Lebanon Road. The business was just west of Lumaghi Heights. Froehrich and his family lived upstairs. (Courtesy Floyd and Bernice Sperino.)

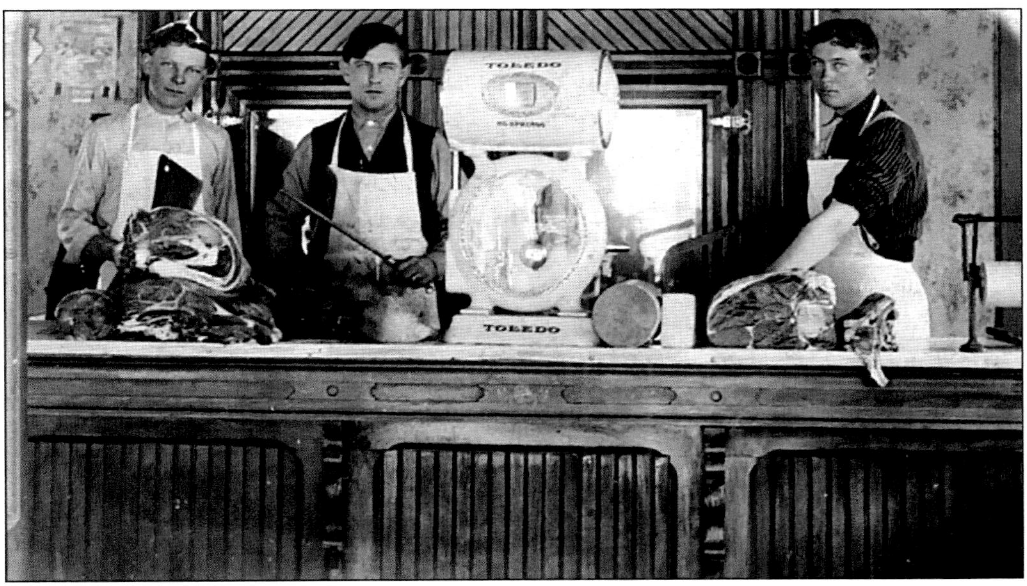

The Albrecht Meat Market was in business at 112 East Main Street *c.* 1908 to 1913. Ben Behle, son of Christian and Elizabeth Behle, is pictured behind the counter on the left. The other men are the Albrecht brothers. A few years after this picture was taken, Earnest Albrecht was listed in the 1916 Collinsville Business Directory as a Prudential Insurance agent.

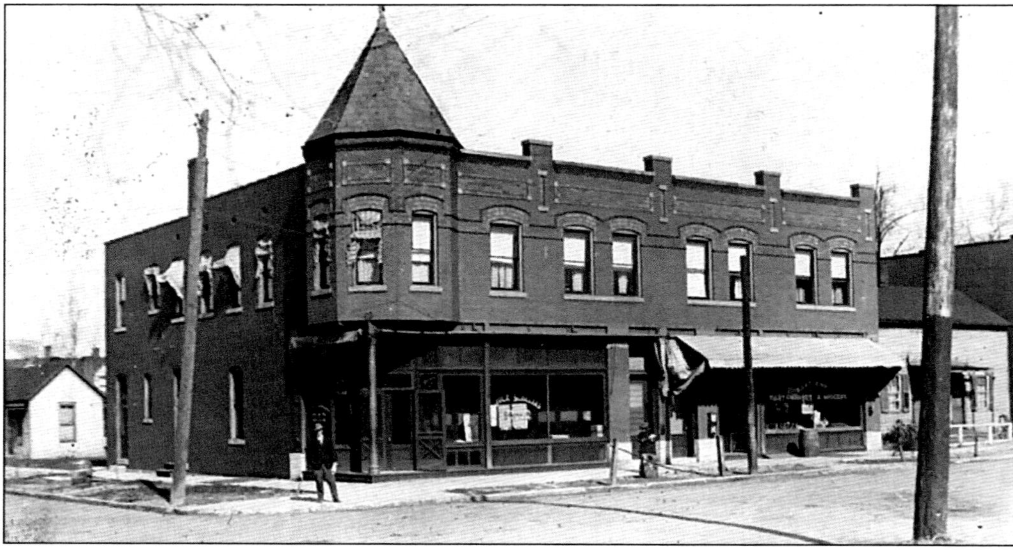

A saloon and grocery store have been the occupants of this building on the northeast corner of Main and Chestnut for nearly a century. In 1903, Charles Gindler opened the East End Market that included delivery wagons and a "refrigeration plant." Collinsville Packing Co., a butcher shop and grocery, run by Frank and Joe Patek, was located here for 18 years at a later date. This picture shows the 1911 Jule Schiller Saloon. A long-time occupant was the East End Tavern operated by Tony Villioco. The turret is no longer on the remodeled building.

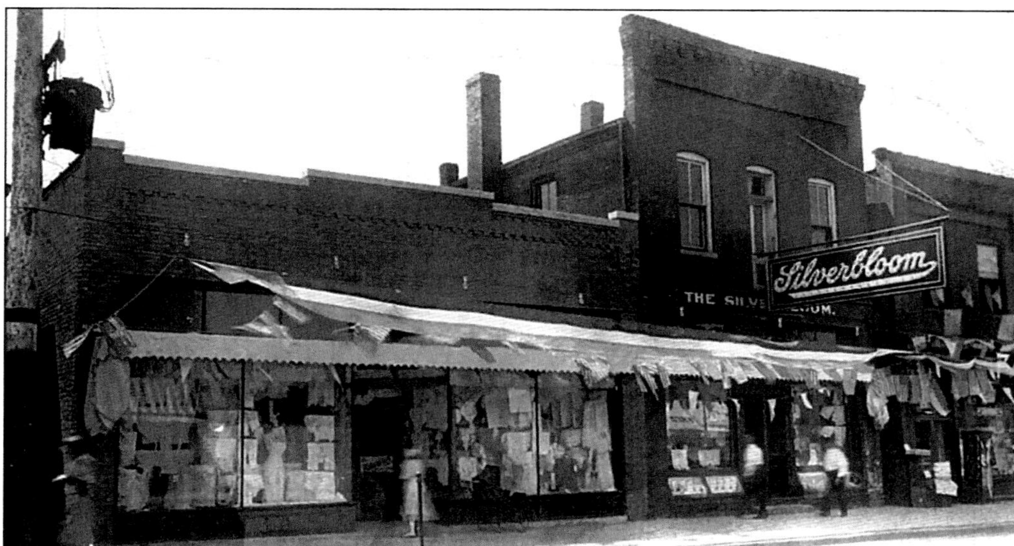

The Silverbloom at 118 West Main was opened by Louis Blumberg who was born and educated in St. Louis. Earlier Blumberg worked for Silverburg Co. of St. Louis. The name "The Silverbloom Dry Goods" became simply "Silverbloom." Its motto was "the house of quality." Throughout the years, William, brother of Louis, assisted with the running of the business. After being in business for 40 years, this store and five other Blumberg stores in the area were sold to P.N. Hirsch Co. in 1947.

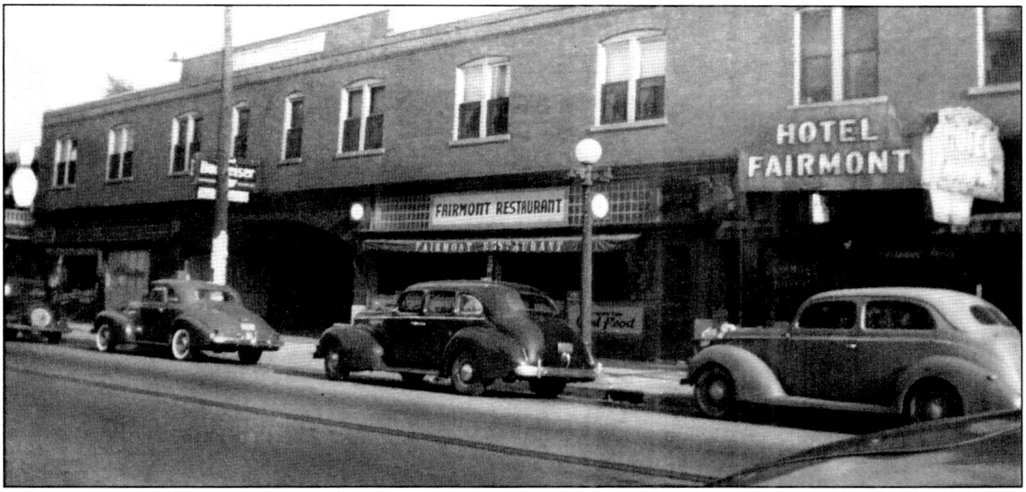

The three-story, 50 room Fairmont Hotel was located at 326 West Main Street. In the early 1920s, Ike Schwartz, the original owner, had the edifice constructed using an arcade concept. It housed a hotel, restaurant, and shopping mall. Eventually the shops were transformed into Arcade Ballroom that included a bar and dining room. The building also contained a 10 lane bowling alley. After the building was vacant in 1983, it was torched by two young men. There were 58 firemen from several neighboring fire districts at the blaze; four firemen were injured.

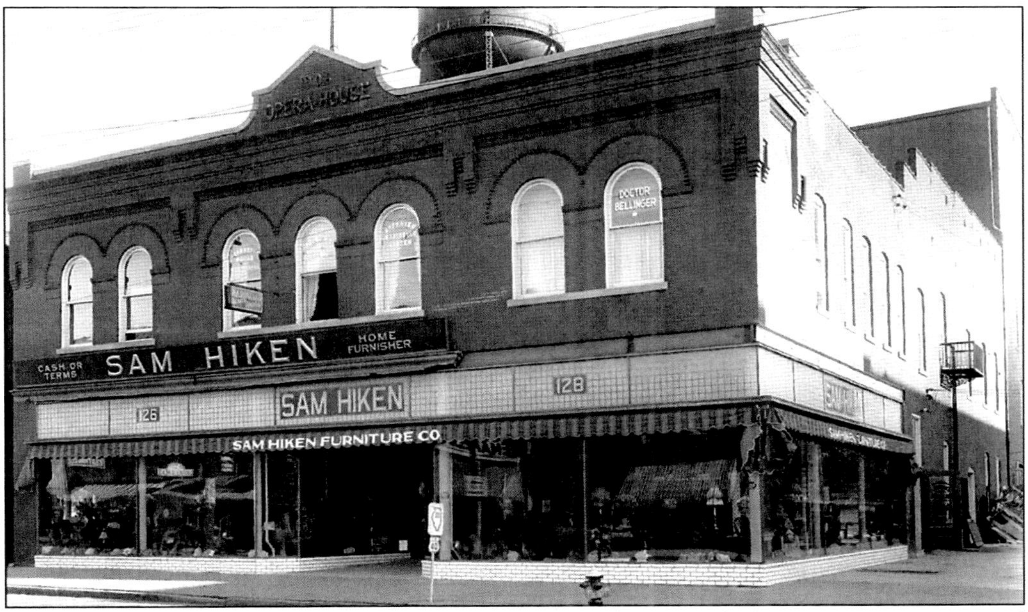

The Sam Hiken Furniture Co. on the southeast corner of Main and Clinton Streets, is pictured in the 1906-constructed Opera House. This store was in business from 1916 to about 1930. The Opera House had been the town meeting place for entertainment before Miners Theatre was built in 1918. There were two other Hiken family furniture stores in Collinsville. Sam and Harry bought out Cicero Ogle in 1912. This store, Hiken Brothers, was in the 100 block of West Clay until 1926 and moved to 205 West Main where it operated until 1972. Sam's son Leo had a furniture store from 1945 to 1968 located at 109 East Main Street.

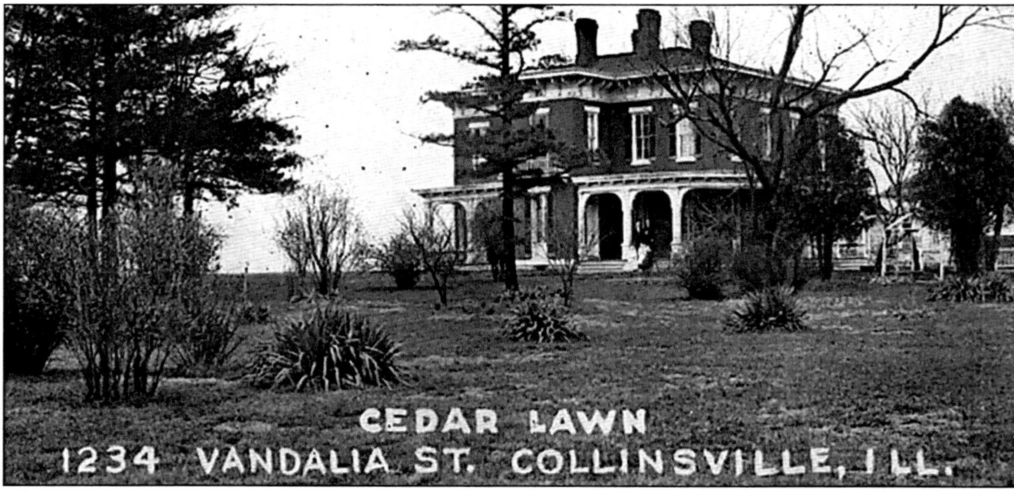

This residence at 1234 Vandalia Street was built as Judge Daniel Dove Collins' third home in Collinsville. It is not clear whether or not he was related to the original town founders of the same name. Collins was the first president of the Village Board and organized the Collinsville Plank Road Company. For a year or two around 1935, the Collins' house was transformed to Cedar Lawn Tourist Camp and was under the supervision of Florine Bowker. D.D. Collins was Florine's maternal grandfather. At various times, Mrs. Bowker taught school, assisted her husband with his paint and wallpaper store on Main Street, sponsored the Baraca class at the Presbyterian Church, and was the organist there.

Greetings from

Cedar Lawn

Cheery Atmosphere—Good Food—Good Beds

Recreations: Rest and Be at Home. Garage, Saddle Horse Accommodations

---

RATES: ROOM AND BOARD

Per Couple Monthly, $100—Single $65
Per Couple Weekly, $35—Single $20
Transient with Breakfast, double $3.50
Transient with Breakfast, single $2.25
Meals A-La-Carte or American Plan
CHICKEN DINNERS — 85 CENTS

Parties and Private Dinners Given Special Attention. Under Personal Supervision of

FLORINE E. BOWKER

FOR RESERVATIONS CALL MAIN 503

Slogan: Smile, Bless You Smile

For a number of years before Cedar Lawn was in business, Mark Henson, Florine's father, owned the Collins' home. At one point Henson, a teacher, had been Mayor of Granite City and later Madison County Superintendent of Schools. The rooms in this house constructed about 1875, were 18 feet square and 14 feet high; the bricks were made on site. The building stands today and is the VFW Home. It was purchased by the organization in about 1948. It is now a one-story structure containing a bar, meeting room, and community hall.

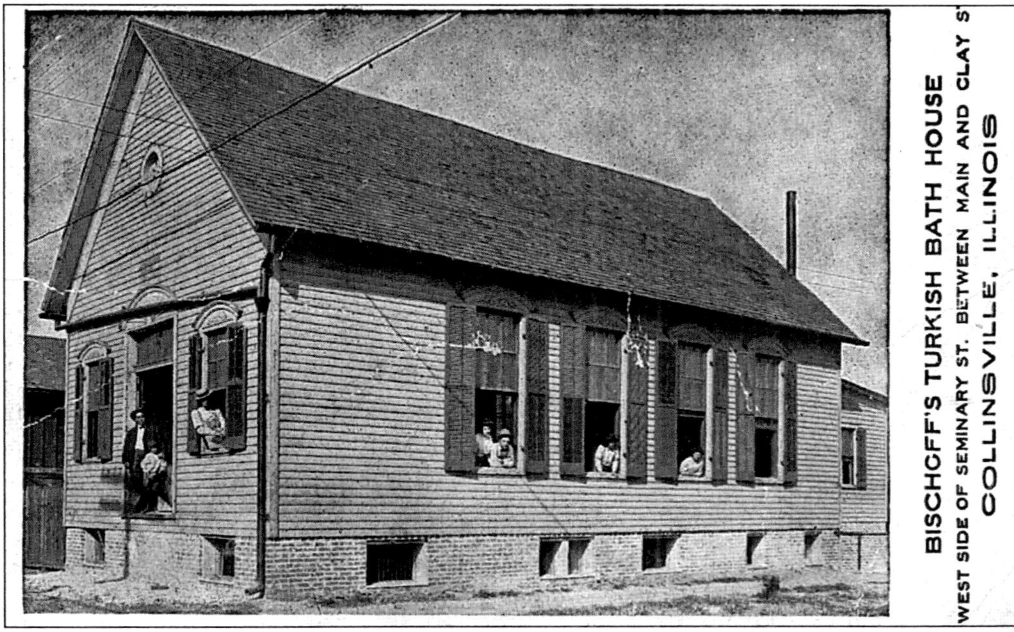

The building shown was the German Evangelical St. John's Church from 1895 until 1907. It was moved from the north side of Clay Street near Seminary to the west side of Seminary between Main and Clay. It had become Bischoff's Turkish Bath House and Bottling Works. Bischoff's soda had been popular for years and carried the motto, "not how cheap but how good." The Theodale Milling Co. was located here from the mid-1920s to the mid-1950s. The structure no longer stands.

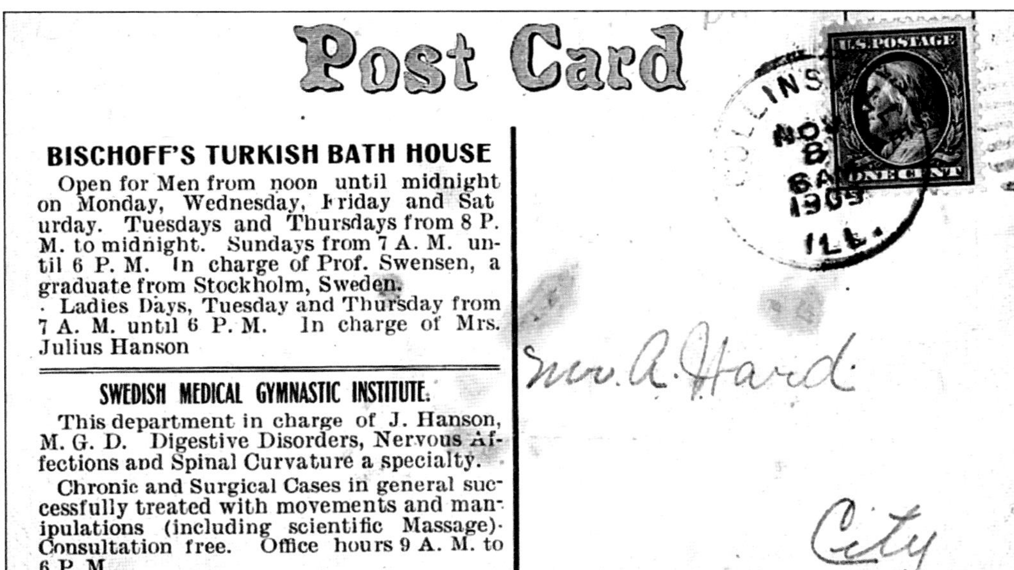

In addition to the interesting images on the front, the backs of the postcards on page 62 and 63 provide useful information as well. Postcard collectors scrutinize the following areas on the back of the card to enhance their knowledge: advertising, cancellation, postmark, address, message, return address, date written, and even the script and signature.

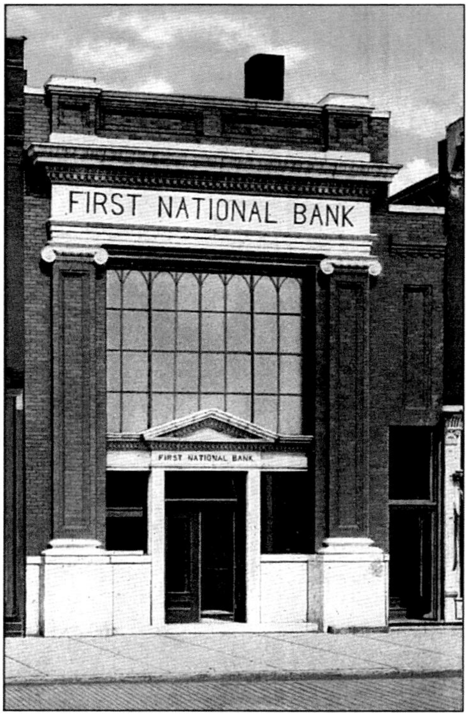

In 1886, James I. Dilliard, father of now-deceased Irving Dilliard, helped organize the Bank of Collinsville, a privately operated bank, for Belt Brothers Company. Dilliard also became the manager of the bank at 123 East Main Street. William Fletcher, father of baseball great Arthur Fletcher, was an organizer and president of the First National Bank of Collinsville. It was chartered in 1902 and immediately acquired the assets of the Bank of Collinsville. The new bank took the same location as its predecessor, and in 1916, the building was completely remodeled.

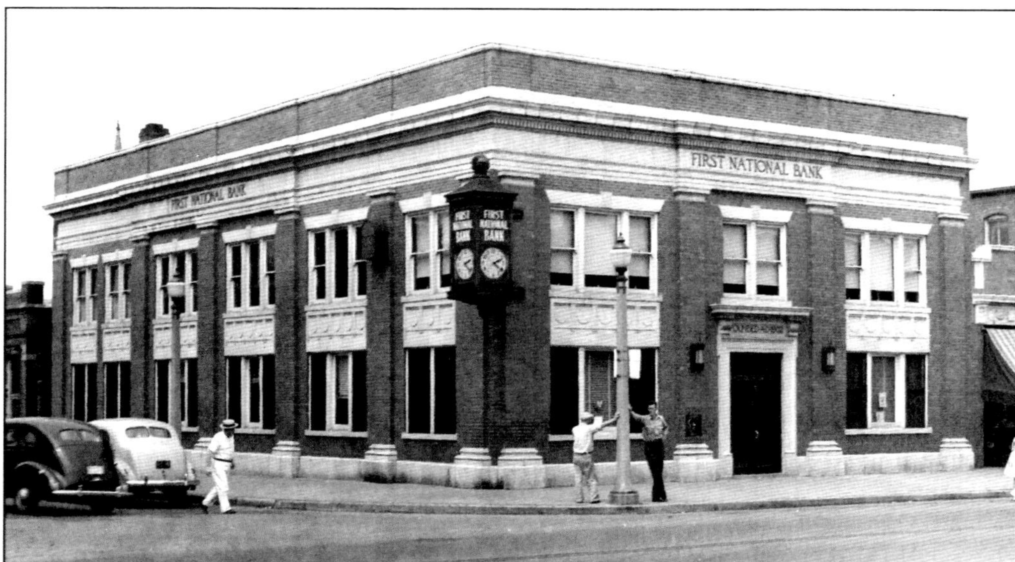

The bank pictured at the current location, 201 East Main, was constructed in 1929 and was extensively remodeled in the late 1960s. Since 1987, the name of the bank has been the United Missouri Bank (UMB). In 1936, Homer Butterfield opened a jewelry store at 205 East Main, the location that Anne Kaveny's Mary Ann Shop had vacated. In 1954, he purchased the former bank building, shown at the top of the page, to house his business. The building remains and business continues as son Jack and his family operate Butterfield Jewelers here. (Courtesy UMB.)

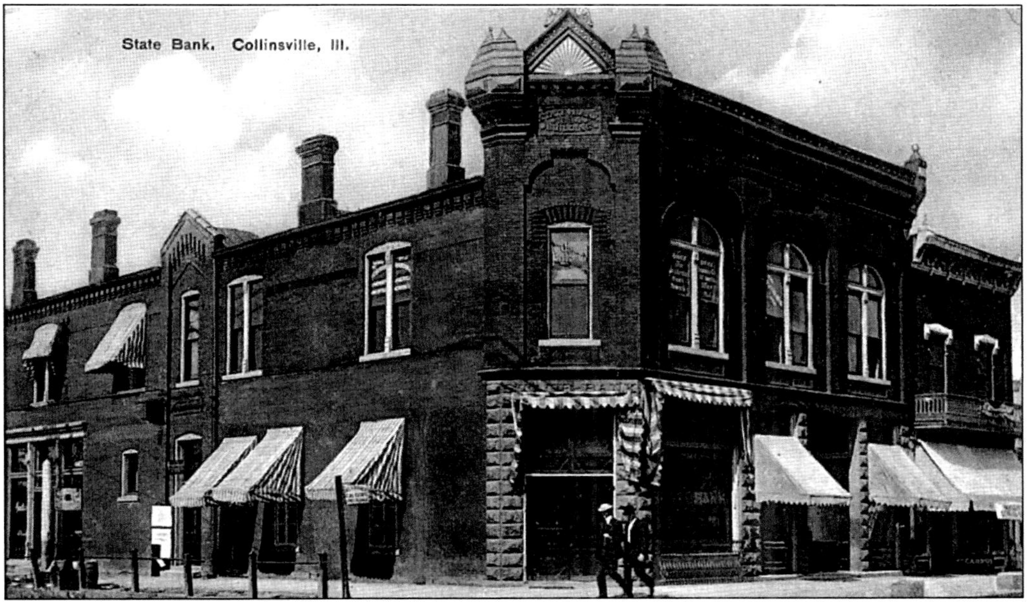

Chartered in 1891, the State Bank was the first publicly owned and state supervised local bank. The bank pictured was situated on the northeast corner of Main and Center streets and featured Victorian architecture including an imposing tower and elaborate cornices. Wilbur C. Hadley helped organize the bank and became its president; he remained there for 30 years. The telephone exchange was on the second floor. After the bank moved, Fredman Brothers Furniture was located here for several years. In 1933, a fire gutted the building. The Will Rogers Theatre, Teen Town Youth Center, Jere's, Glik's, and Isle of U are businesses that followed in this location.

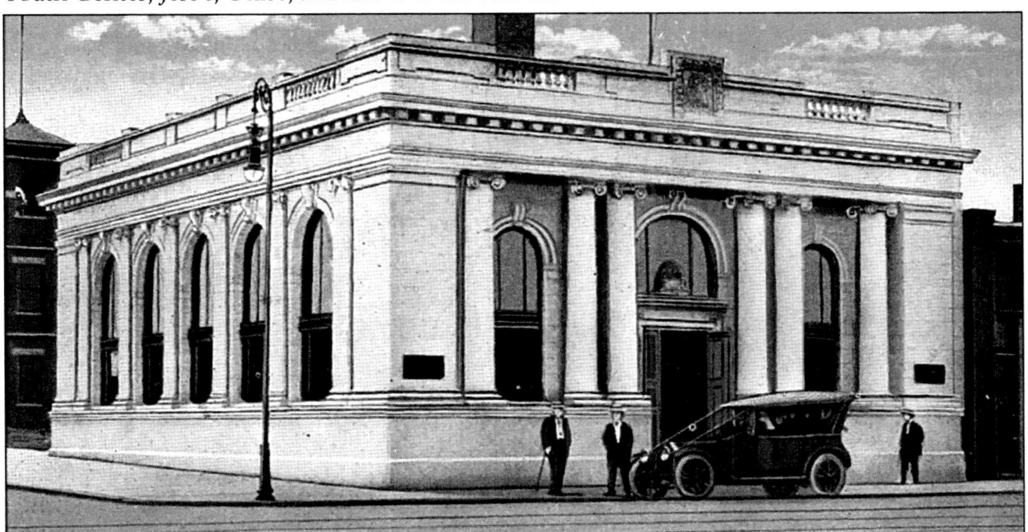

In 1916, the State Bank of Collinsville was moved into the facility pictured on the southwest corner of Main and Center. This edifice has limestone exterior walls and marble interior walls. The architect of the building was Robert G. Kirsch who also designed Miners Institute and the Madison County Courthouse. The bank had been renamed United Illinois Bank, Central Bank, and most recently US Bank; however, the building is vacant at this time.

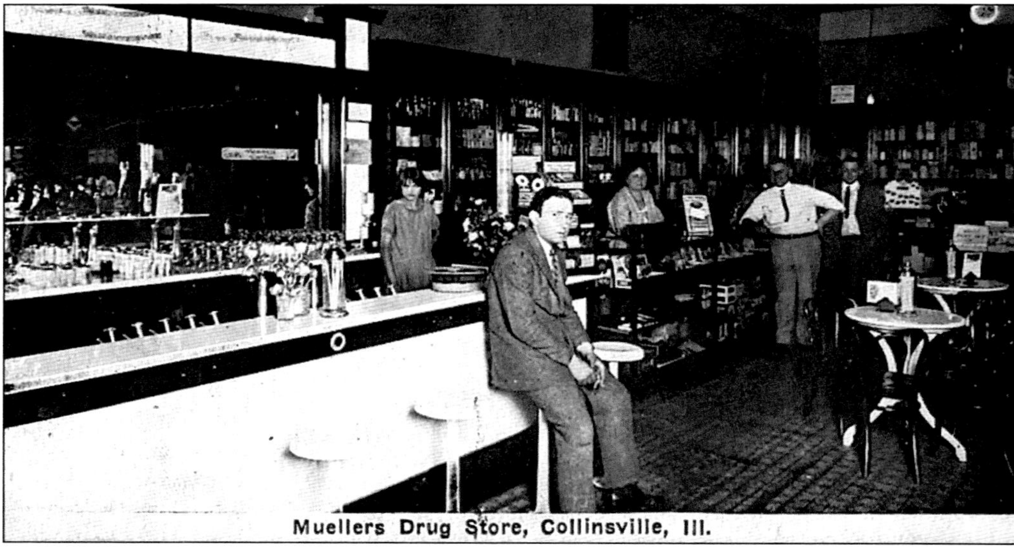

Christ Mueller initially operated a drug store at 206 West Main Street. According to Lucille Stehman in her book about Collinsville, he sent postcards announcing the April 15, 1911 opening of his soda fountain. Mueller had moved to the southwest corner of Main and Seminary by 1916. In about 1922, he relocated to 100 East Main where the store remained until 1937. Pete Schmacker and his confectionery followed Mueller to the 300 West Main location. Ostle-Campbell purchased the 100 East Main business in the mid-1930s.

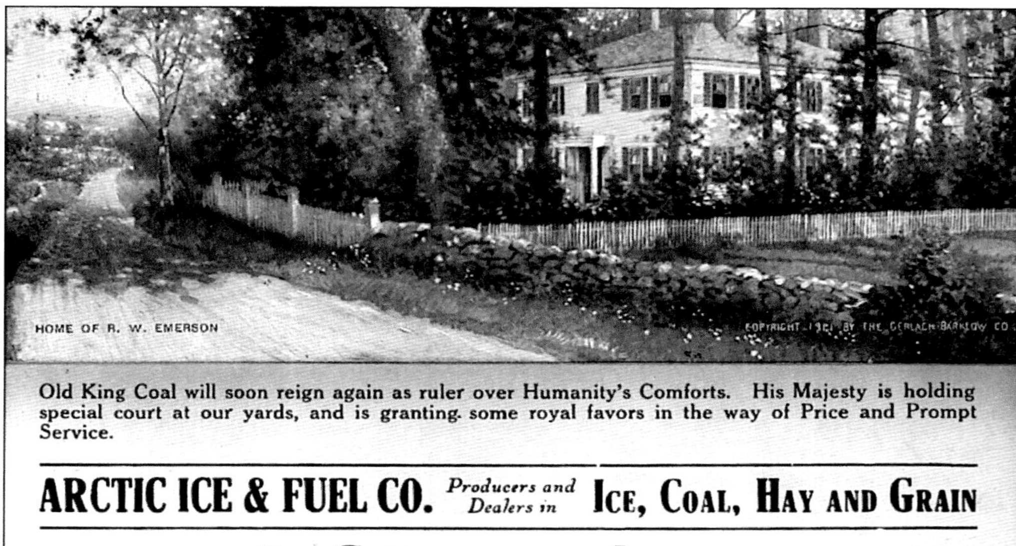

In 1903, the Abbey Coal and Mining Co. was formed. It became the Abbey Coal Co. in 1911. The Long Coal, Ice & Refrigeration Co. was established in 1907. Jesse Long was the president of both companies, and in 1912, was selling ice and coal under the name of Artic Ice and Fuel. The firm, considered one of the largest and most complete ice plants in Southern Illinois, also featured cold storage. In the early years the retail office of Artic was located at 103 West Main, and the ice was manufactured at 609 South Clinton.

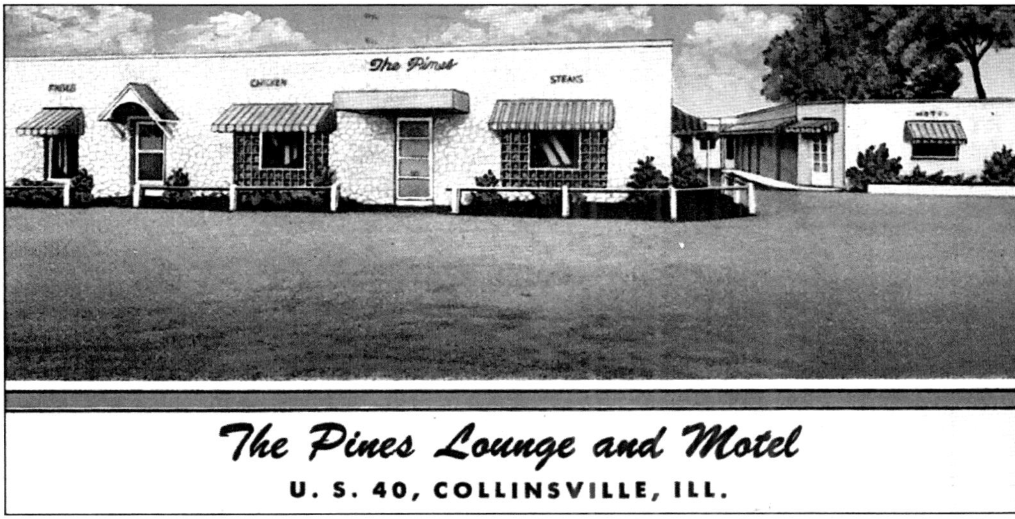

The Pines Lounge and Motel was located on Cuba Lane (Route 40) when it opened in about 1948. Today the lounge is L.J. Ducks and the address is listed as 416 Belt Line Road. Pleasant Street is on the west side of the lounge where the motel stood until 1978. This postcard is a bright and colorful linen. Linen postcards are a domestic creation; the paper stock has a rough or textured finish to the touch and looks woven. They were common in the 1940s and 1950s. The colors appear gaudy, at worst, bright and art deco-like, at best, because of the manner in which the dyes adhere to the paper stock.

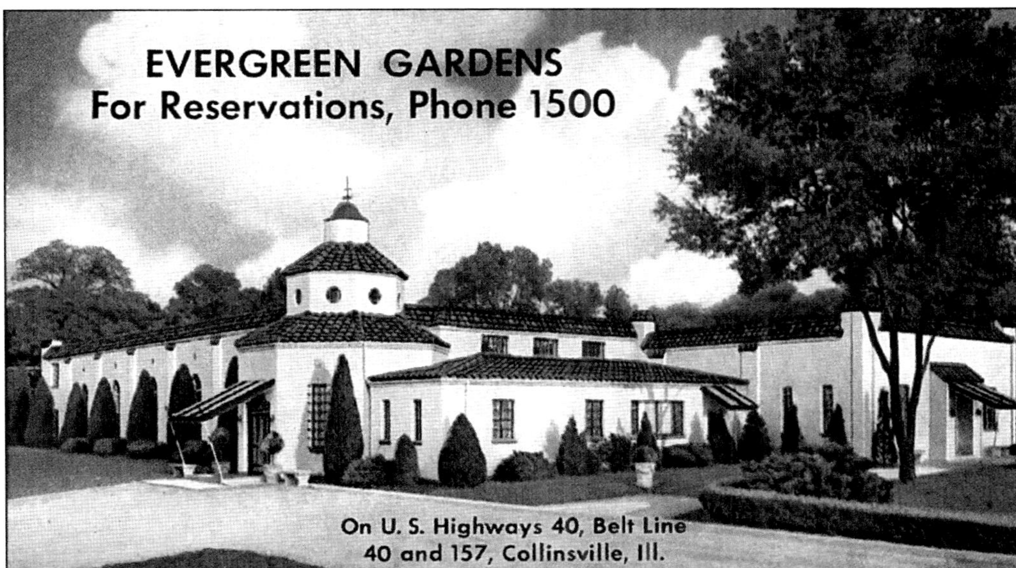

The Evergreen Gardens Restaurant and Night Club was located at the foot of the bluffs at 1701 St. Louis Road. On the back of this picture postcard, management proclaimed this establishment was the largest and finest nightclub in the Midwest. This 1940s cabaret had nationally known entertainers and in 1948-49 was named Katsina's Evergreen Café. In the 1950s, it was used as an office for G.S. Suppiger. Over 40 years ago the building was converted to the First Church of the Nazarene. The building rests on the area that was once a depot for the interurban cars.

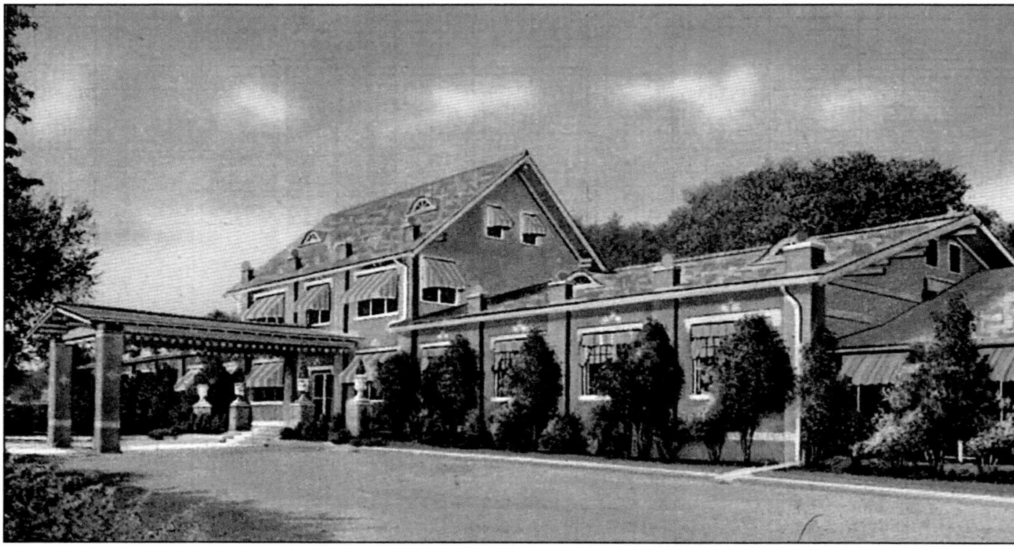

The images on these two pages are from a postal folder advertising the Mounds Country Club in the late 1940s. The Mounds Country Club and Garden was located on Highway 40 (8011 Collinsville Road) just east of Monks Mound. The two-story center section of the Mounds Club was an inn and part of Schmidt's Mound Park before the turn of the century and into the 1920s. After additions and refurbishing, the club opened as a dining, dancing, and gambling venue.

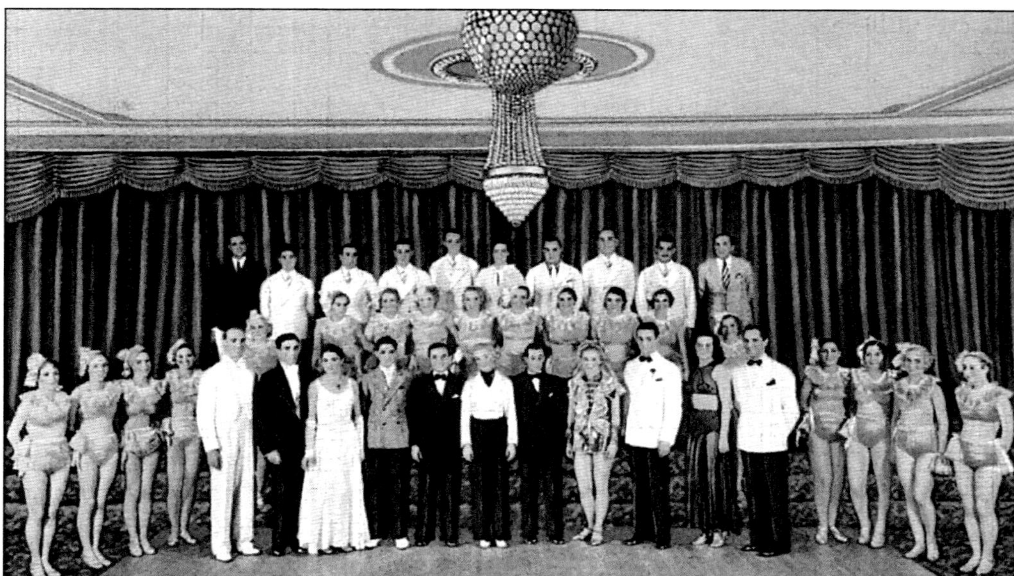

The lavishly furnished emporium premiered with a flourish on April 6, 1929, to 300 hand-picked guests who had received engraved invitations. Many arrived in chauffeured limos. They were greeted by parking and checkroom attendants, plus doormen in full dress. Crystal chandeliers and gilt frame mirrors adorned the east wing that was for dining, dancing, and cabaret entertainment. The west wing was the casino that had ankle deep carpets, terra cotta walls, mahogany gambling tables, and slot machines. Employees consisted of a rogue's gallery of underworld figures.

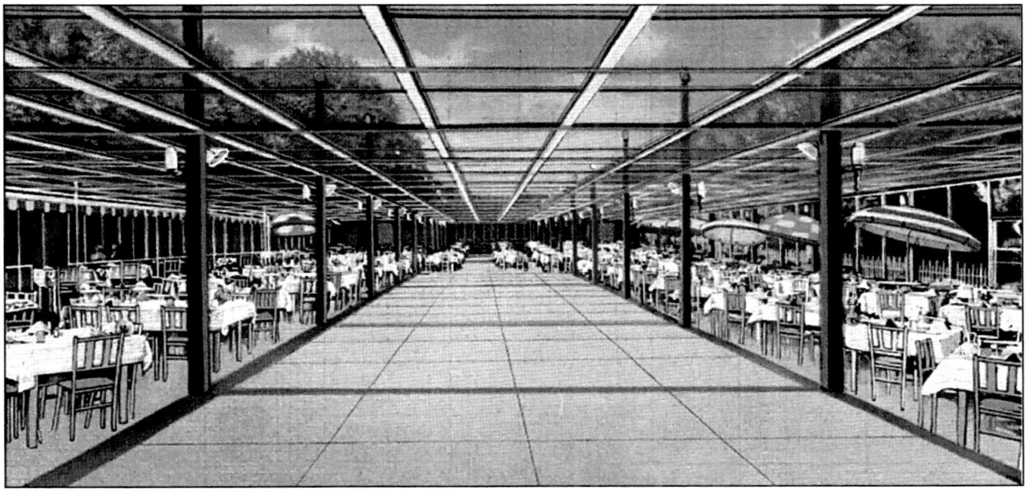

The original owners were Harry Murdock, a twice-convicted bootlegger who was later convicted for income tax evasion, Frank Waller, a known East St. Louis bookmaker, and William (Bow-wow) McQuillan, an East Side gangster who was later arrested on a narcotics charge. Frank "Buster" Wortman was thought to be the controlling partner during much of the club's existence. According to Virginia Irwin of the *St. Louis Post-Dispatch*, "It was considered the most elaborate and wide open gambling house south of Chicago. It was patronized by society figures, businessmen, members of the racetrack fraternity, prosperous bootleggers, and the cream of the East Side underworld."

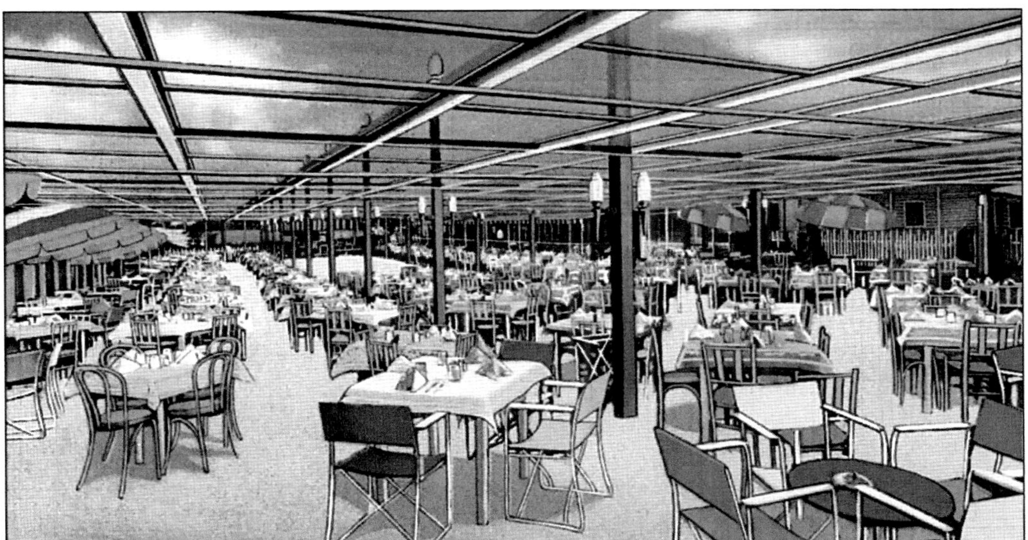

Entertainment included well-known figures like Sophie Tucker and Rudy Vallee. This advertising postcard folder from the later years emphasized that the food and entertainment were under the supervision of Jack Langer, and that the establishment could accommodate 2500 people. After the Mounds Club closed the final time in the mid-1950s, the building became the office for the Grandpa's Discount Store that had been constructed next to it. In 1958, it was razed to make room for a parking lot for the store.

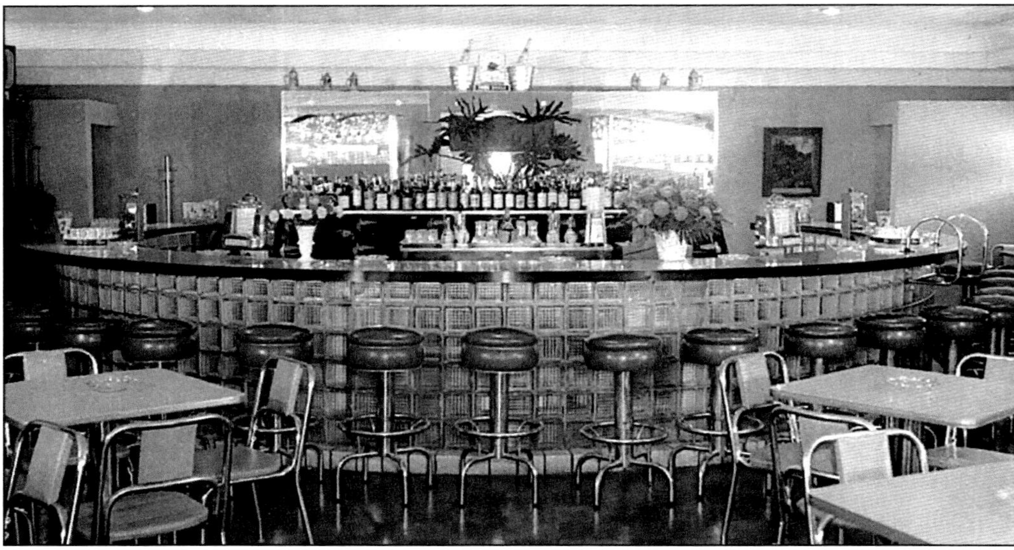

This establishment opened in about 1947 as Circle Cafe and Tap Room and was operated by H. Maack, and then Everett Beckman. The chrome finish postcard captures the interior of Saggio's Tap Room and Dining Room at 410 St. Louis Road as it appeared in the mid-1950s. John Saggio operated this bistro from 1953 to about 1959. The lounge, one of Collinsville's busiest, remains as Horseshoe Sports Bar. This building, along with other businesses and homes, stands on the site that was Abbey No. 1/Hardscrabble Coal Mine from 1904 to 1938.

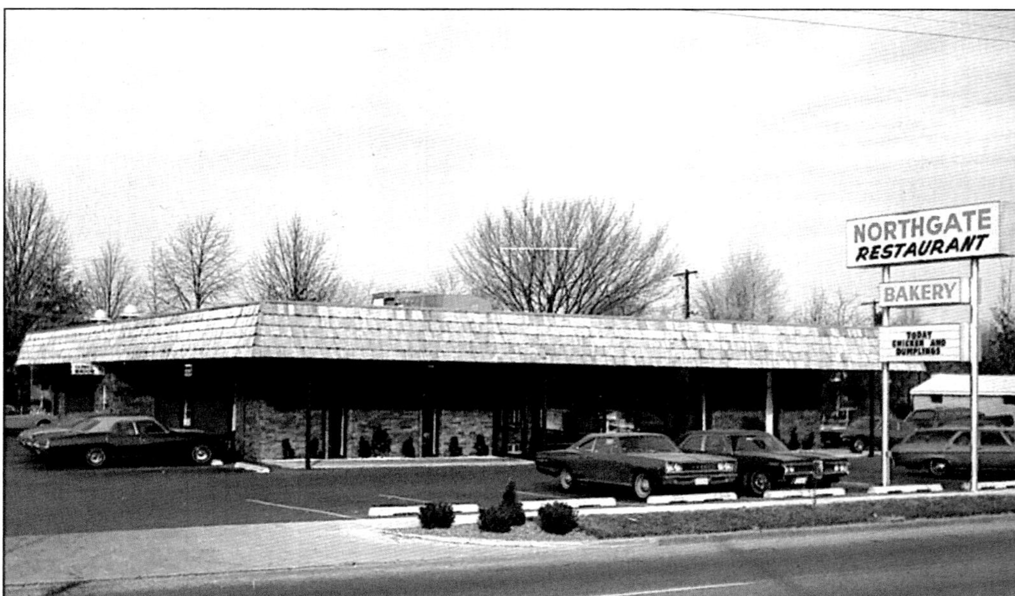

Northgate Restaurant is pictured as it appeared in 1973 in a new building at 1497 Vandalia Street. In about 1952, Leo Case opened Case's Northgate Drive-In across the street at 1492 Vandalia. A short time later the name changed to Palm's Northgate Restaurant. Jimmie's Restaurant, June's Northgate Restaurant, Mane Attraction Hair Studio, Collinsville Discount Furniture, and Northgate Small Animal Hospital (since 1996) have been more recent occupants.

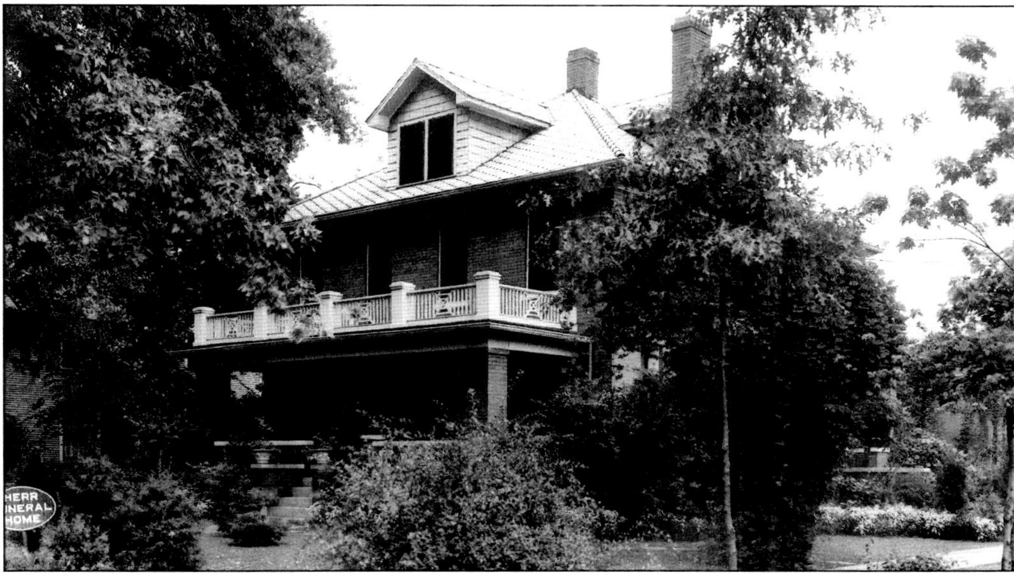

The Herr family has been in the funeral business for five generations. In 1914, V.A. Herr Sr. moved to Collinsville to assist funeral director John E. Schroeppel. In 1916, he became the owner of the business that was located at 118 North Morrison. A few years later, he moved to 300 East Main. In 1928, the house shown was purchased from Peter Grieve Jr. to become the site of Herr Funeral Home which remains today, though remodeled and expanded numerous times.

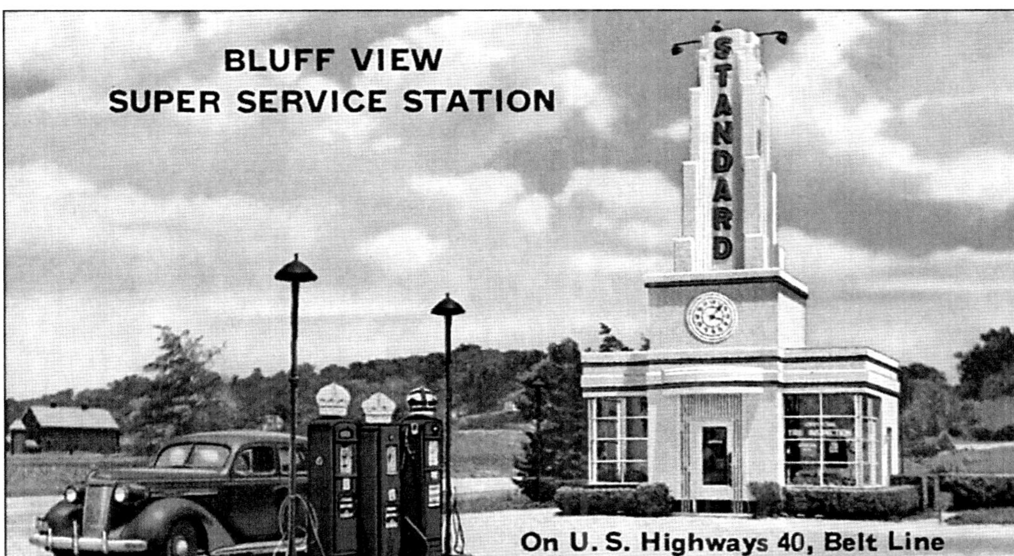

Bluff View Standard Service Station is pictured as it appeared in the mid-1940s. It was located at the busy intersection of Collinsville Road (U.S. Routes 40 and 66) and Bluff Road (Route 157). Louis Kropp operated the station from about 1945 to 1950. "Best transient service in the Middle-west, including quick lunch and clean restrooms" was advertised on the back of this vividly colored postcard. Ramon's Eldorado Restaurant has been at this 1711 St. Louis Road location since 1974.

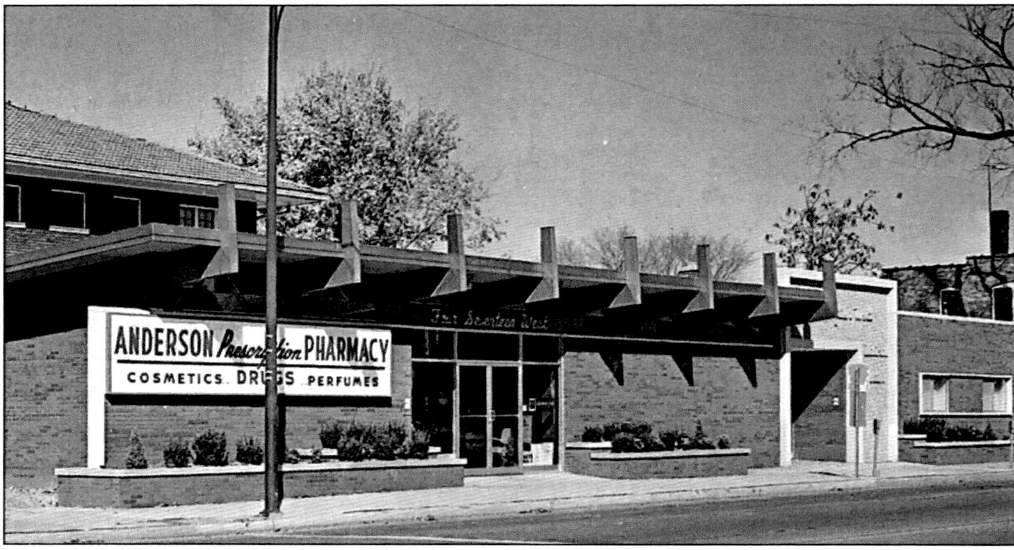

In 1903, Henry Schoettle opened a drug store at 105 East Main Street. It was purchased in 1922 by Kurt Wendler; in 1927 Wendler moved the business to 131 West Main. In 1935, he moved across the street to the Opera House building at 128 West Main; the store was completely destroyed by fire in 1945. He reopened at 114 North Morrison and Bernie Evers worked with him as an apprentice in 1946. C.W. Anderson purchased the pharmacy in 1950, and in 1964, he moved to 417 West Main. It became Evers Pharmacy in about 1975 and remains in business.

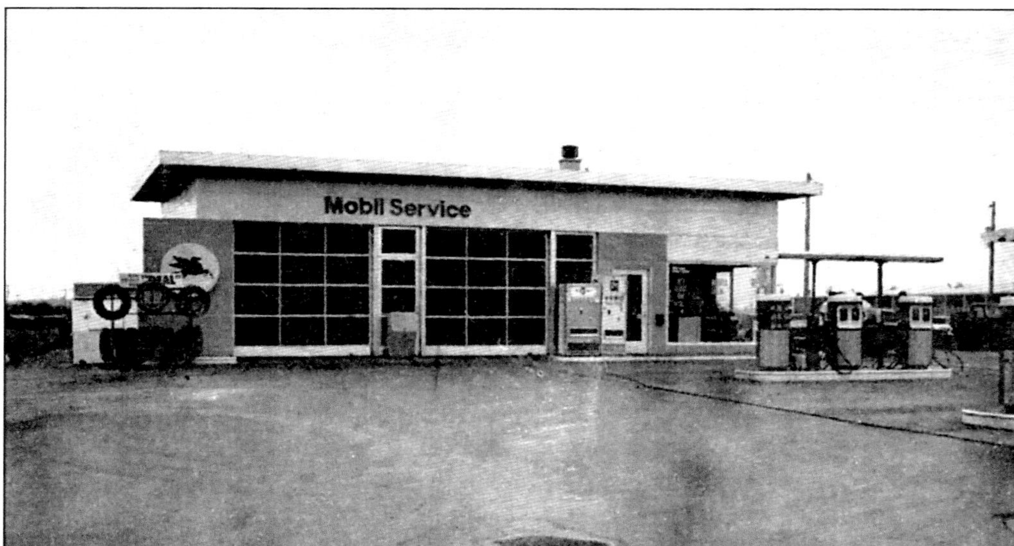

John's Mobil Service Center at 2000 Vandalia Street was at this location from 1972 to 1976. John Finley, who previously had a station at 299 North Bluff, was the proprietor of the business that solicited these services on the postcard shown: "towing, brake work, oil change, muffler and shocks and complete 'SUN' tune-up." Al Tognarelli followed Finley as the proprietor of the station that became known as Al's Mobil Service. Today the business is Megeyese's Service Center, a Citco station.

In about 1911, this postcard was used for advertising to display samples of wallpaper. Henry Volk and William Ackermann, painters and paperhangers, began their business in 1892 at 313 West Main Street. They carried a full line of wallpaper, paints, oils, and glass. After the death of Ackermann, Volk ran the business until his retirement. Then ownership was taken over by William Ackermann's son, Henry. He remained in business until the early 1960s.

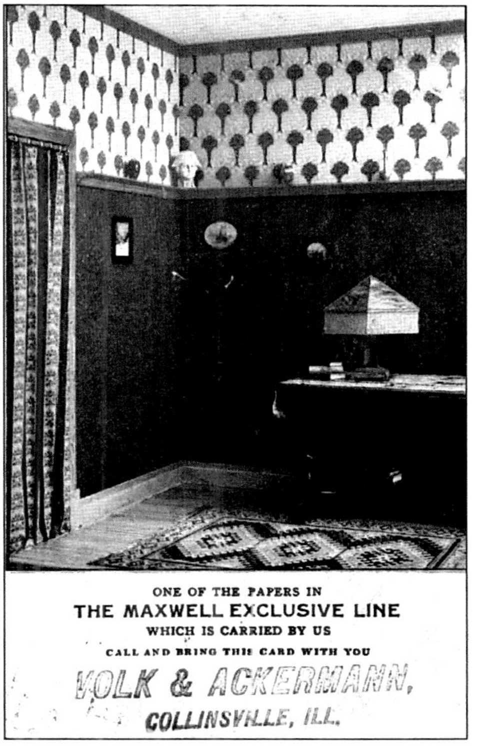

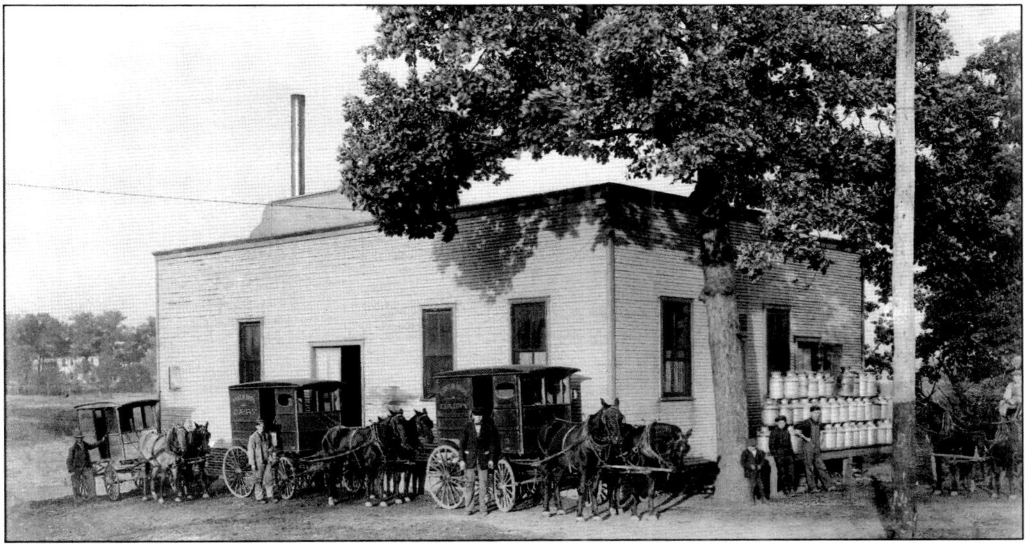

The Luker Bros. Dairy was on the northeast corner of Spring and Summer Streets. The brothers, Rudolph and Martin, were in business from about 1912 to 1915. In 1915, Rudolph sold out to Henry Bantz as did Martin a year later. In 1923–24, Collinsville Home Dairy was at this location. It later moved to 107 South Chestnut and became East End Dairy. Also at this location from 1930 to 1952, Louis Johann had a food processing plant. At different times tomatoes, nuts, squab (pigeon), and dog food were canned here. (Courtesy Ralph and Marian Haury.)

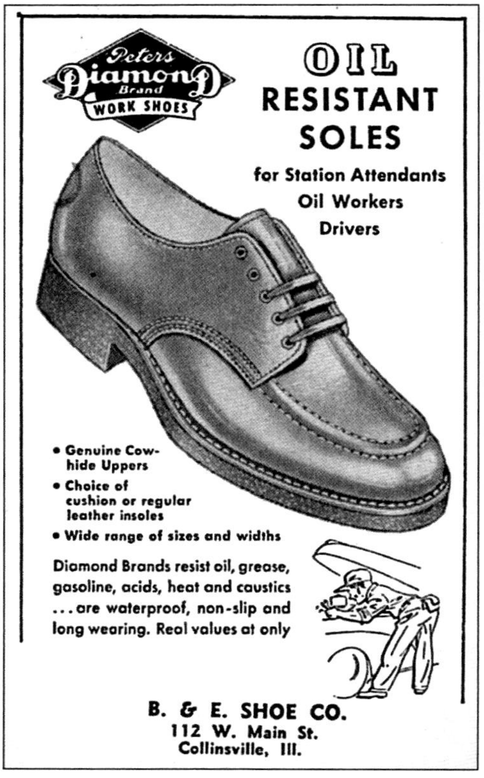

The B. & E. Shoe Co. was at the same 112 West Main Street address for forty years. The proprietors were Arthur Bendel and Theodore Eigenbrodt. Pictured is an advertising card printed on a government postal (penny postcard). It shows the product (shoe), the logo (Peters), and lists the attributes of the product, but does not state the price. By today's standards, this shoe looks more like a dress shoe than a work shoe as advertised.

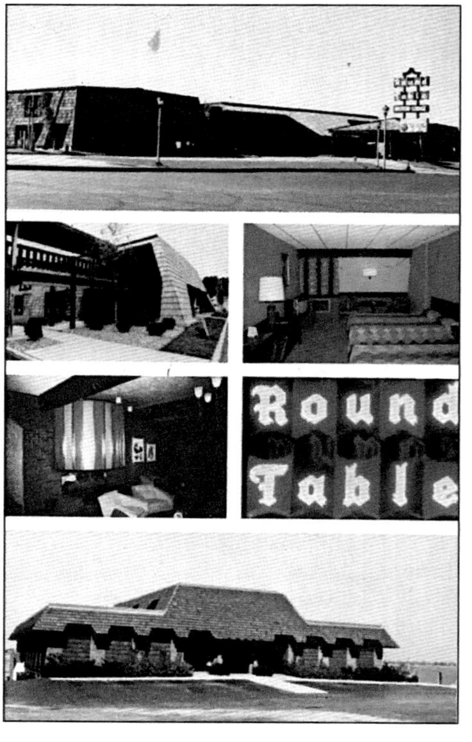

The business advertised on this postcard is the Round Table Lodge and Restaurant. It was situated one-half mile south of I 55-70 on the corner of Mall and Bluff Road (Route 157) where Lenny's Carpets and Floor Center stands. The restaurant pictured near the bottom of the postcard was in business from 1969 to 1981 at which time it was destroyed by fire. The 82-room motel became the Best Western Round Table Motor Lodge, then Round Table Professional Center and is now an apartment building.

The Morris Agency was founded in 1934 by Lossie E. Morris and C.C. Morris. This real estate and insurance sales business was located at 224 West Main Street. In the mid-1950s it moved to 101 West Main where it shared facilities and management with Union Savings & Loan. In about 1985, Morris Agency moved to 514 West Main, where it remains today. This real photo advertising postcard could be considered a collectible Friday-the-13th item.

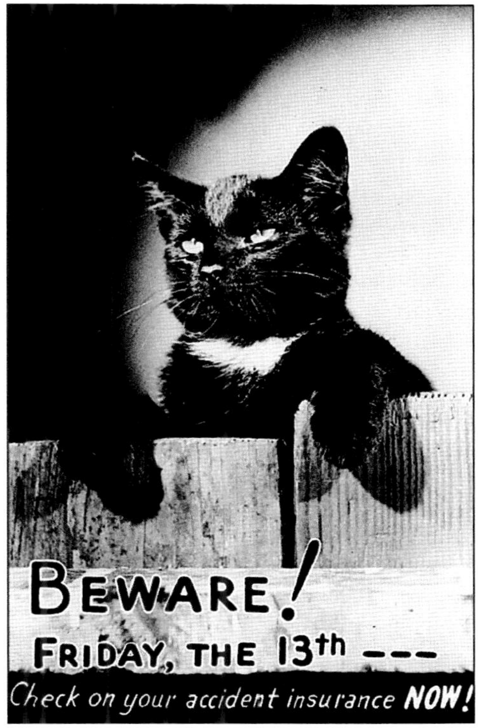

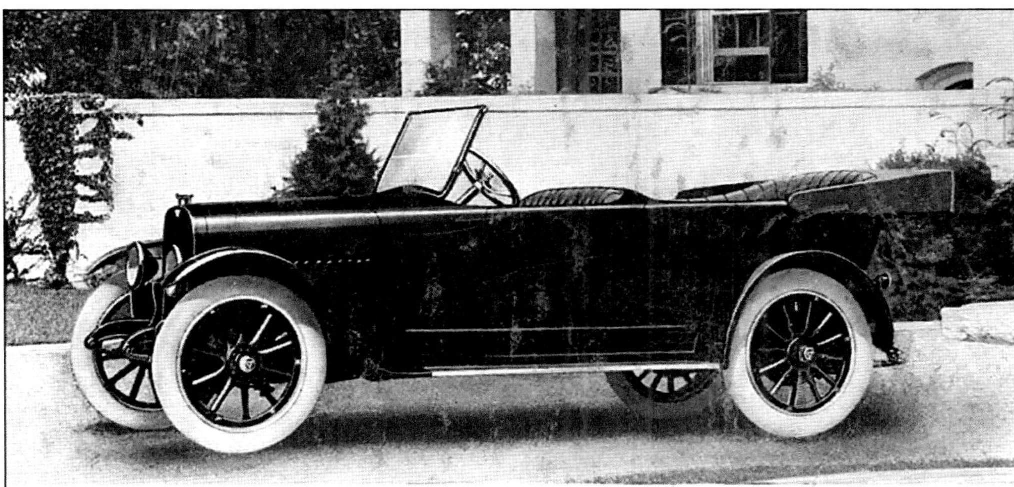

The New Hudson Super-Six Phaeton (7-Passenger). Price $1375, f. o. b. Detroit
Also built in Touring Sedan, Cabriolet, Limousine, Town Car and Roadster

Bernhardt-Niehaus & Co. sent this postcard in 1910. It advertises the Hudson super-six, seven-passenger, Phaeton that could be purchased for $1,375. The firm began in 1890 as Bernhardt Bros. before it became Bernhardt-Niehaus in 1898. It was located at 116-122 Vandalia Street and remained in business until the mid-1930s. Owner Fred Bernhardt went on to operate Collinsville Transfer. William F. Niehaus was mayor from 1927 to 1931.

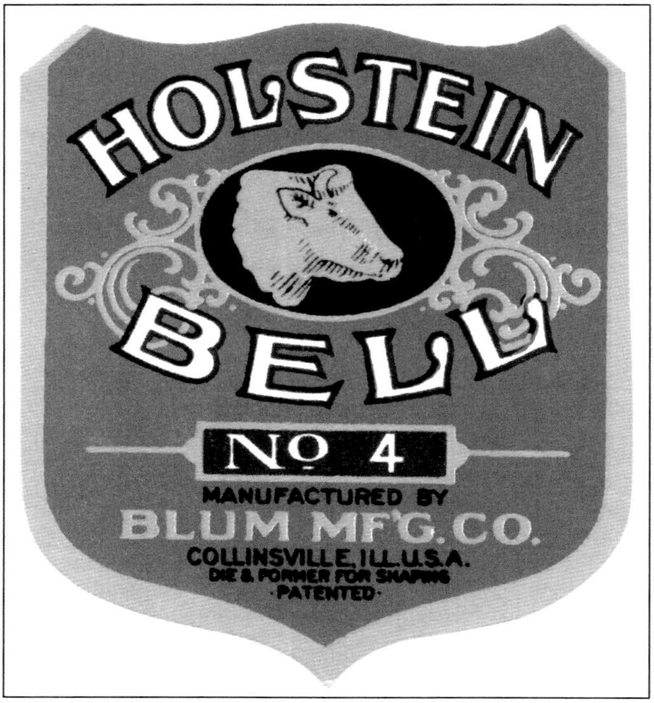

Cowbells were manufactured in Collinsville from 1849 to 1955. In 1849 Joseph Moore, a blacksmith, and his brother James began making cowbells. His son, Isaac, the town's second mayor, took over the trade in 1870 after the death of Joseph. In 1876, Christian Blum purchased the business; his son Henry continued to manufacture cowbells as did his son Henry Jr. Pictured is a label of the Blum Stock Bell Co. that was located on Goethe Street.

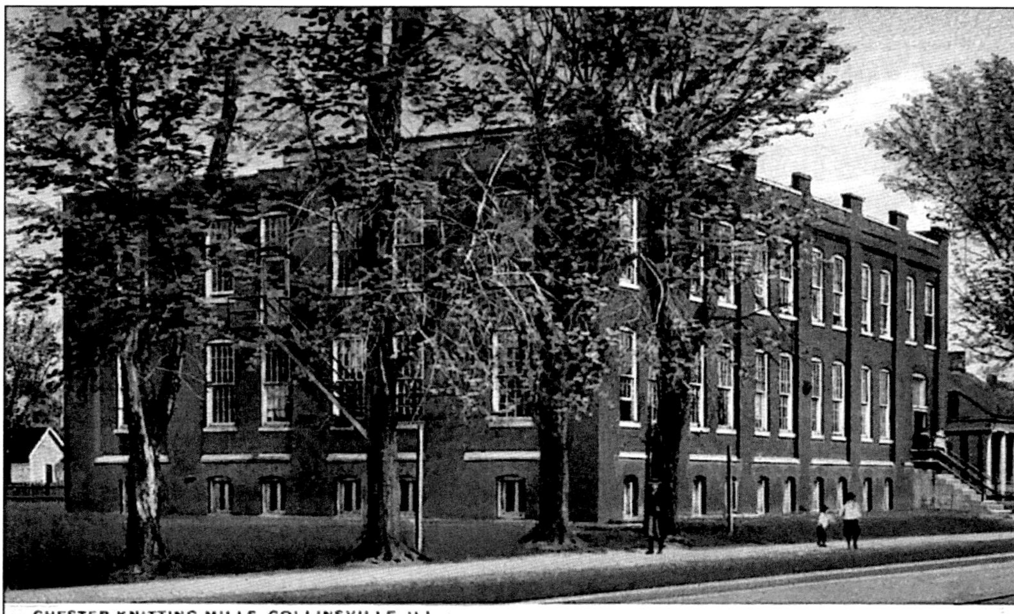

The pictured factory at 701 West Main was constructed in 1915. Stockings and dresses were made at various times by the Chester Knitting Mills, the Crown Millinery, Forest City Manufacturing, and the Martha Manning Co. at this site. In 1920 employees produced 4,947 dozen stockings a week. Although the wages were low, the factory produced jobs for Collinsville residents for more than 40 years. Main Street Apartments occupies the building today.

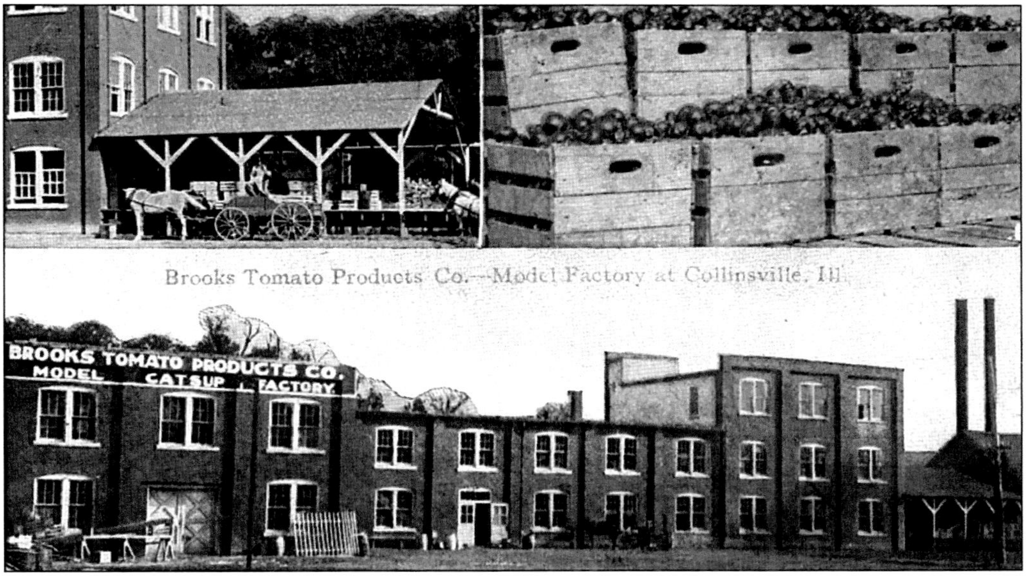

The complex shown, with additions and different configurations, had been a food processing plant since the early part of the 20th century. Before this plant at 800 South Morrison became Brooks Catsup Co., it was the Triumph Catsup and Pickle Co. In 1933, the Brooks company was purchased by G.S. Suppiger; however, the products still carried the Brooks label. For a while after the catsup processing operation shut down, Hawaiian Punch fruit drinks were canned there.

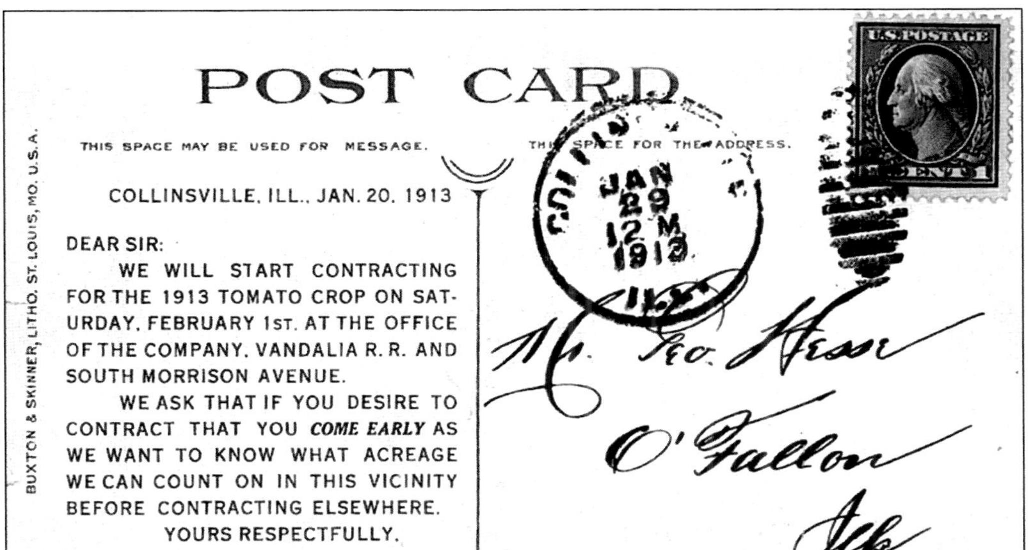
POST CARD

THIS SPACE MAY BE USED FOR MESSAGE.

COLLINSVILLE, ILL., JAN. 20, 1913

DEAR SIR:

WE WILL START CONTRACTING FOR THE 1913 TOMATO CROP ON SATURDAY, FEBRUARY 1ST. AT THE OFFICE OF THE COMPANY, VANDALIA R. R. AND SOUTH MORRISON AVENUE.

WE ASK THAT IF YOU DESIRE TO CONTRACT THAT YOU *COME EARLY* AS WE WANT TO KNOW WHAT ACREAGE WE CAN COUNT ON IN THIS VICINITY BEFORE CONTRACTING ELSEWHERE.

YOURS RESPECTFULLY,

BROOKS TOMATO PROD. CO.

BUXTON & SKINNER, LITHO. ST. LOUIS, MO. U.S.A.

THIS SPACE FOR THE ADDRESS.

U.S. POSTAGE

JAN 29 12 M 1913

Mr. Geo. Hesse
O'Fallon
Ill.

P.J. Ritter bought the business in 1959 and later sold it to Curtice-Burns. In the days before many people had telephones, the plant would communicate with the tomato growers by postcard and newspaper. Older residents have fond memories of the aroma of catsup cooking and the sight of pickup trucks and autos, factory-bound, loaded with boxes and baskets of tomatoes in both front and back seats and trunks. The building is currently owned and used by Bethel Eckert Enterprises as a warehouse.

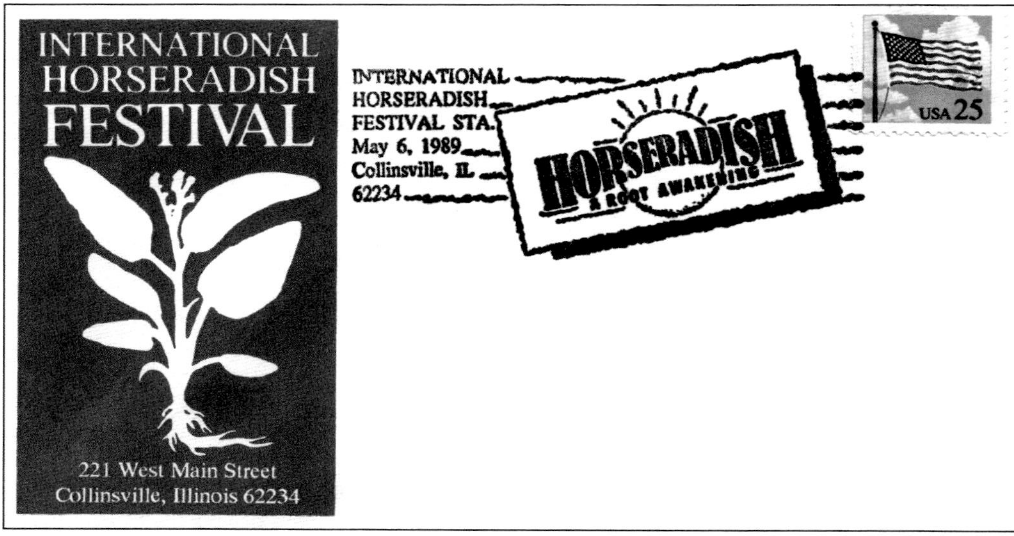

A large part of the world's horseradish supply is grown in this area. Collinsville has been called "the horseradish capital of the world." The river basin west of Collinsville is known as the American Bottom. The soil is rich in potash, a chemical nutrient on which the plant thrives. Collinsville celebrates this heritage each year by hosting an International Horseradish Festival.

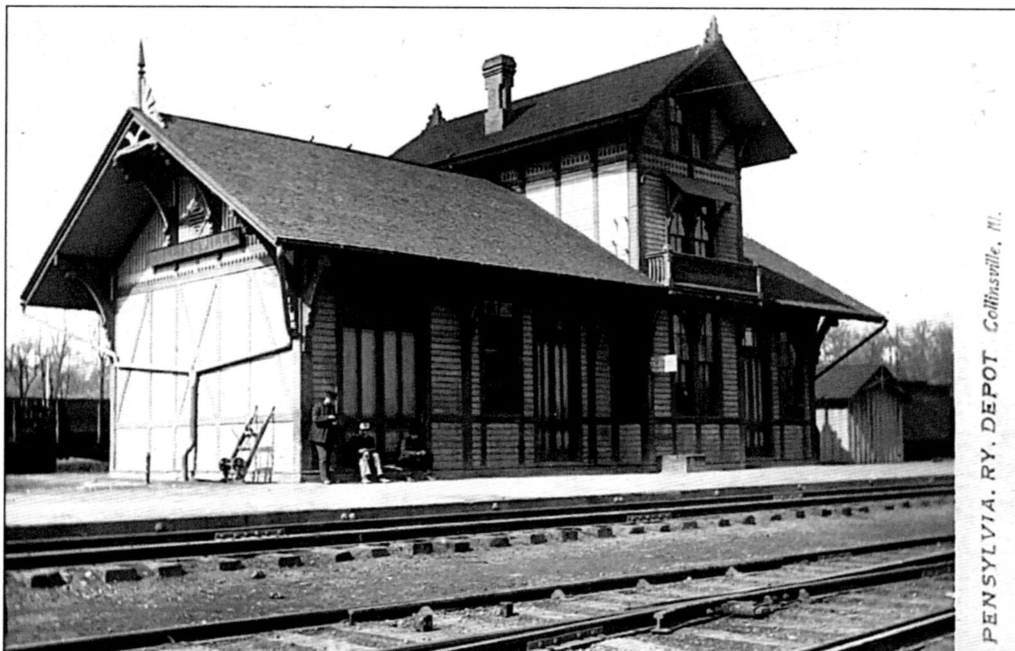

The Vandalia Railroad came to Collinsville about 1867 and the depot was constructed in 1871. The availability of the railroad enhanced industrial development. In 1903, the Vandalia line built a double track to East St. Louis. The Vandalia line became the East St. Louis, Vandalia, Terre Haute Railroad, and later the Pennsylvania Railroad. After then becoming Penn Central, which eventually declared bankruptcy, the name changed to Conrail and is now CSX.

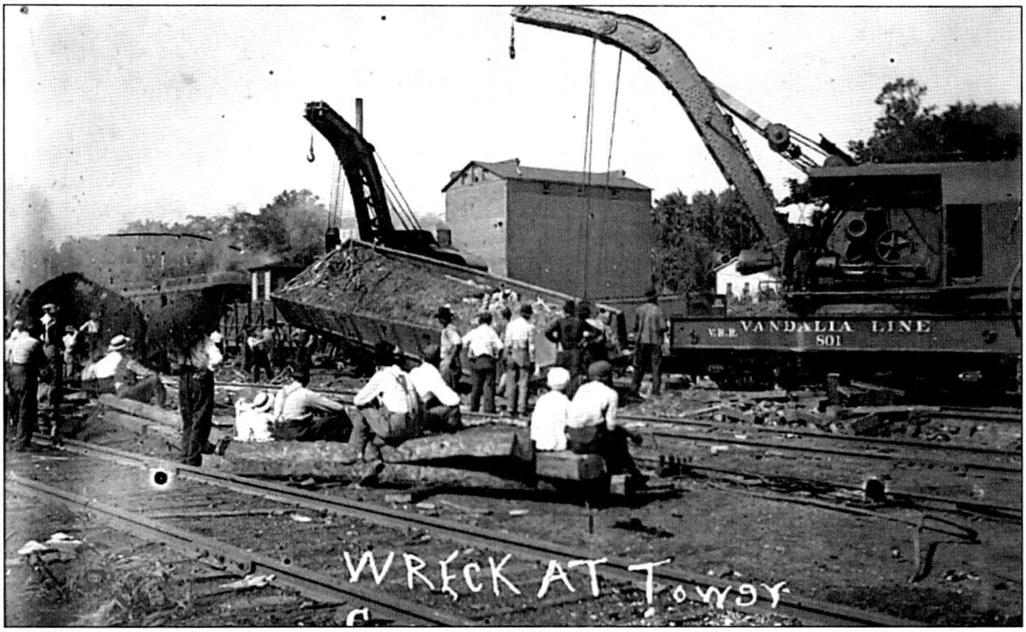

The two real photo postcards shown on this page are views of a train wreck that occurred in Collinsville. On August 4, 1911, at 6:09 p.m., extra train No. 236, pulling a string of loaded coal cars from Lumaghi Mine, was hit and derailed by freight train No. 95.

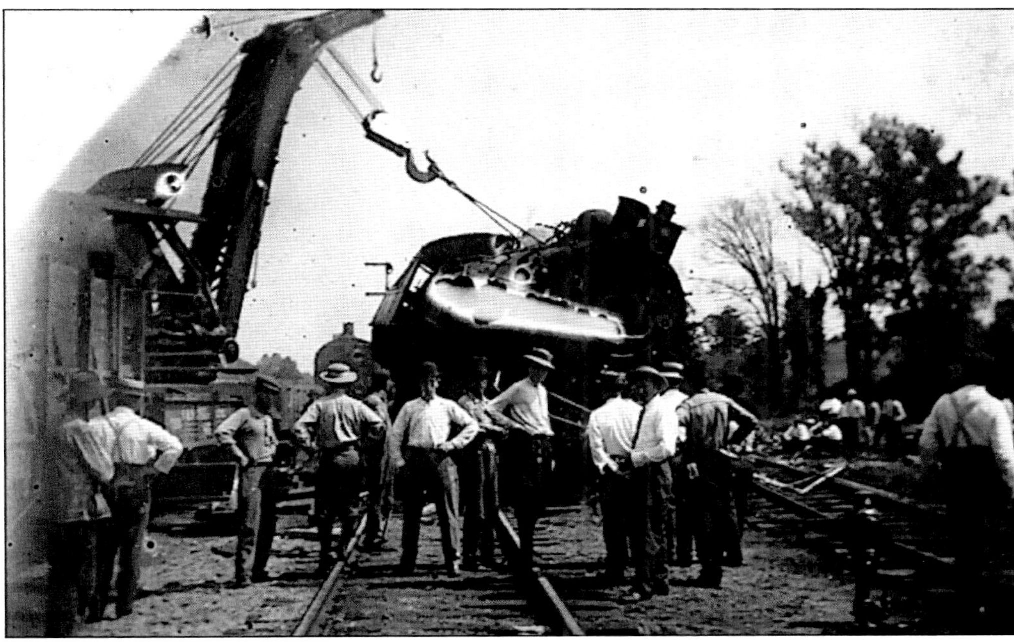

Four employees jumped to safety immediately before the collision. Train No. 236, whose destination was East St. Louis, was entering the main line when it was struck. Freight train No. 95 was traveling west at a high rate of speed. The brakes were applied, but it could not stop before the collision. Numerous railroad cars were demolished, but no one was injured.

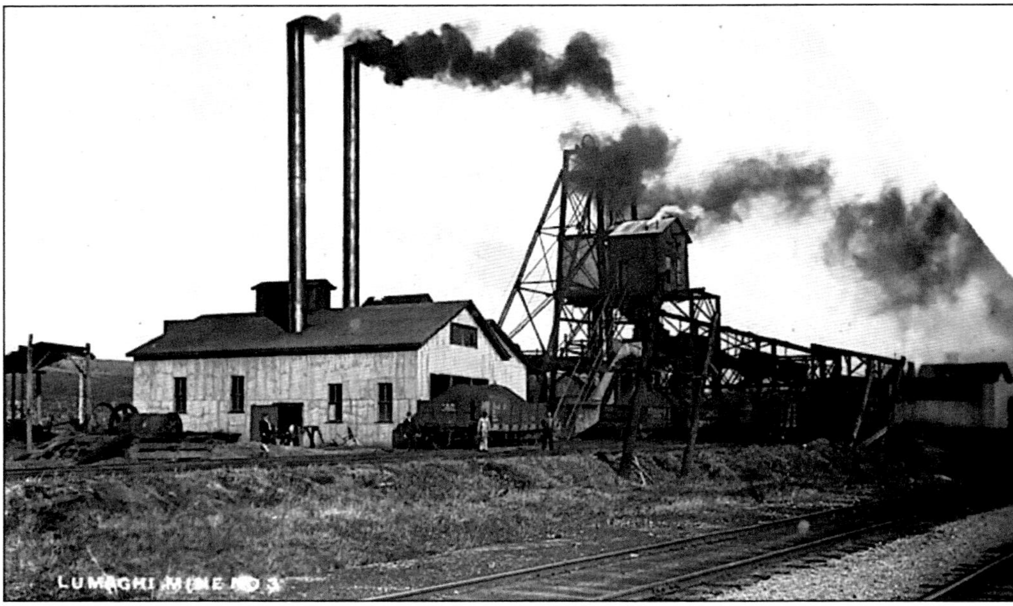

The coal mining industry generally thrived from 1900 to the early 1920s. The Lumaghi No.3 Mine (shown) was on the south side of Lebanon Road and railroad tracks just east of Quatto Hill. During World War I, 60,000 United Mine Workers 1eft the mines to serve in the military. In 1920, Madison County had 26 shipping mines, and six of them were Collinsville mines.

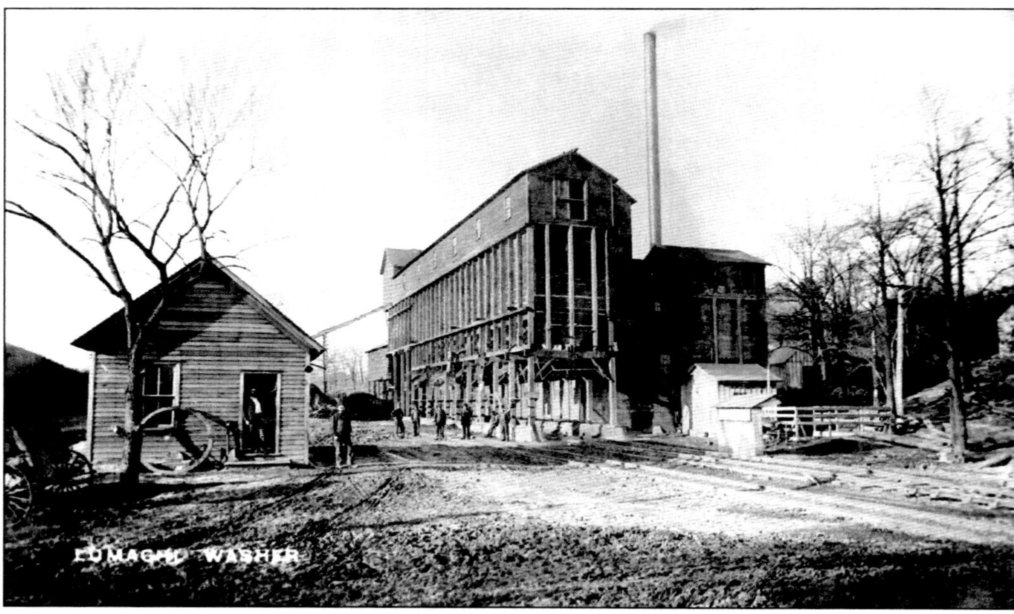

It is believed that this Lumaghi washer was first used in 1937. In addition to the quality of the coal, the safety of the miners was a crucial issue. The Madison County Coal Report of 1920 listed 10 fatalities and 210 non-fatal accidents. In 1977, a sign was placed at the sports complex on Old Route 40 commemorating 60 Collinsville coal miners who died in mine accidents. (Courtesy Steve Mueller.)

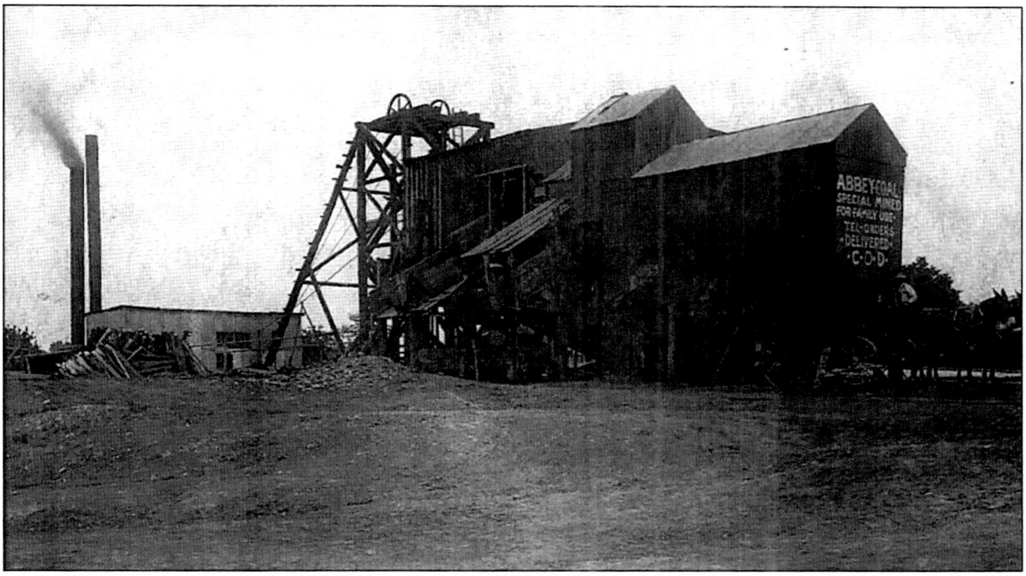

An especial distinction was found in the Donk No. 1 Mine (area known as Cuba north of town). In 1912, it was the only mine in the state that had an underground hospital or chamber for emergency care. Dr. John Siegel was the mine physician. The mine was commended by the state inspector. This is the Abbey No. 4 Mine just north of Reed Avenue at Railroad Street. According to the message on the shed, they produced a grade of coal that was usable in the home.

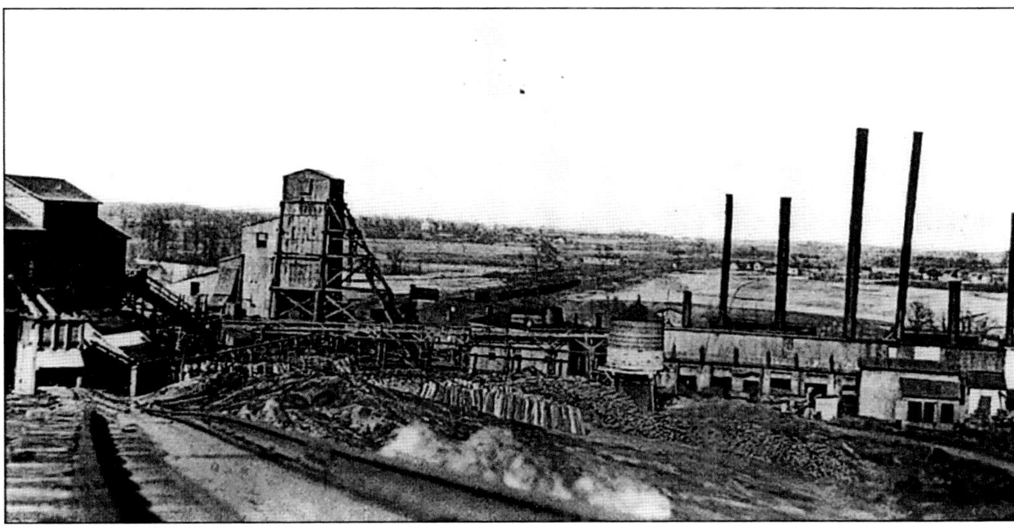

The Consolidated Coal Co. No. 17 Mine was sunk in 1904 and closed about 1926. The mine was located one-half mile east of Route 159 (south of Collinsville) on Bethel Mine Road. The mine was owned by Jay Gould, coal mine magnate from the East, and had a daily capacity of 17,000 tons. Peter Grieve Jr. was the local manager and with his brother-in-law, Al James, had an office at 103 South Seminary. The mine was serviced by the Vandalia Railroad that had a spur from the trunk line on the southeast side of Collinsville. Workers who resided in town would take a heated boxcar ride to the mine. Off in the distance in the center of the image, the old Bethel Baptist Church can be seen. (Courtesy of Belleville Labor and Industry Museum.)

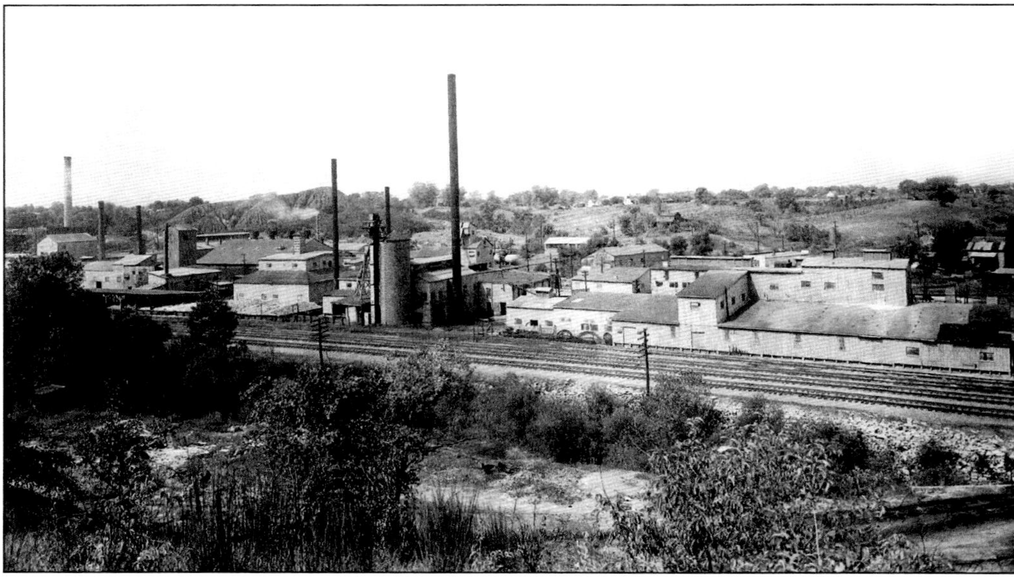

Pictured is the St. Louis Smelting and Refining Co. (the Lead Works) that was assembled in 1904. The 225-acre location northeast of Collinsville (Pine Lake and Collinwood area) was chosen because of the transportation network and its proximity to an unlimited supply of coal. In 1917, the company had a 386-foot smokestack constructed at a cost of $75,000. With a work force between 225 and 425, the plant functioned continuously until 1933 when it closed.

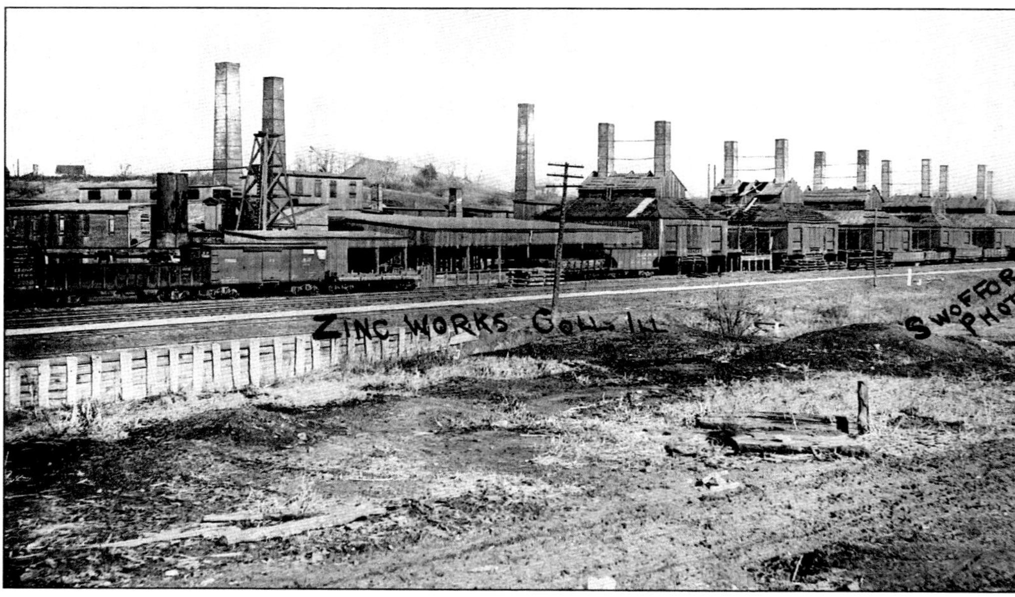

Dr. Octavius Lumaghi sunk his first coal mine in about 1869; a few years later, he began this zinc works. It was just east of the coal mine so that the fuel supply was near. The plant prospered for many years and is reputed to have employed 1500 men in 1912. It changed ownership a number of times until Glidden Co. provided some years of stability. The plant closed in 1953, and Glidden contributed land to the City that was developed into Glidden Park.

Five

Landmarks

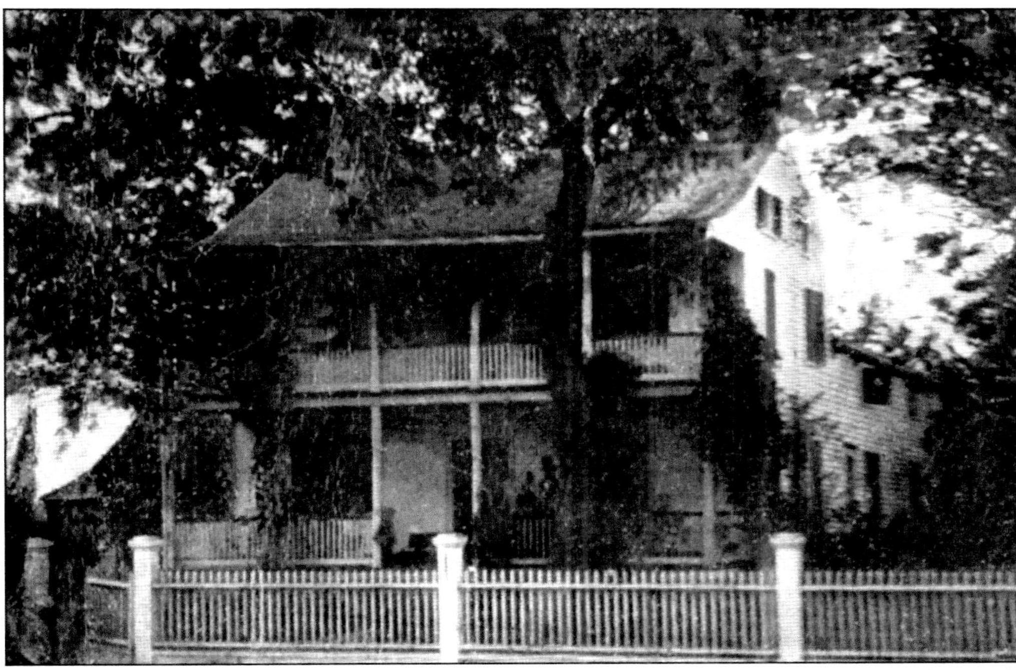

The Collins Homestead was built by the Collins brothers on land they purchased from John Cook. Completed in about 1822, the house stood on the northwest corner of Church and Aurora streets. The family of Elizabeth A. Collins Reed, daughter of William Burrage and Elizabeth Wilt Hertzog Collins, and her children and grandchildren were the last of the family to occupy the house. The house was razed in 1960; an apartment complex currently occupies the site.

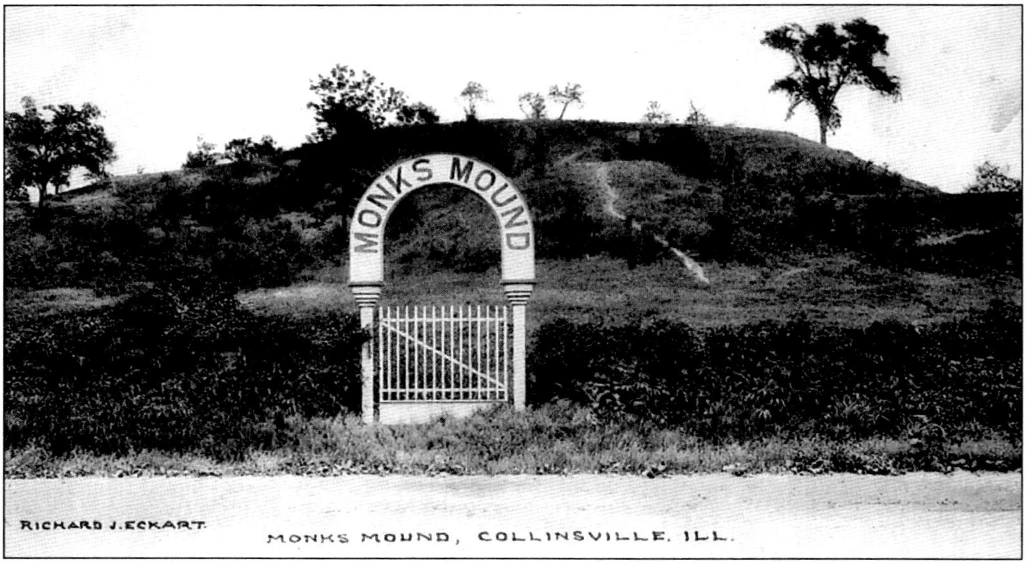

Monks Mound is the largest prehistoric earthen construction in the New World. This 100-foot tall four-tiered platform was built in stages over a period of 300 years. Its base covers more than 14 acres and contains about 22 million cubic feet of earth. The soil was dug with tools of stone, wood or shell and carried in baskets by the mound builders to the area under construction. It is believed that the principal ruler of the Indians lived at the top of the mound where he conducted ceremonies and governed the city below. It was named Monks Mound with reference to the French Trappist Monks who lived nearby in the early 1800s.

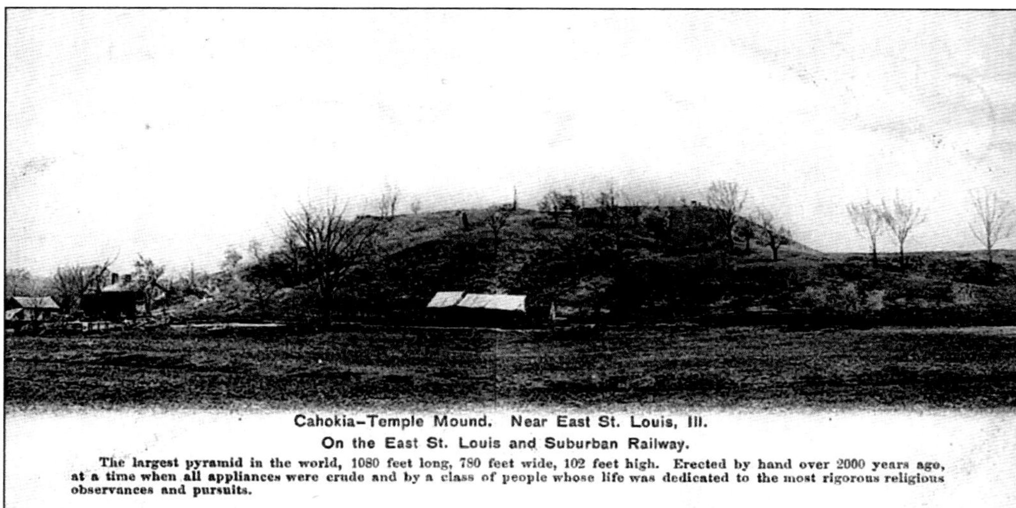

Today the Cahokia Mounds historic site is a 2,200-acre area that preserves the central section of the largest prehistoric Indian city north of Mexico. It is recognized as a United Nations World Heritage Site and National Historical Landmark. The park is located three miles west of the bluffs and six miles east of the Mississippi River in the American Bottom. Cahokia borders Collinsville on the east side, is near the confluence of three rivers and is at a merging area of four ecozones. Old Route 40 (Collinsville Road) bisects the property and to its north is I 55-70.

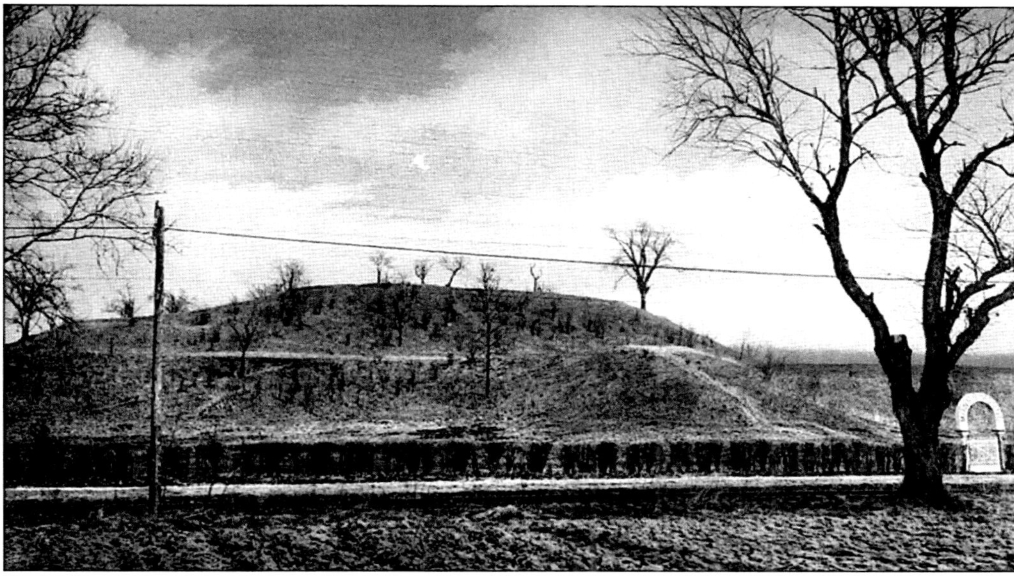

Although the original name is not known, this prehistoric urban center is called Cahokia. In the mid-1800s that name was given it to honor the historic Illini sub-tribe, the Cahokia. Prior to that, it had been known as the Cantine Mounds because of a French trading post that once stood near Monks Mound. Cahokia is, at times, referred to as "the City of the Sun" to recognize the sun symbolism on certain artifacts, the existence of sun calendars on the site, and belief that these Indians may have honored the sun as a Deity or spirit.

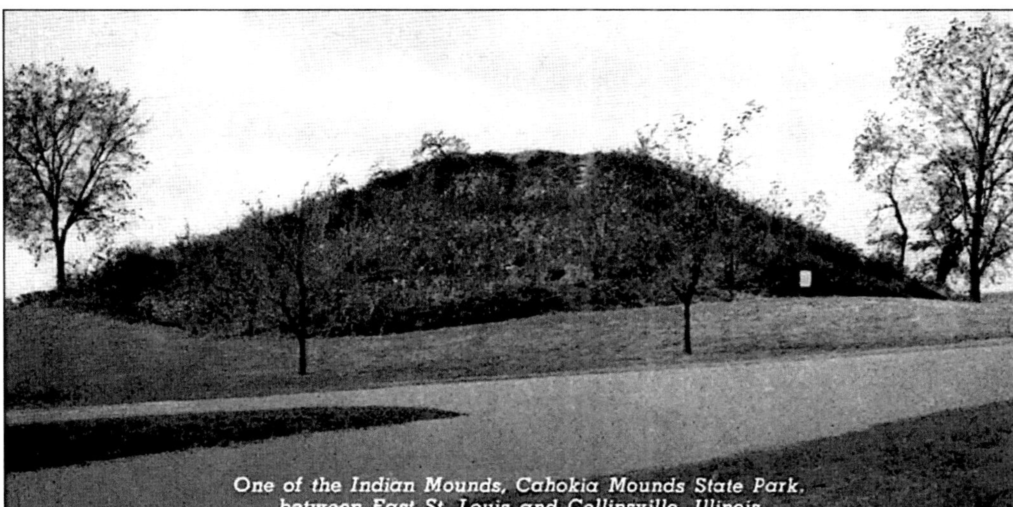

Cahokia was once a large prehistoric Indian city that covered 4000 acres or nearly six square miles. The area and distribution of mounds are roughly diamond-shaped with Monks Mound at the center. There were approximately 120 mounds. The city may have had a population as great as 20,000 people. Beginning around A.D. 700, Indians of the Late Woodland period inhabited Cahokia. After A.D. 900, the Mississippian culture developed and flourished here over a period of several hundred years before the gradual decline in population began around A.D. 1200. By A.D. 1400, Cahokia was abandoned.

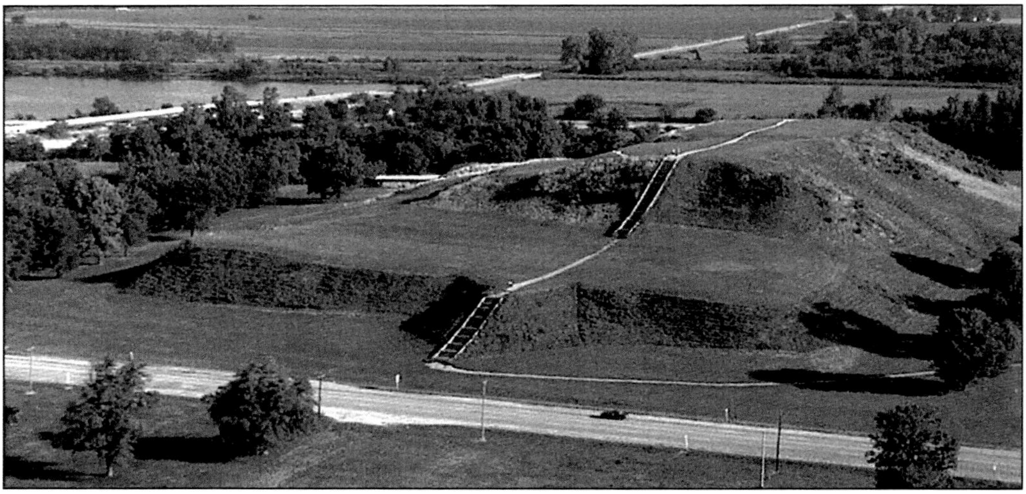

In the latter part of the 19th century, interest and support grew for preserving the mounds. Since 1860, Thomas Ramey, a member of the Illinois General Assembly, had owned much of the land on which the mounds stood. During the 1890s, he lobbied the state for Cahokia's preservation, as did other organizations and individuals in the early 1900s. Warren K. Moorehead, the first archaeologist to do field work at the site, championed the cause for preservation. He stated: "The mounds are to America what Stonehenge is to England." Finally, in 1925, the state purchased 144.4 acres, including Monks Mound, from the Ramey family for $52,110. Cahokia Mounds State Park was created.

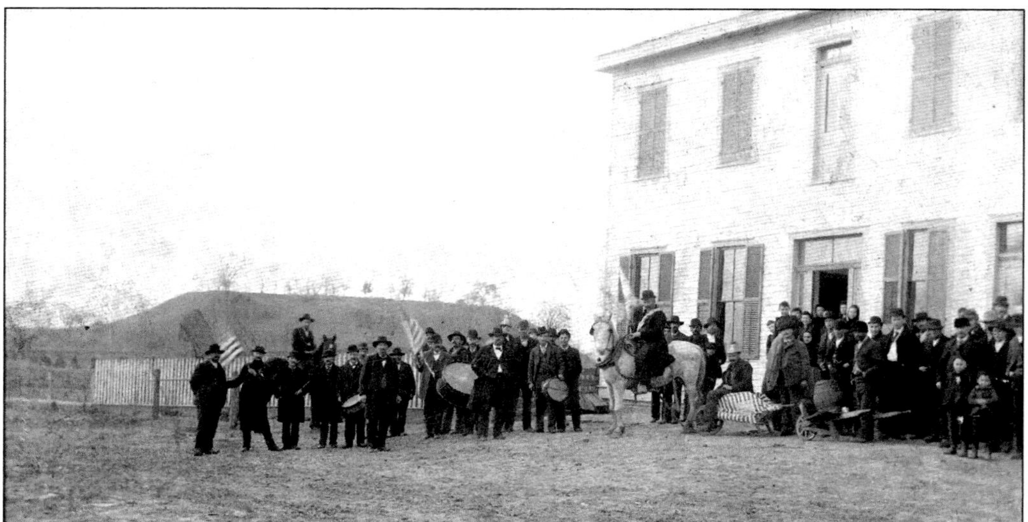

The c. 1890 picture above and the three on the next page are images of Schmidt's Mound Inn and Park located one-quarter mile east of Monks Mound. The images on page 87 are all parts of a single elongated photograph. They depict a celebration on October 25, 1914 by the Edwardsville Moose Club on the grounds of the Schmidt facility. It also shows the interurban and rock road (later Route 40). The Inn was to become the center section of the Mounds country Club when it opened in 1929. (Courtesy Bill and Lois Metzger.)

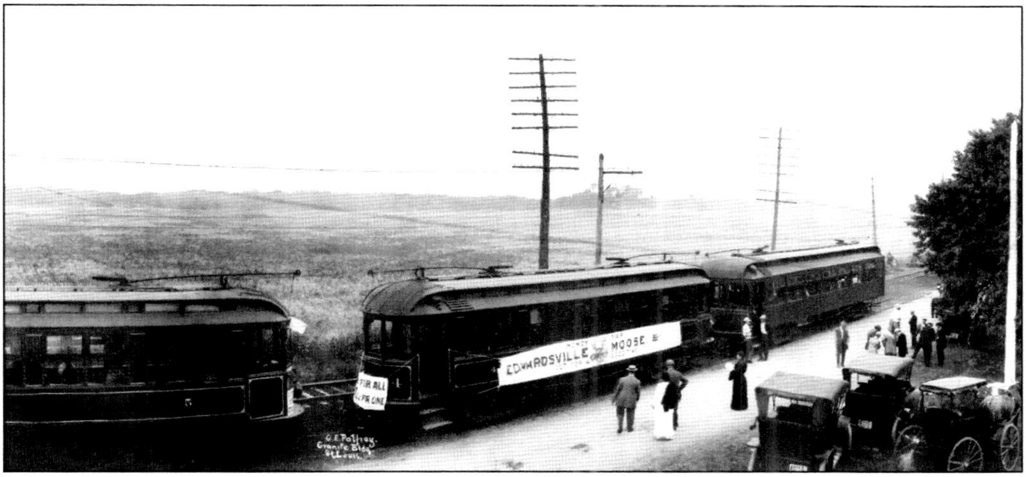
EDWARDSVILLE
MOOSE
FOR ALL
C. E. Pottroy
Granite Bldg
St. Louis

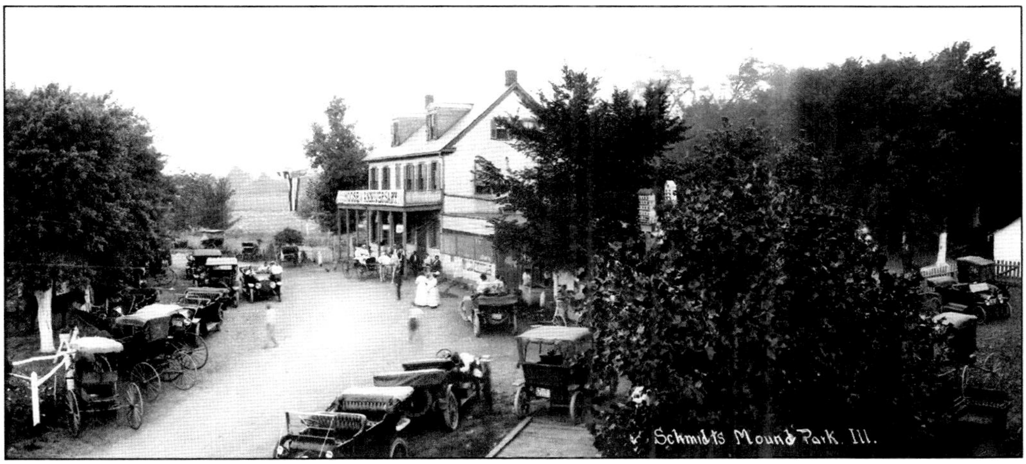
Schmidt's Mound Park. Ill.

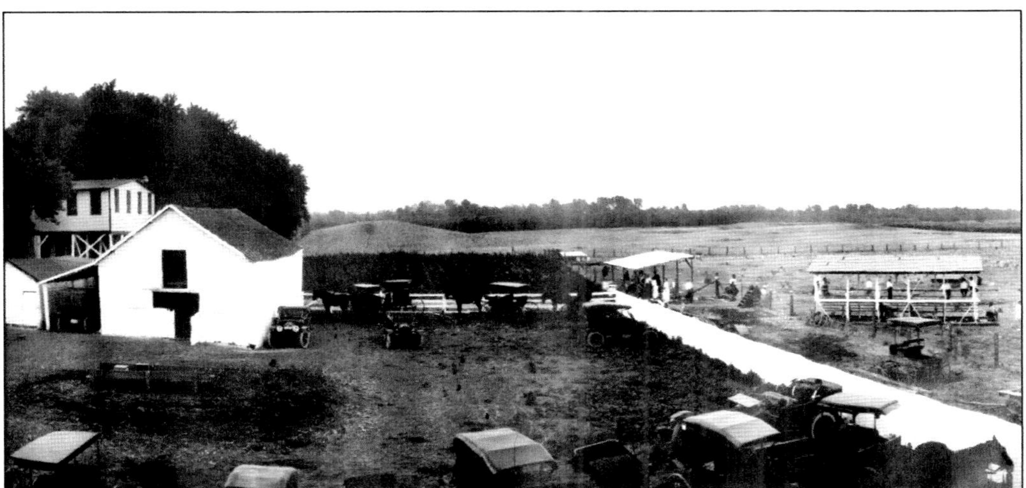

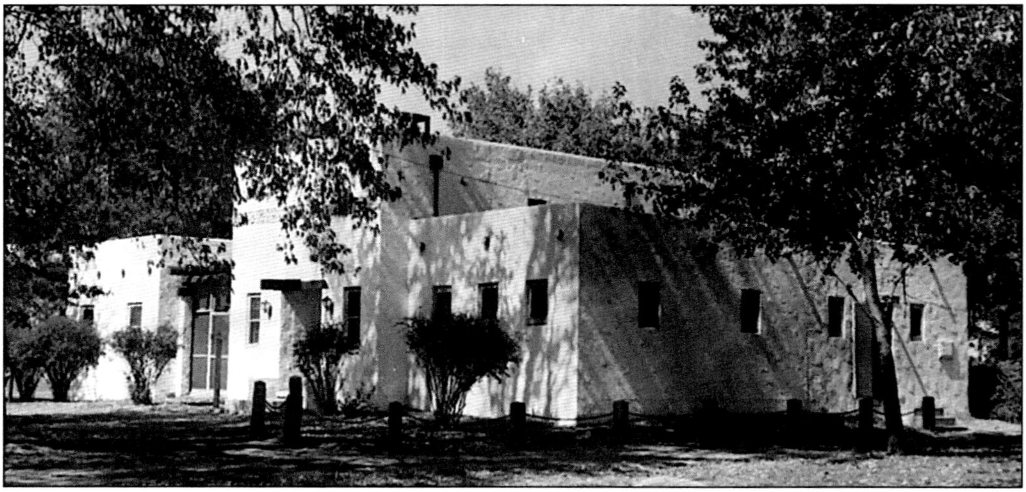

The Southwestern style structure housing the museum and living quarters for the park ranger was built about 1930 on the spot where the Ramey house stood. The driveway and parking area of this facility are where the farm buildings were located. After the state purchased the land from the Ramey family, the farmhouse was moved to the east side of the mound. Starting in the early 1970s, the state developed and expanded the former ranger's residence into a fine small museum.

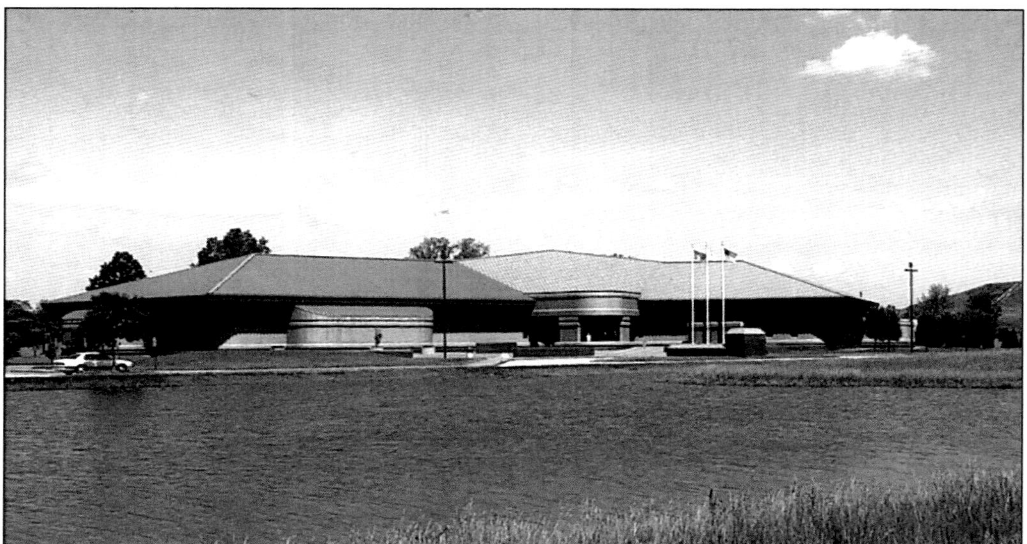

The Interpretive Center, a state funded $8.2 million facility, was completed in 1989. This 33,000 square-foot building uses state-of-the-art design concepts and technologies to present the story of Cahokia. The primary purpose of the building is to help visitors learn about Cahokia with exhibits, artifacts, dioramas, and audio-visual presentations. It also provides a setting for various events throughout the year, including films, lectures and special programs. Southern Illinois University at Edwardsville conducted excavations of the proposed site of the Interpretive Center prior to construction.

The World's Largest Catsup Bottle is located at 800 South Morrison (Route 159). The 70-foot high water tank with a 100-foot support tower was built in 1949 for G.S. Suppiger, maker of Brooks catsup. It held 100,000 gallons of water and was to provide water for the plant and for fire safety. The bottle cap is eight feet in diameter. This structure is recognized as an excellent example of mid-20th century roadside Americana. It was named to the National Register of Historic Places in 2002. (Courtesy of Michael Gassmann.)

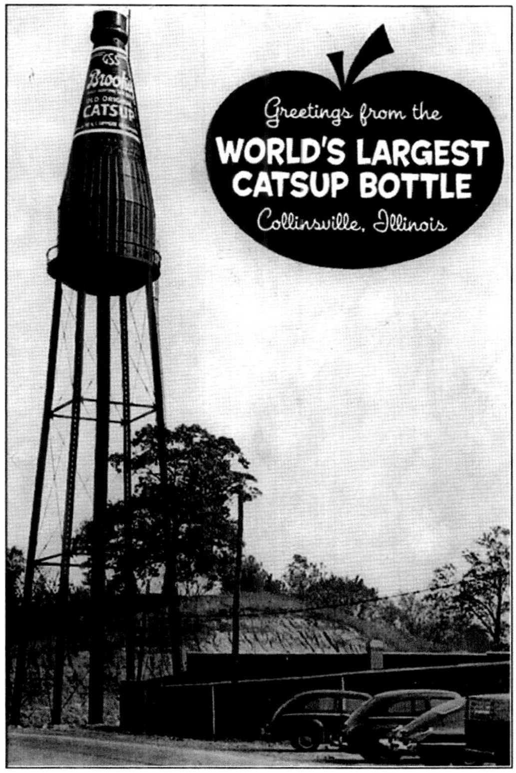

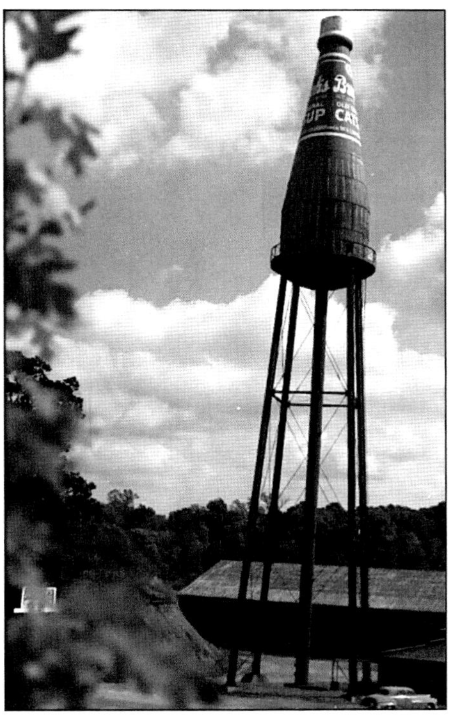

W.E. Caldwell (now Caldwell Tanks, Inc.) was the designer and builder of the tank and tower. One of Caldwell's more recent creations is the "Earffel Tower," the Mickey Mouse water tank erected for Walt Disney World in Florida. The real photo postcard image shown was probably snapped shortly after the tower was completed or in the early years. Apparently, there were never commercially printed picture postcards of the gigantic catsup bottle until recent years.

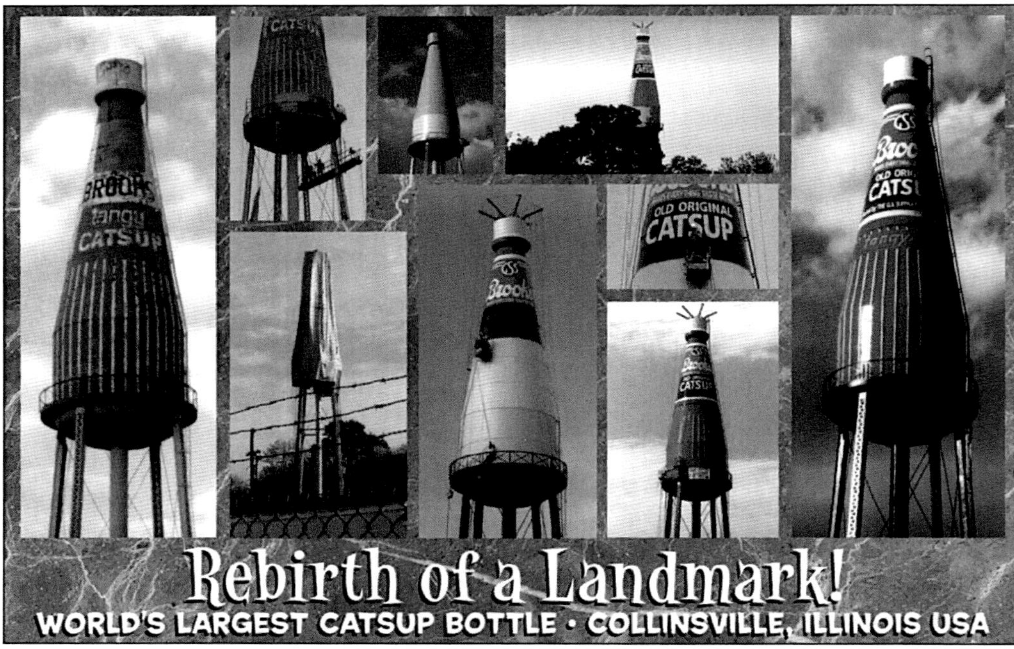

In 1993, the catsup bottle water tank and tower had begun to show its age. Community activists under the leadership of Judy DeMoisy organized residents to do something about the timeworn structure. The Catsup Bottle Preservation group collected S68,000 in 19 months. Although the catsup factory has been closed for many years, Brooks Foods contributed $10,000 towards the $77,000 needed to restore the landmark. The unveiling of the restored structure was held on June 3, 1995. (Courtesy of Michael Gassmann.)

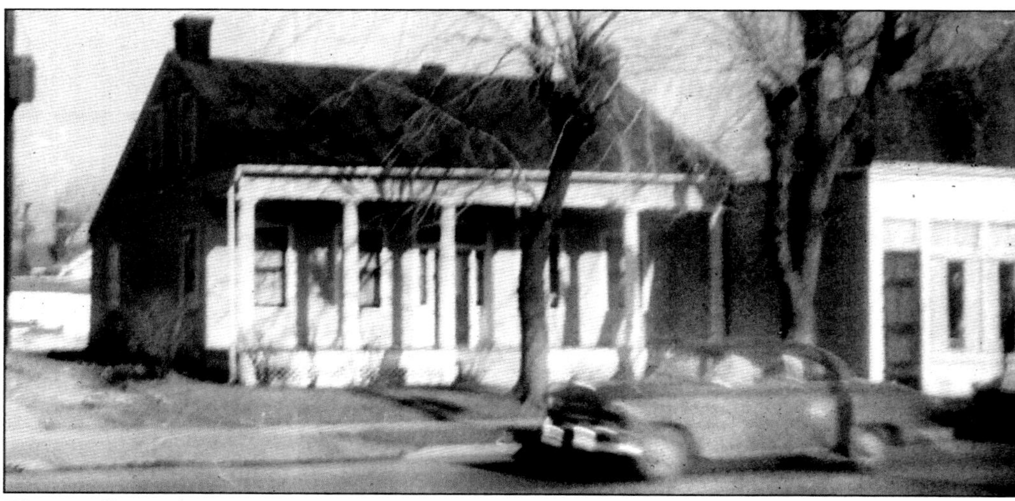

This small Greek Revival home was built by Daniel Dove Collins, the first village president, in about 1845, after his marriage to Elizabeth Anderson. It originally stood on the northeast corner of Main and Center streets and is now located at 621 West Main. Irving Dilliard gave the house to the city in 1998; it is currently being restored. The house was placed on the National Register of Historic Places in 2002.

Six

Sports and Leisure

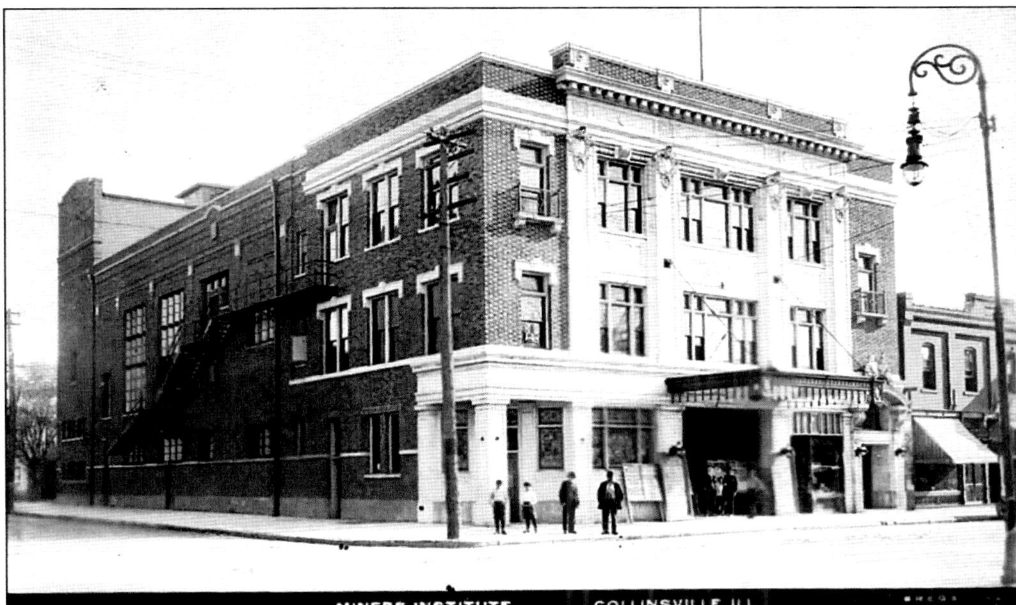

The Miners Institute at 204 West Main Street was constructed in 1918 by Henry Eberhardt for $139,993. Three buildings had to be removed from the site before construction could begin. Robert E. Kirsch of St. Louis was the architect. Each coal miner contributed one percent of his wages to finance the cost and the United Mine Workers of America made the original loan to facilitate the financing. Besides housing the theater, there are meeting rooms on the second floor and a banquet hall on the third floor. In its day, the locals had their office here, and the theater provided a place for the union membership to assemble. Two local coal miners, Matt Pigford and Alfred Bailey, posed for the statue over the entrance to the upper floors. The building is on the National Register of Historic Places. In 1988, after the movie theater had closed, a local support group was formed in an effort to save the structure. The group is active today.

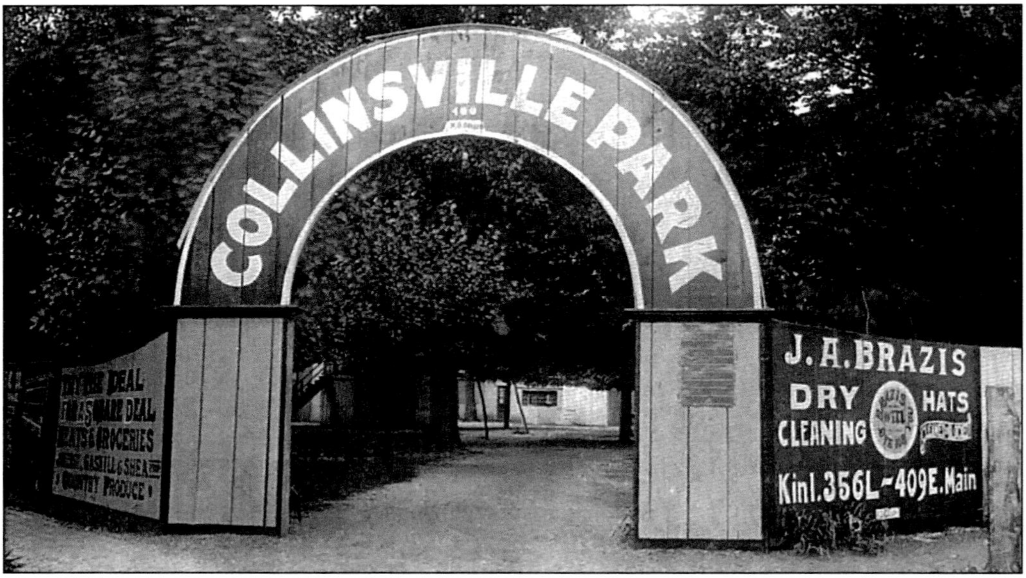

The well-known Collinsville Park (and Ballroom) facility was originally known as Becker's Grove. It opened in the 1880s as a place to have band concerts and picnics. It was owned by John Becker, Collinsville's first mayor. In August of 1902, an estimated 8,500 people attended the first annual picnic of the Merchants Association at Becker's Grove. In this era, the typical parade route was to travel west on Main Street to Hesperia and then north to the park.

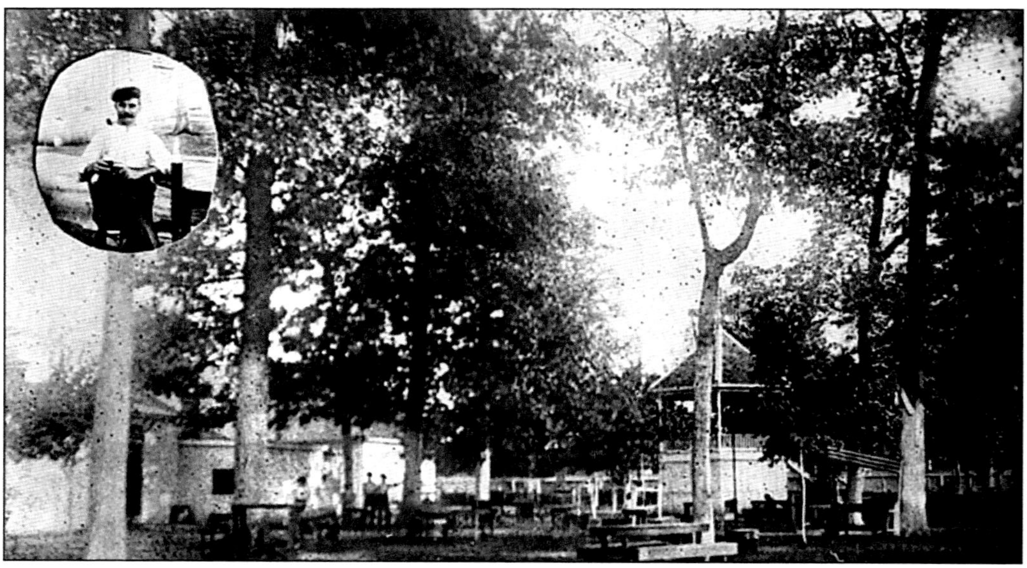

In 1903, Victor Vigna (inset upper left corner) purchased the park. It was named the Victor Vigna Park Collinsville Pleasure Resort. His park eventually provided an open dance pavilion and a tent theater where free movies were shown. In addition to providing a place for church and school picnics and socials, there were special events like a Wurst Markt and Farmers' Chicken Fry & Harvest Home Festival. In 1911, special presentations included appearances by Billie Plumlee and his Company and the Buckskin Ben Amusement Co.

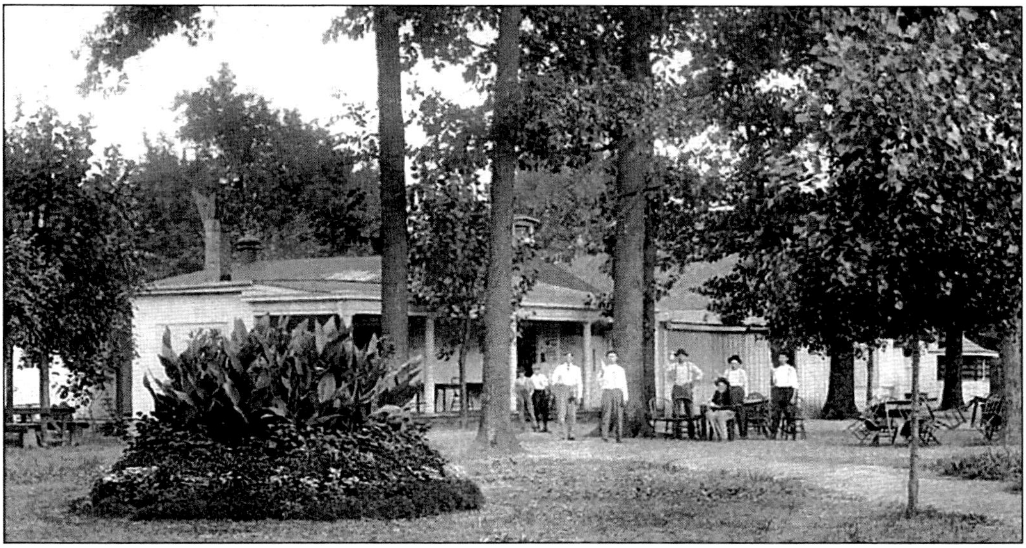

As times and ownership changed and Prohibition was repealed, a dance hall and ballroom became the center of activities at Collinsville Park. In the 1930s and through the 1950s, Collinsville Park Ballroom was a stopping place for the big bands or name bands between St. Louis and Chicago. Many area folks enjoyed dancing and listening to the music of Russ Morgan, Artie Shaw, Guy Lombardo, Tommy Dorsey, Stan Kenton, Vaughn Monroe, Les Brown, and Harry James. Frequently crowds numbered over 1,400 people.

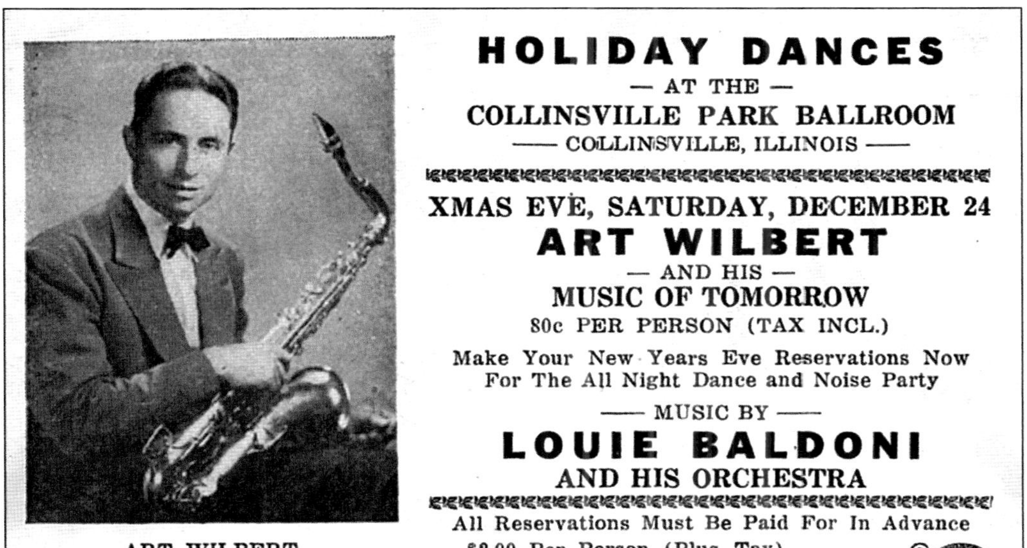

The ballroom also spotlighted local talent, as this postcard indicates. Other local bands that were popular are Dick Jurgens, Bill Berutti, and Joey James. Owners Pete Zinke and Al Danni were responsible for the success of the establishment during its mid-century run. Business declined after the big band era when younger audiences embraced a new sound. The Collinsville Park Ballroom was destroyed by fire on December 29, 1980. In its place stands a large complex of multi-unit apartment buildings named Collinsville Park West.

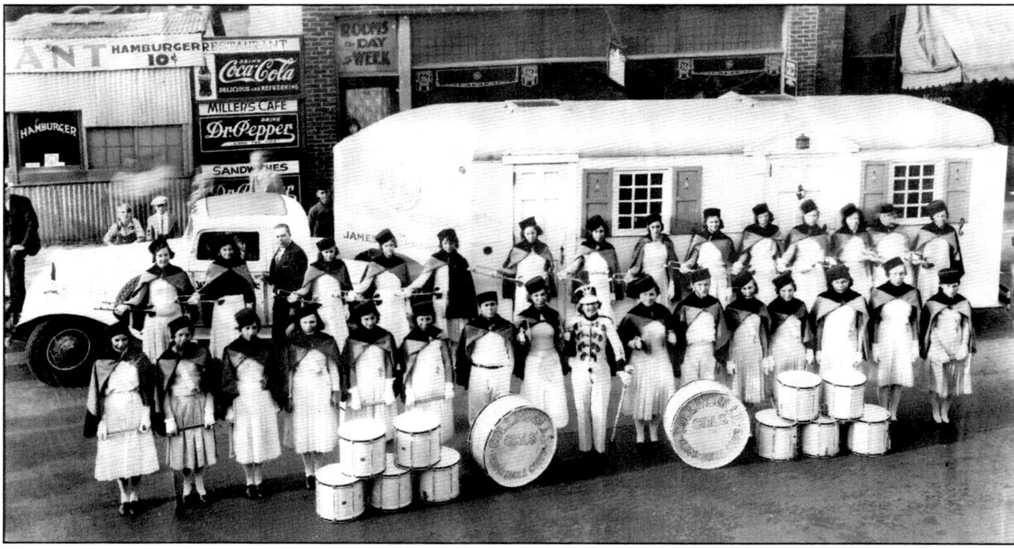

This photo with the interesting signage shows members of the Collinsville Girls' Drum and Bugle Corps after a performance in Wood River. Abbie Kneedler organized the group and was its Drum Major. In 1918, the corps appeared at local parades and farewells for members of the military. In the 1933 competitions, the corps was the state and national champion of its class. An engraved baton representing the 1936 Illinois State Fair performance, and a commemorative quilt listing members' names and the places they performed in 1937 can be found in the Collinsville Historical Museum. The group was active from 1918 to 1942.

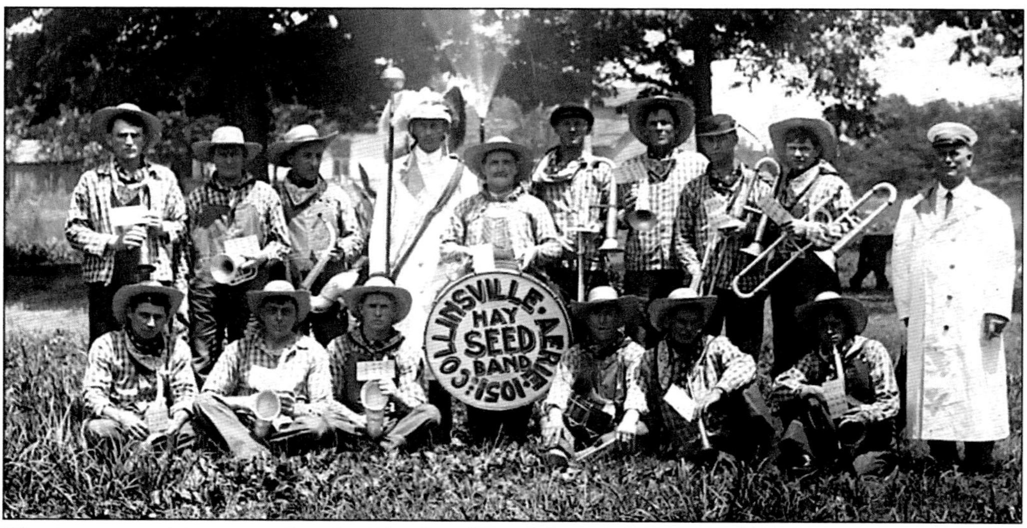

The image on this postcard is the Hay Seed Band that was sponsored by the Fraternal Order of Eagles, Aerie 1051. According to Frank Patek, an early musician, Collinsville had its first band in 1884. Henry Dewald had a 12-piece band and gave fiddle lessons in his barber shop on Main Street. The Stringtown Band was organized by Charles and Bill Long in about 1890. Frank Schmacker and Frank Futcheck also had an early band. John Koch had a municipal band at the turn of the century to about 1925, and the Music Makers played for dances at the Bunker Hill Club at 205 Juda Avenue.

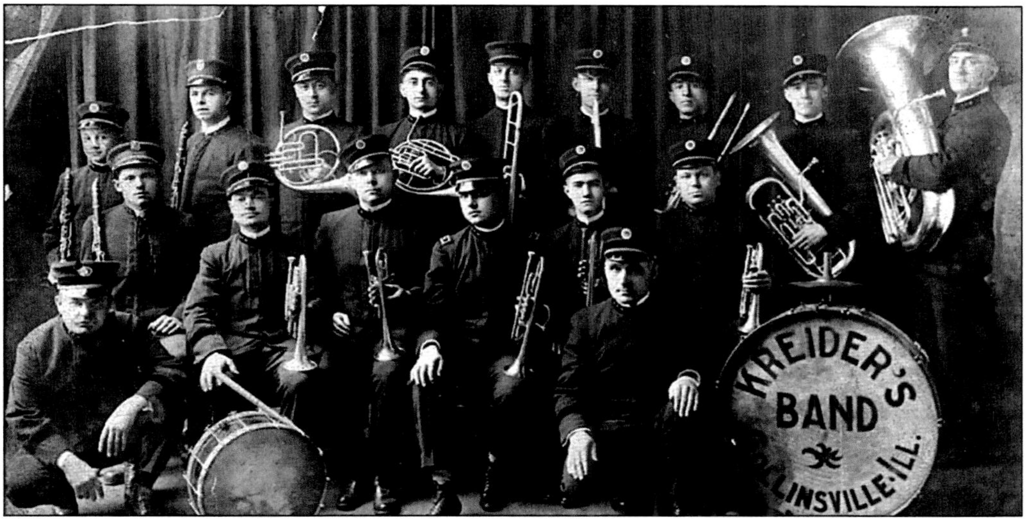

Franklin C. Kreider attended Catholic grade school and Collinsville Township High School. He became an accomplished violinist. He also studied cornet and other instruments. He and his wife Louisa operated the Rhein-Kreider School of Music at 106 1/2 East Main. The bands that he organized played in parades and at World War I ceremonies at City Hall Park. In January of 1919, a month or so after the opening of Miners Theatre, Kreider was hired to lead an orchestra that provided music to enhance the silent films. On this postcard, Kreider is the cornet player fourth from the left of those seated. His father is kneeling beside the bass drum.

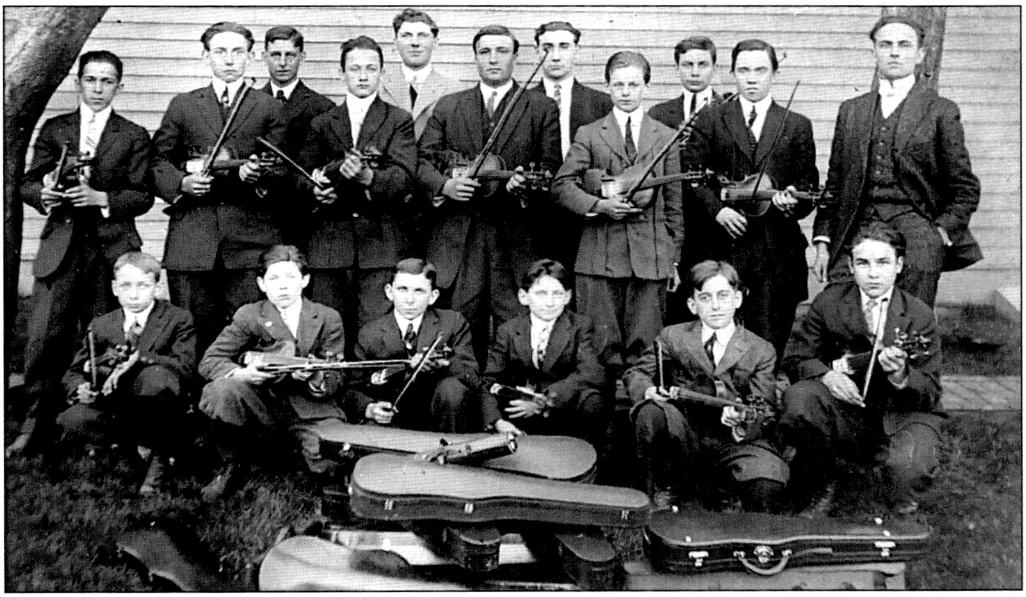

A photo of a youthful Franklin Kreider and his violin class is shown. He is on the far right of those standing. Kreider organized the CTHS Band in the 1930–31 school year. Within a few years, the band had received national honors. Kreider was a pioneer of instrumental music education in the public schools. He retired in 1962 and died in 1981. The auditorium in Webster School was dedicated to his memory in 1985 and named the Franklin C. Kreider Auditorium. "Prof" Kreider instilled a love of music in the lives of many students and musicians.

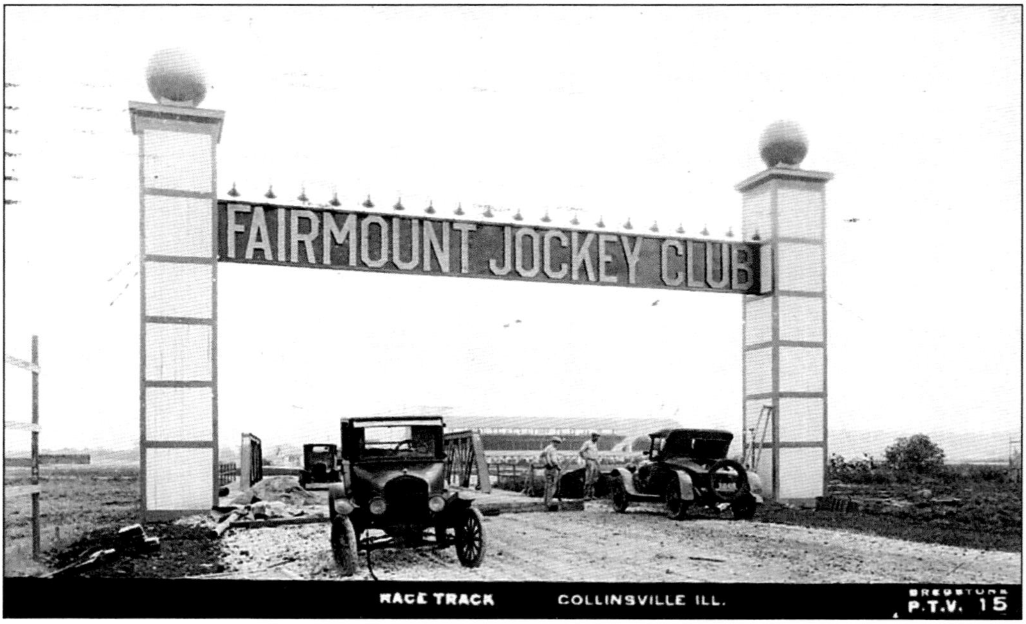

Fairmount Park Jockey Club, built on what was previously Edwards' hog farm, opened on September 26, 1925. Despite a heavy rain, 9,000 people attended. Seth's Alibi won the feature race and paid $4.70 for a $2.00 subscription. In those days, betting was illegal but so-called subscriptions towards the winner's purse could be made with appropriate returns for those contributing. The first major derby was a race in 1926 with a purse of $25,000. A horse named Haste, ridden by "Dandy" Earl Sande, edged out Baggenbaggage for the win. Haste finished second that year in the Kentucky Derby.

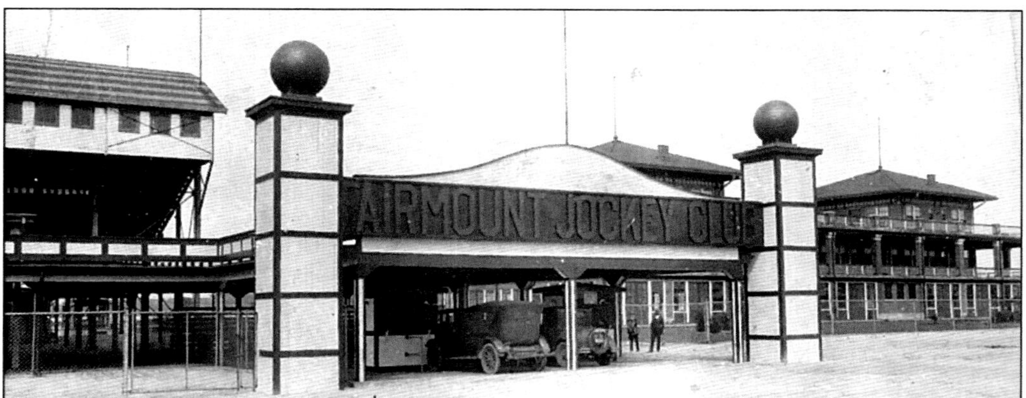

C. 1900, an earlier racetrack was built in Collinsville by R. Guy and William Kneedler on the Kneedler farm that comprised much of the current Meadow Heights. It was used for both track and field and horse racing. It later became known as League Park and was used by the top local baseball teams as well as the high school sports teams. About the same time that the one-half mile Kneedler track was coming into use, another track was developed by A. Sumner on the north end of Sumner Boulevard in Maurer Heights.

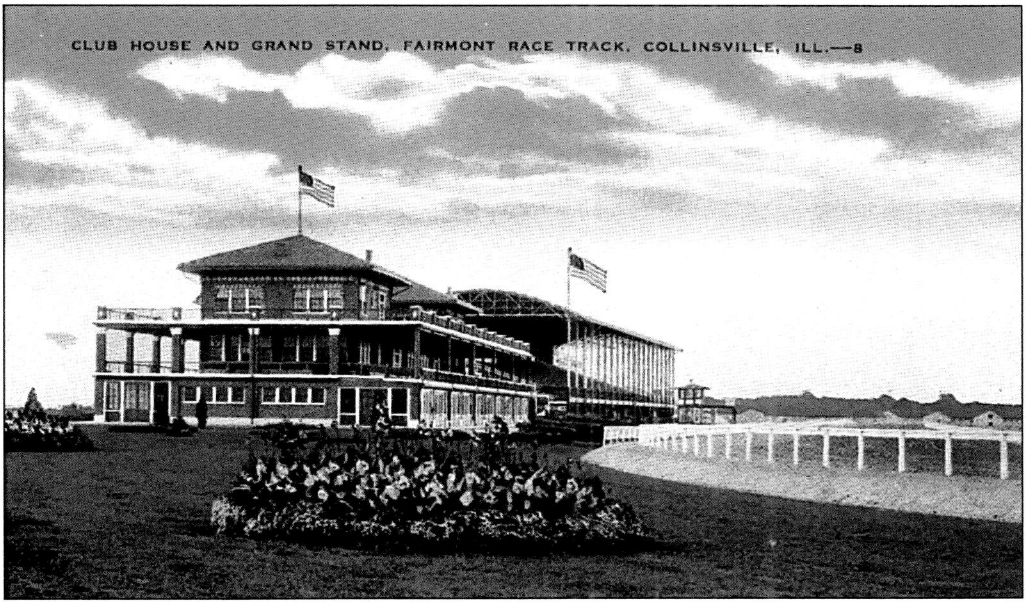

Fairmount Park offered racing under the lights for the first time in the nation's history in 1950. Although the cost was $100,000, it reversed a decline in revenue and began a money-making trend for race tracks across the country. Harness racing was the first under-the-lights racing; night thoroughbred racing followed within a few years. As late as 1952, the appearance of star jockeys Eddie Arcaro and Johnnie Adams was noteworthy, but generally the early years were the glory years of Fairmount Park. The top jockeys have been Earl Sande, Steve Brooks, Clarence Meaux, and Dave Gall.

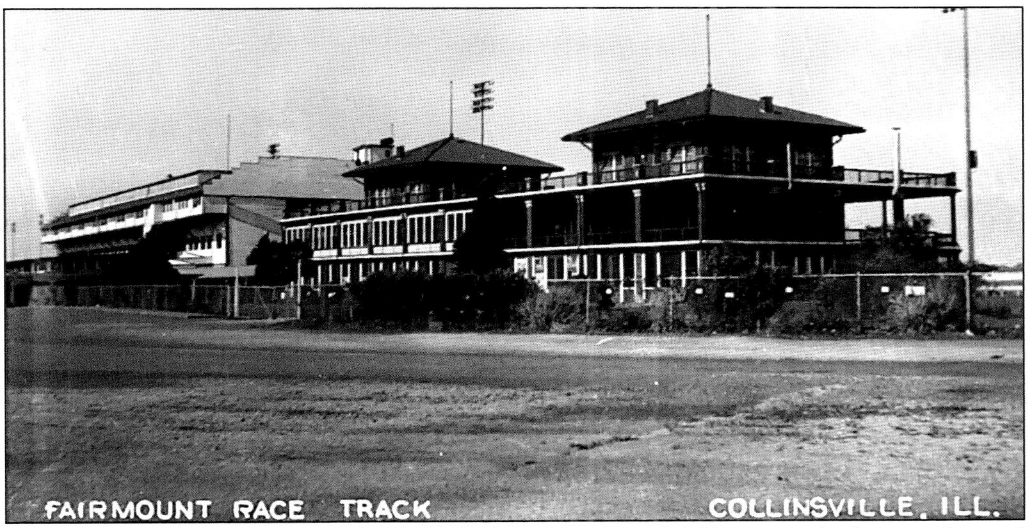

On September 7, 1953, the year before Cahokia Downs opened, Fairmount had a record crowd of 13,898 who bet a record $525,138. Tornadoes took the grandstand roof off in 1952 and again in 1953. In 1954, Fairmount Park was sold to a syndicate from Huntington, West Virginia, for $2 million. In 1966, a ventilation system was installed in the grandstand. It was remodeled, but remained primarily wood.

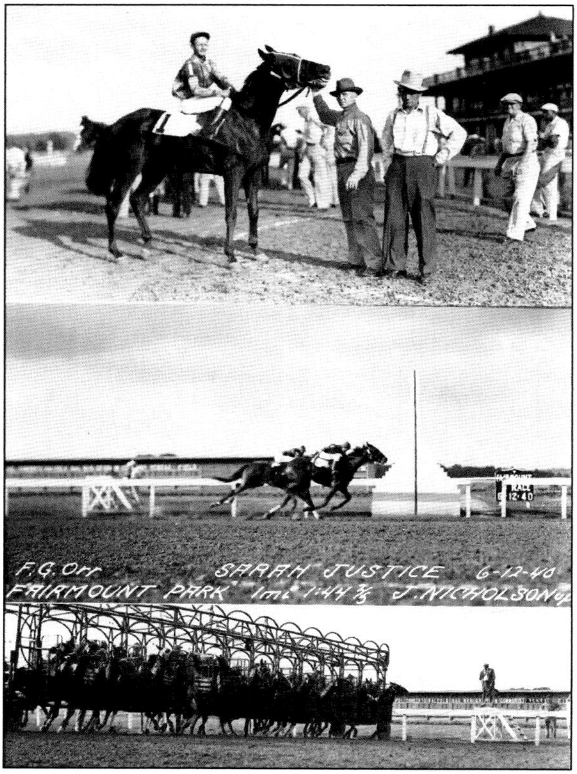

The top photo of this Fairmount race on 6-12-40 shows the winning horse (Sarah Justice), winning jockey (J. Nicholson), groom (Emmett O'Brien) and trainer/owner (Frank Orr) in the winner's circle. The middle image shows the finish line and indicates the length of the race (1 mile) and the winning time (1:44 2/5). The bottom part of this series shows the eleven horses as they burst out of the starting gate. (Courtesy of Darlene Orr Knoebel.)

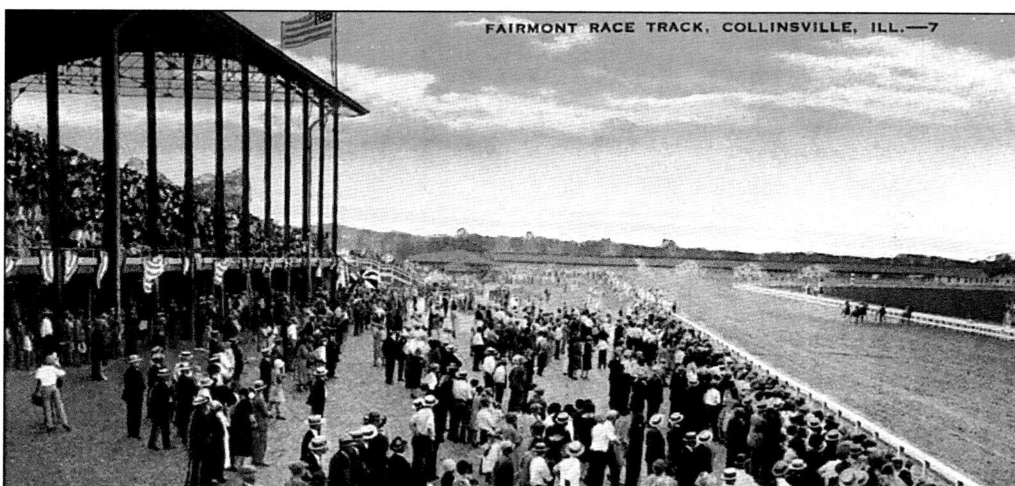

At its apex, Fairmount employed 500 people, including owners, trainers, jockeys, stable help, ticket sellers, and concessionaires. In 1969, Ogden Corp. of New York acquired the track as part of a deal reported to have a cost of $20 million. Ogden had agreed to acquire all the holdings of Edwards Enterprises that included other racetracks in West Virginia and Maine and several bath, tennis, and golf facilities. In August of 1972, 18 thoroughbreds perished in a barn fire. In 1974, Fairmount was annexed to the City of Collinsville and three years later connected to the city sewer system.

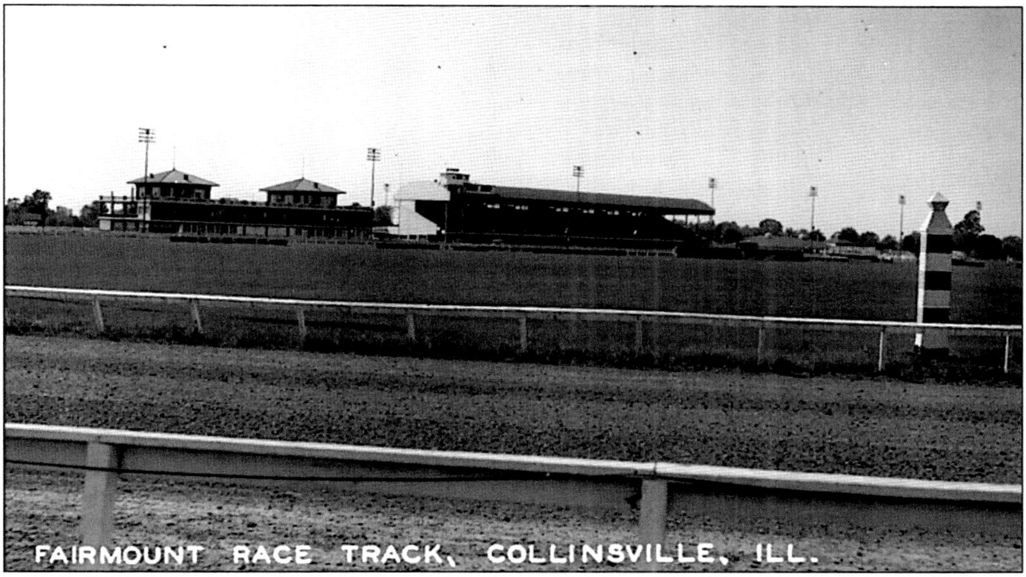

Coincidentally perhaps, there was a big fire on April 15, 1974, during a contract dispute. The fire broke out in the middle of the afternoon a day before the Illinois Racing Board was going to make a decision on the impasse. Seven nights of the 75-date season had already been missed because Ogden Corporation and the Horsemen's Benevolent and Protective Association couldn't agree on how to split the commissions and breakage from wagering.

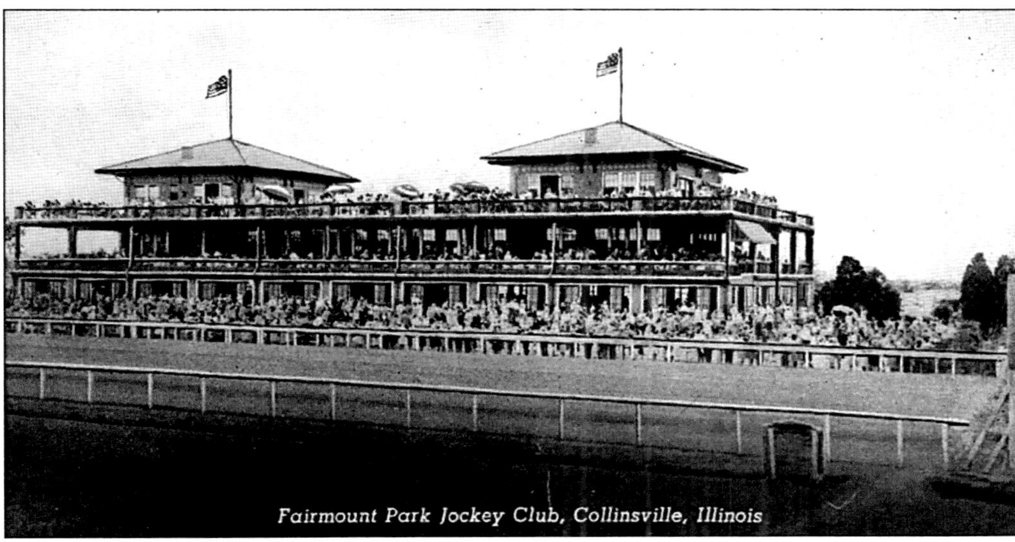

Collinsville firemen were overwhelmed by the size of the fire and made a desperate attempt to save the nearly fifty-year old grandstand. There were ten fire engines at the fire. Fortunately there was only one injury, that person being a fireman. Over 1,000 horses in nearby barns were not harmed. It was estimated that there was $6 million worth of damage to the structure and equipment; the computers alone were valued at over $1 million. Fairmount then ran its meets at nearby Cahokia Downs until 1976 when it reopened.

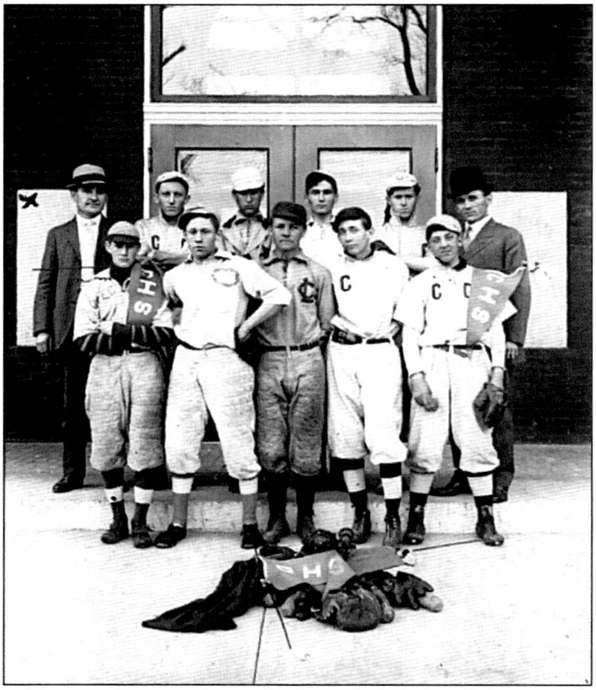

This real photo postcard is undoubtedly an early Collinsville Township High School baseball team. The picture was taken in front of the high school. On the back of the postcard is inscribed only "1909-1910, never were beaten." The only identified player is Mathew Welch, fifth from the left in the back row.

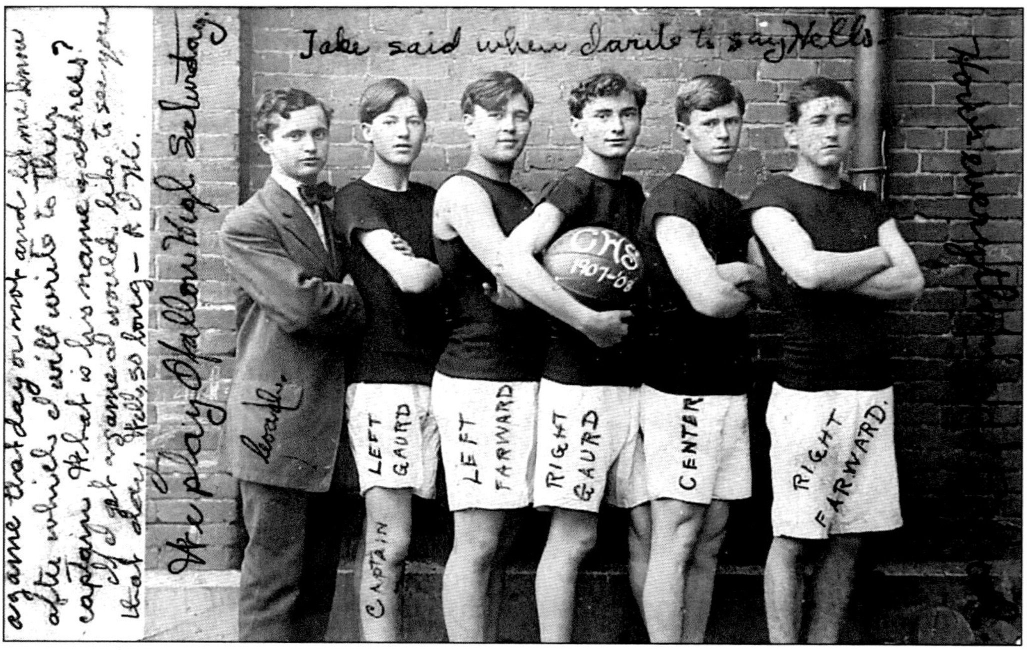

In 1907 Bliss Dee, the school principal, was responsible for initiating and coaching the first boys' basketball team at CTHS. The 1907-08 team shown won eight games and lost four. Team members are (from left to right): Coach Bliss Dee, Ralph Mabbs, Gayle Windsor, Uen Harrison, Mat We1ch, and John Snadden.

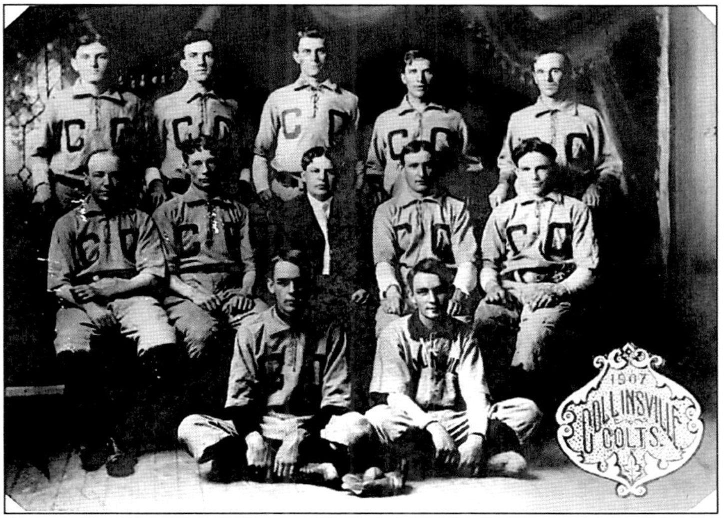

This is a real photo postcard showing the 1907 Collinsville Colts baseball team. The names of the players are unknown. Louis Lumaghi Sr., Collinsville mayor from 1901 to 1905, was a pitcher and manager of the Colts for a while. He had also been a member of the Reds. The Colts were formed in 1885; organized baseball was introduced to Collinsville in 1878. The name was initially the Lumaghi Colts and later the Collinsville Colts. It was said of the early Colts: "They were a hard-boiled team made up of youngsters who had cut their eye teeth on a lump of coal and worked underground from age 12."

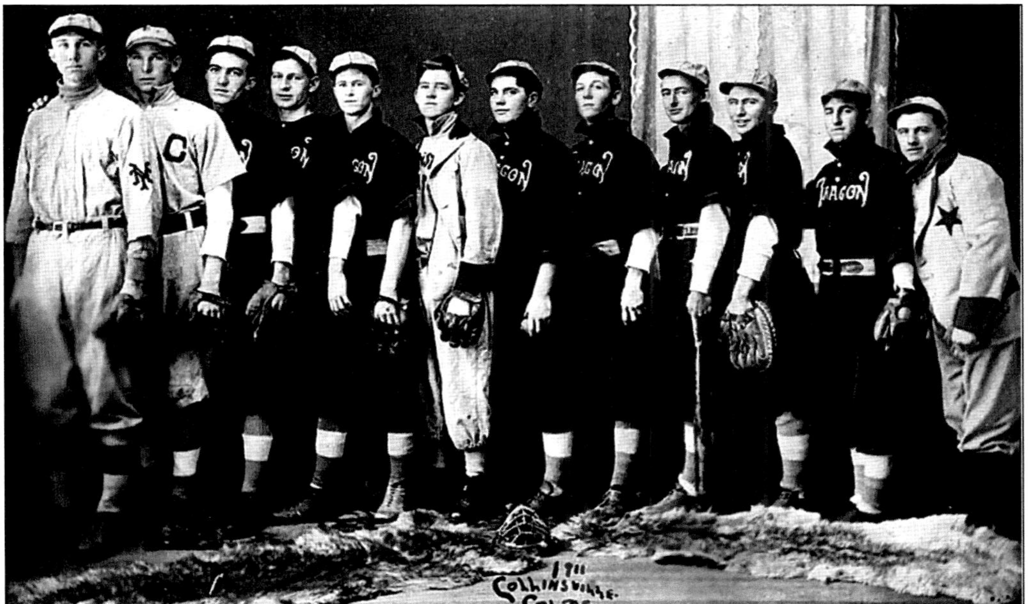

This is an image of the 1911 Colts. They are (from left to right): Ferd "Fifty" Wilbert, George Needle, Bill Jokerst, Mickey Shannon, Mat Welch, unidentified, Bill Staten, "Choppy" O'Hara, ? Lawhead, and ? Fischer. The remaining two are unknown. Some of the names of the early teams were the Caseyville Mutuals, Mueller Stars, Dutch Hollow Ku Kluxers, and Horseshoe Bitters (Hardscrabble Mine team). The Collinsville Reds were formed in 1898; they dominated the Trolley League for a number of years. Arthur Fletcher, associated with major league baseball for 39 years, was a product of the Reds and perhaps the best player ever to come out of Collinsville. After the Reds broke up, the Maroons became the dominant team.

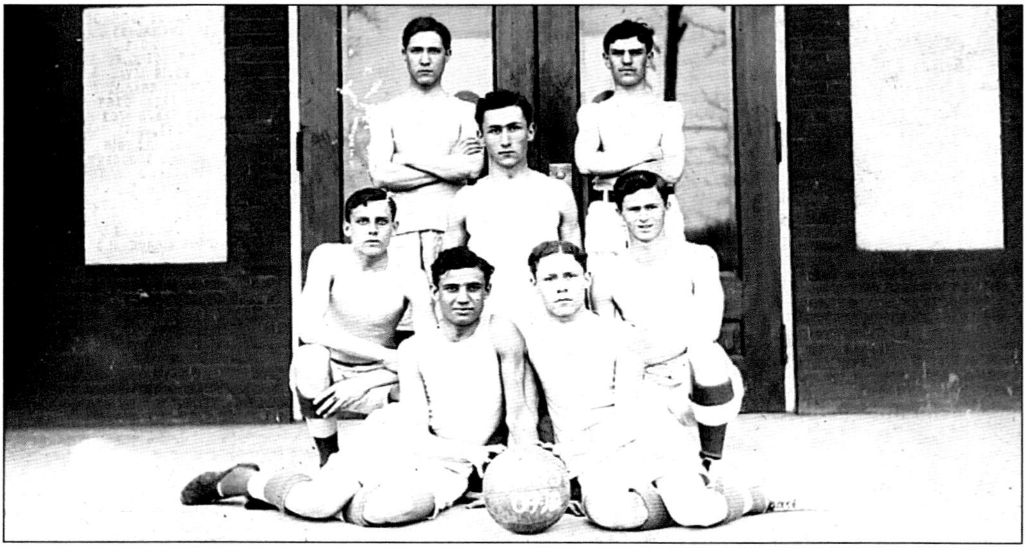

The 1909-10 Collinsville Township High School basketball team pictured had a record of 12 wins and 4 losses. It was coached for one year by R.C. Sayre. Players are pictured, from left to right: (front row) Jules Field and Roy Johnson; (middle row) Elmer Harrison, Walter Lepp, and Mat Welch; (back row) Bill Johnson and unidentified.

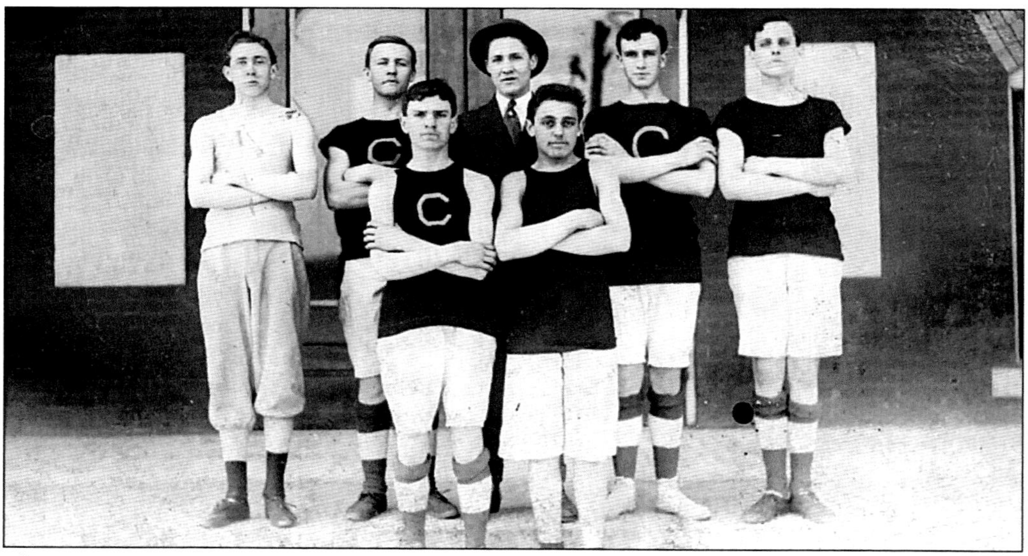

This is a *c.* 1910 real photo postcard; the team and players are unidentified. The picture was taken in front of CTHS. According to Frank Pitol, in his comprehensive book on Kahok basketball: "During the 1909-10 season the first organized league was introduced. It included Belleville, East St. Louis, O'Fallon, Lebanon, Edwardsville, and Collinsville. Collinsville tied with Lebanon for the championship but lost the playoff game which was played in the Louisiana Hall in St. Louis."

Pictured is the 1910-11 CTHS basketball team (from front to back): (nearest) Jules Fields, Earl Francis, Roy Johnson, and George Holding; (back row, from left to right) Max Colbert, Coach William Green, and Elmer Harrison. William Green coached for two years. This team was 13 and 3, and the following year it was 15 and 3. Pitol recounted: "The score of a 1910 game found in the Granite City newspaper has Collinsville on the short end of a 91 to 13 score. This still stands as the worst defeat for a Collinsville team. The previous week Collinsville defeated Belleville 78 to 8."

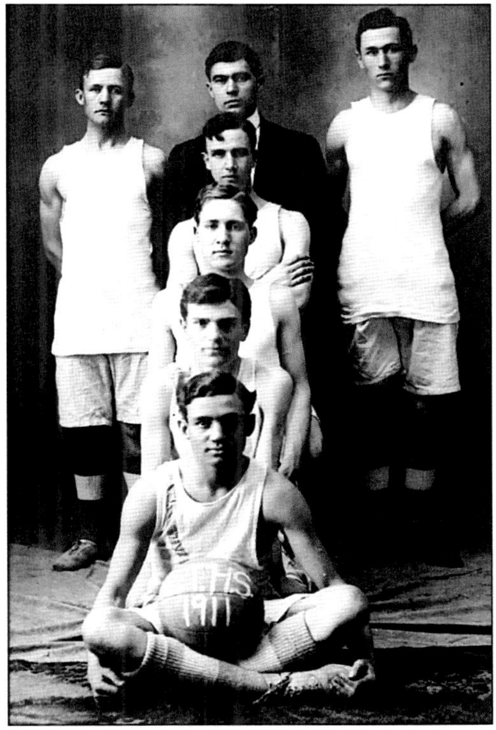

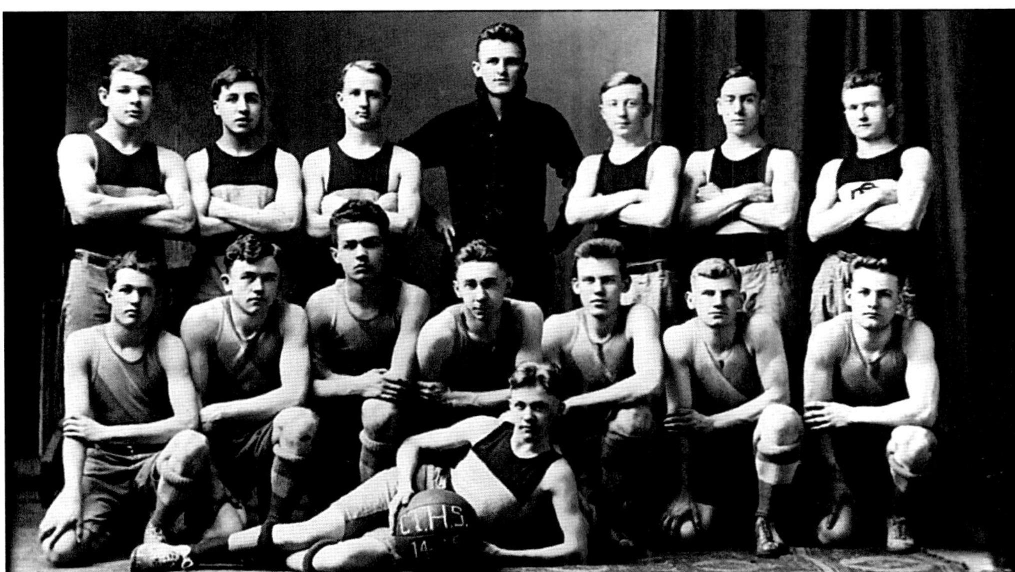

T.J. Beck coached for two years at CTHS compiling a 38 and 16 record. Concerning this team that compiled a 21 and 9 record and played tough teams, Pitol states: "The 1915 team stands as one of the best teams to wear the Collinsville uniform." The 1914-15 CTHS basketball team is pictured here, from left to right: (with the ball) Roy Jenkins; (front row) A. Kneedler, Homer Dillon, Milburn Dorris, Tony Gaizat, Erwin Brede, John Willie Martin, and Elton Brayford; (back row) B. Lewis, Hubert Kneedler, B. Ludweg, Coach T.J. Beck, A. Needam, Fred Kaveny, and L. Brewer.

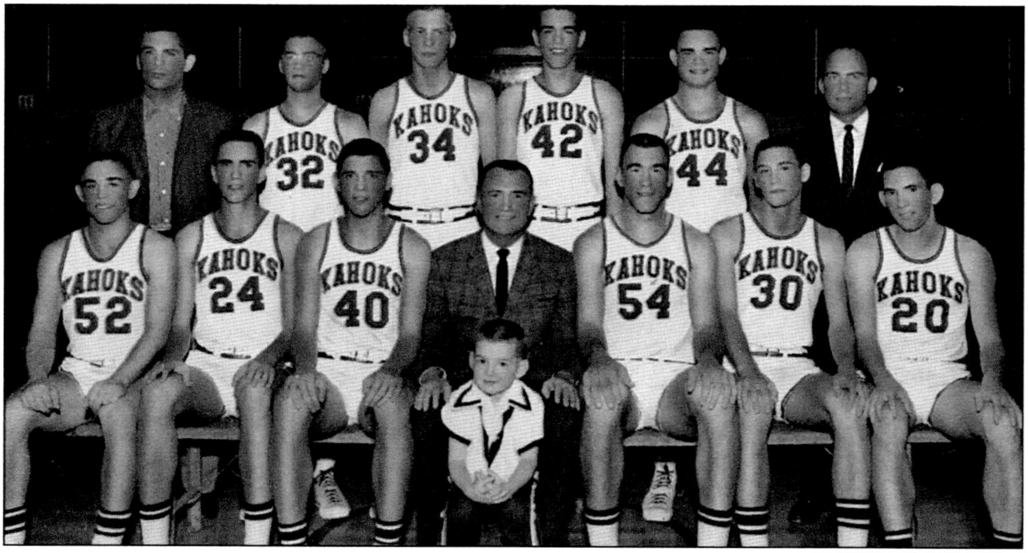

Members of the Collinsville High School 1961 Kahoks undefeated basketball team are pictured from left to right: (seated) Bob Meadows, Ron Mottin, Fred Riddle Jr., Coach Vergil Fletcher and his son Mark, Bogie Redmon, Bob Basola, and Bob Simpson; (standing) Assistant Coach Bill Hellyer, Than Byrkit, Ron Matikitis, Joe Brennan, Harry Hildreth, and Assistant Coach Bert Weber. The 1961 and 1965 state championship teams have been placed in the Illinois Basketball Hall of Fame. Both postcards on this page were produced for Home Federal Savings and Loan Association of Collinsville.

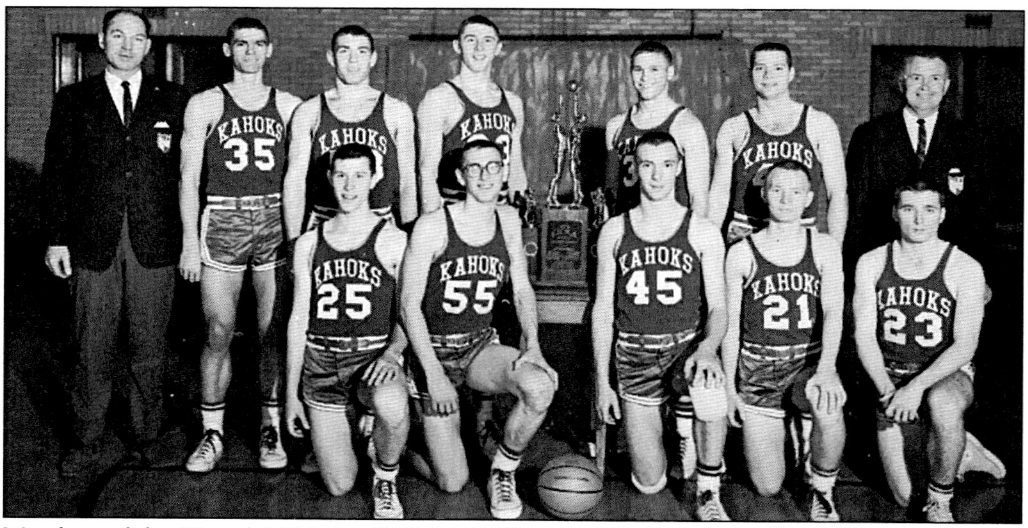

Members of the 30 and 2 Kahoks 1965 State Champion Basketball team are shown from left to right: (kneeling) Bruce Evans, Mike Vincent, Dennis Arnold, Keith Zeisel, and Mick Belobraydic; (standing) Assistant Coach Frank Pitol, Harry Parker, Don Birger, Dennis Pace, Jack Darlington, Steven Gauen, and Coach Vergil Fletcher. Coaching in Collinsville from 1946 through 1978, Fletcher's teams won 747 games while losing 110. He is a selectee of the Illinois Basketball Hall of Fame and the National Basketball Hall of Fame. In June of 2004, Vergil Fletcher was inducted to the National High School Athletic Coaches Association Hall of Fame.

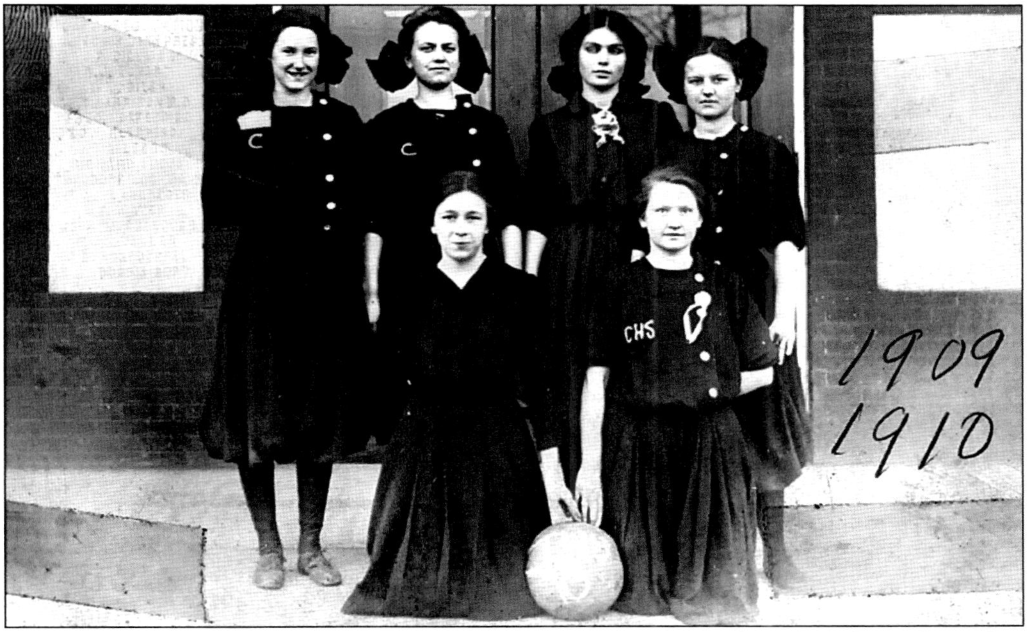

According to Frank Pitol, author of *The Wonderful World of Collinsville Basketball*, "Collinsville's first basketball can be traced back prior to 1907, but boys weren't doing the playing. The girls started playing the game as early as 1903-04. Most of the boys were reluctant to take up basketball, as they considered it a sissy game." This is a picture of the 1909-10 CTHS girl's basketball team. From left to right are: (kneeling) Babe Martin and Kate Schmidt; (standing) Myrtle Welch, Blanche Powell, Alice Williams, and Gertrude Fletcher.

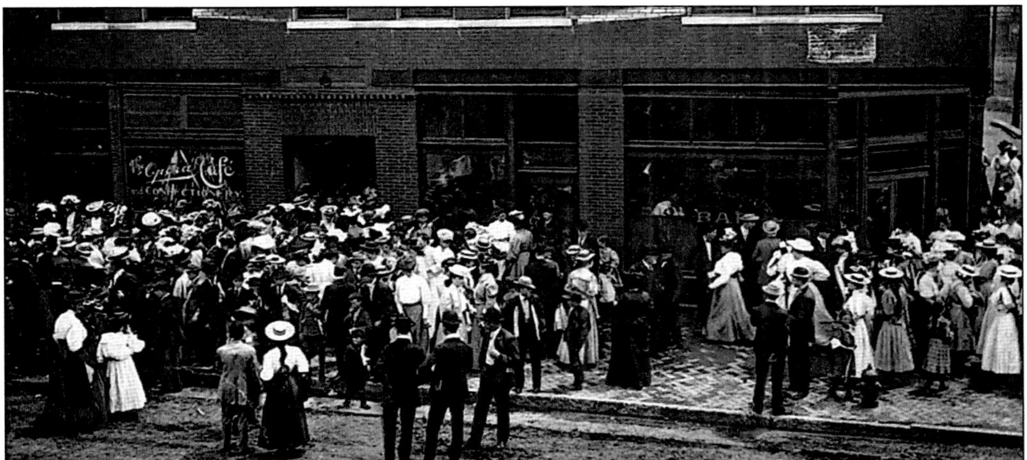

High School Meet, May 10th 1907, Collinsville, Ill.

Titled "High School Meet, May 10th, 1907," this scene was captured in front of the Opera House on the southeast corner of Main and Clinton streets. The Opera House was constructed in 1906 and was the site of many civic, school, and social events. The edifice housed the Opera Cafe & Confectionary, a barber shop, and on the corner, the Opera House Bar.

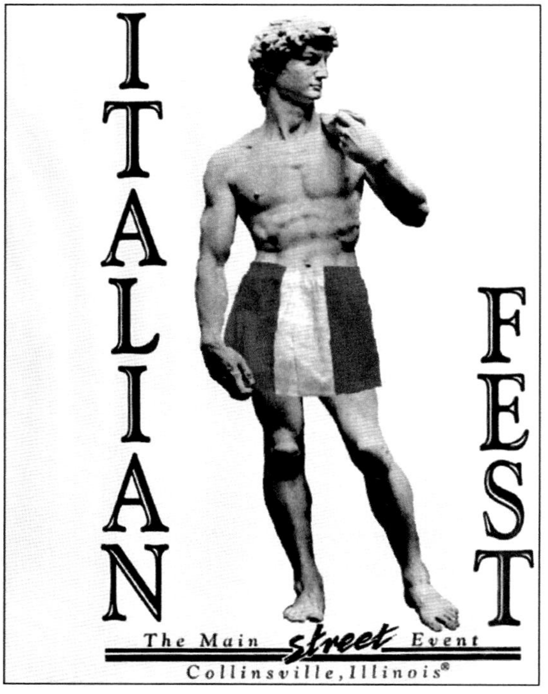

As a result of a 1984 effort to promote downtown Collinsville on Columbus Day, the annual Italian Fest was born. The festival, honoring the city's Italian heritage, has become a tradition on the third weekend of September. Family fun, Italian cuisine, and a variety of entertainment are the ingredients of the gala affair. Activities include a grape stomp, a 5K run/walk, wine-making/tasting, Special Olympics events, a bocce-ball tournament, the moonlight paisan pedal push, and a 100-plus unit parade.

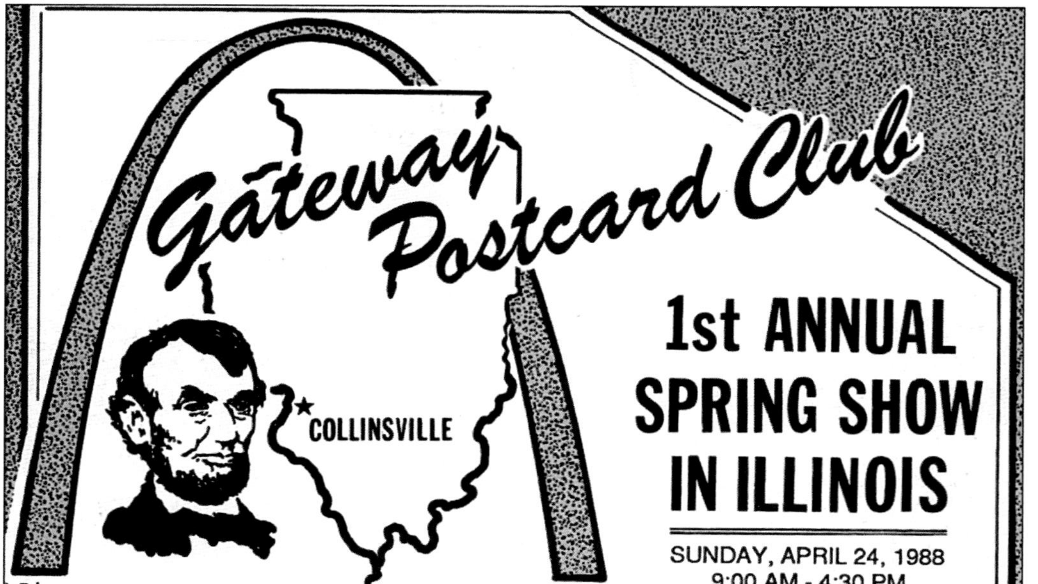

This postcard advertises a Gateway Postcard Club of Greater St. Louis postcard show. The shows feature a display of over a million vintage picture postcards for sale by area and out-of-state dealers. They have been held in Collinsville since 1988 because of the availability of a well-lighted hall and an easily accessible location. Founded in 1974, the Gateway Club meets monthly at the Kirkwood Community Center. It provides a quarterly bulletin, a library, guest speakers, and social activities.

Seven

The Henry J. Marshall Postcard Collection

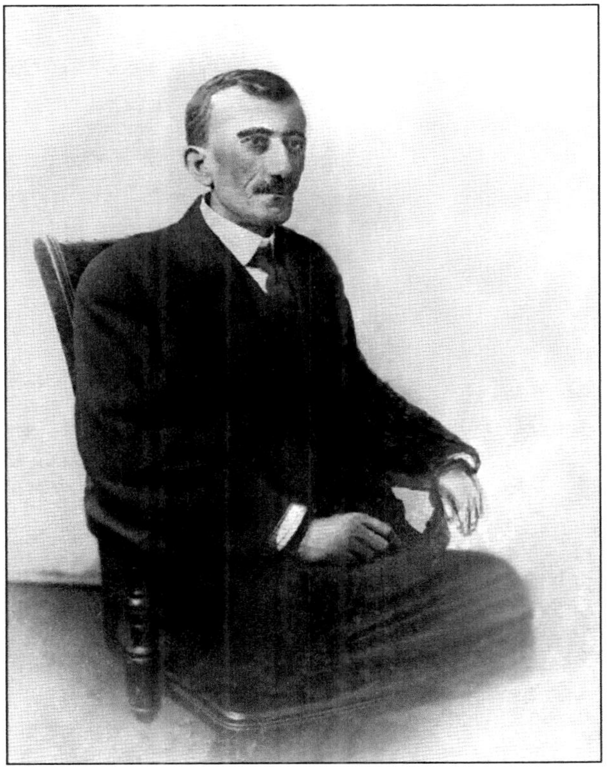

Henry J. Marshall, only child of Joseph and Wilhelmina Marshall, was born in St. Louis c. 1855. The family moved to Collinsville at the outbreak of the Civil War. Henry's father, Joseph, opened Collinsville's first millinery and notion store and purchased other business properties. In 1879, he took his son as a business partner. Henry married Ida Gerk; they had five children while living in Collinsville.

In 1891, Henry J. Marshall sold his business and moved to St. Louis. In 1911, be moved back to Collinsville and had a home built at 820 West Clay Street. The house still stands. Because of poor health, Marshall spent much time in St. Louis near his chosen medical facilities.

By this time, Marshall had become a self-appointed Collinsville historian. He was concerned about the lack of a recorded history of Collinsville.

He researched the history of Collinsville, wrote articles for the *Collinsville Herald* on the topic and openly advocated the creation of a historical society for the collection and preservation of related materials.

According to the *Collinsville Herald* of May 7, 1915, an informal ceremony marked the laying of the cornerstone of the new post office to be constructed at 201 West Clay Street. A copper box containing historical information about Collinsville had been prepared by the late Henry J. Marshall for insertion in the cornerstone. Chairman J.A. Yates read from Marshall's introductory letter: "The contents of this box consist of 107 postal card views of all the old landmarks that I was able to secure up to this date. Among the lot are also the photos of all the mayors and newspapers in the history of Collinsville."

Several days after his father's death, a son of Marshall delivered the copper box to Mr. Yates. He apparently died some time between 1912 and 1915. A duplicate set of these items was to be left with Marshall's family and a third set to be presented to the public library when that institution was established. In late September of 1964, officials removed the copper box from the cornerstone of the vacated post office. The contents of the box were presented to the Collinsville Memorial Public Library. Some years later, the postcards were transferred to the Collinsville Historical Museum.

Marshall had good intentions and made considerable effort to preserve the photographs and data; however, the photos on the postcards were damaged and continue to disintegrate. Most of the brief typed descriptions on the postcard backs remain unharmed. Except for a few obvious errors, we have to take the information as being accurate. The whereabouts of Marshall's family is unknown; the set of materials that the public library was to receive at Marshall's death is a mystery, and the disposition of the original material unfortunate.

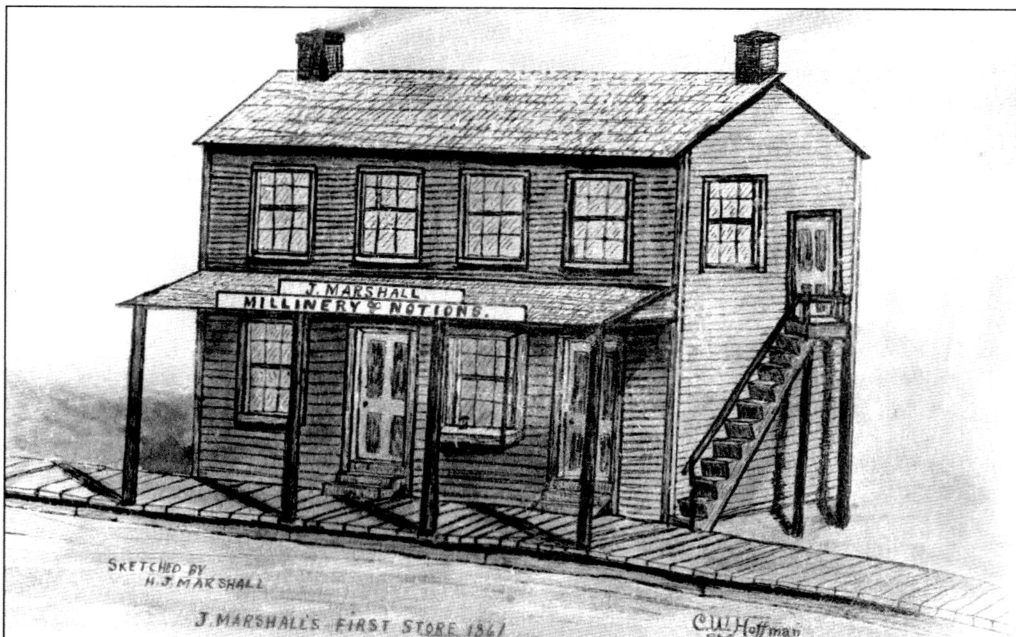

One example of a postcard from the Marshall collection (front side).

According to the 1937 *Collinsville Herald Centennial Edition*: "It is said that the late Henry Marshall who lived for many years on West Clay street kept large numbers of newspaper files and other historical material . . . . . A few years ago the *Herald* called on members of the family now living in St. Louis about the matter and was told that they had several times offered the material to the city, but at the time there was no library and little interest in such matters and they went begging. When the family moved from Collinsville, it destroyed whole trunks full of the irreplaceable documents."

The only items that remain are the postcards; many of them are presented in the following pages. The Marshall photos were enhanced via computer by Ralph Haury. Henry Marshall attempted to do what the Collinsville Historical Museum is in the process of doing, collecting and preserving Collinsville history. Hopefully, we can learn from Marshall's successes and failures; we must appreciate his efforts. Let us be grateful for the materials that did survive. "His one great desire is to preserve the true history of Collinsville for future generations." (Interviewer, *Edwardsville Intelligencer* about Henry Marshall, 1912.) Sources of the postcard images in this section:
(a) Sketched from memory by H.J. Marshall.
(b) Drawn from Marshall sketch by G.W. Hoffman of St. Louis.
(c) Plat litho.
(d) Photo from *Collinsville Herald*.
(e) Photo was enhanced via computer by Ralph Haury.

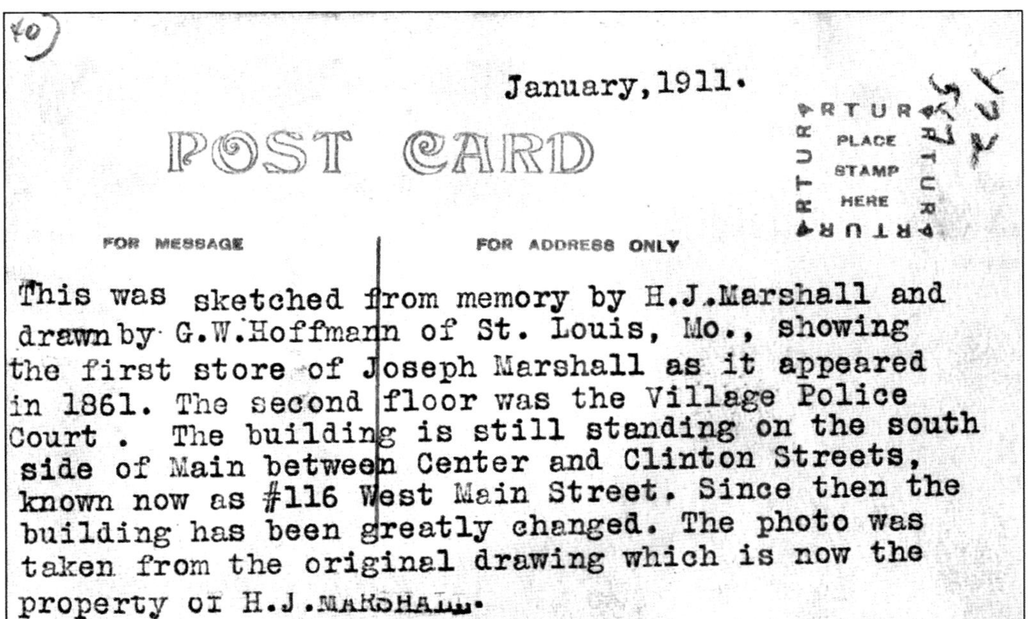
January, 1911.

POST CARD

PLACE STAMP HERE

FOR MESSAGE | FOR ADDRESS ONLY

This was sketched from memory by H.J.Marshall and drawn by G.W.Hoffmann of St. Louis, Mo., showing the first store of Joseph Marshall as it appeared in 1861. The second floor was the Village Police Court . The building is still standing on the south side of Main between Center and Clinton Streets, known now as #116 West Main Street. Since then the building has been greatly changed. The photo was taken from the original drawing which is now the property of H.J.MARSHALL.

The back side of the postcard from previous page.

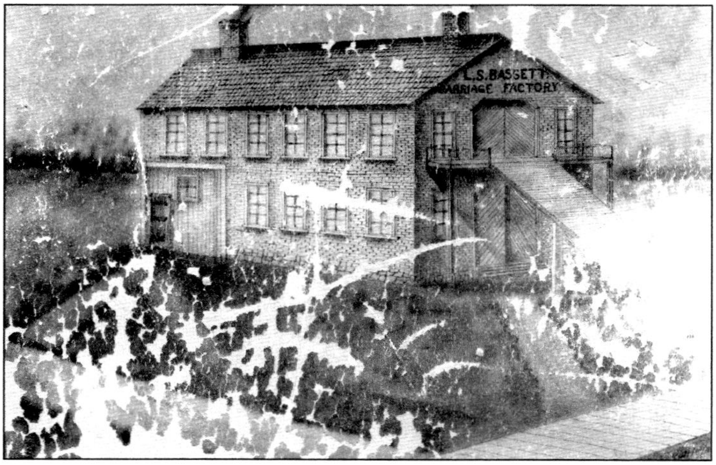

This is an example of an untouched and deteriorating Marshall postcard. In about 1860, the Bassett Carriage Factory was located in the middle of the 200 block of Vandalia Street on the west side. The building had also been used as a temporary school, a turning school, and the Bischoff Soda Company. (a.)

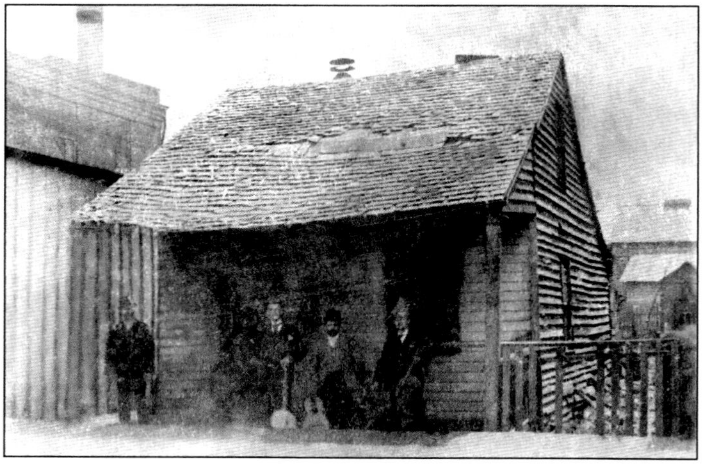

In the early 1840s, this old house, owned by Mrs. A. Walters, was a roadside inn used by farmers on their way to the St. Louis market. It was later owned by "Uncle" Jimmy Owens and in 1856 by C.G. Blum. (e.)

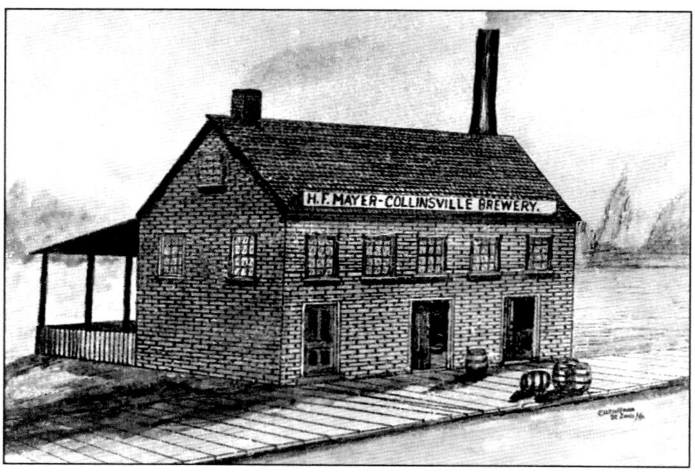

The first Collinsville brewery, owned by H.F. Mayer, was built in 1858. It stood on the west side of the street in the 400 block of Vandalia Street. Early in the 1860s, J. Fix assumed ownership; and in the early 1870s, the building was destroyed by fire. (a, e.)

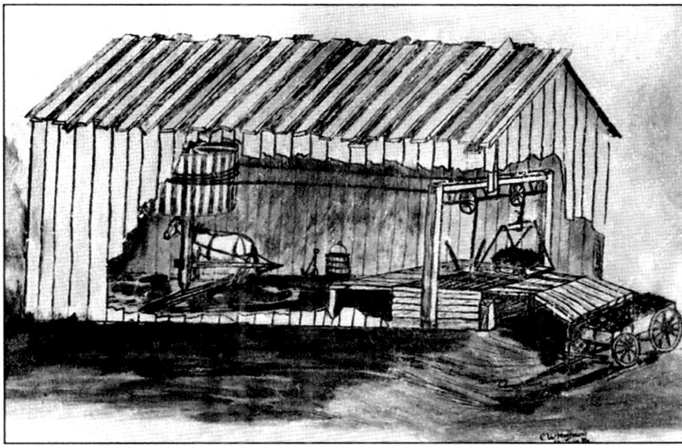

The first Collinsville coal mine was located at the south end of Mill Street on the northeast corner. Peter Wonderly began the coal mine in about 1859; Pat Darmody was the hoister, and the hoist was horse driven. Most of the coal was used to run local mills and factories. (a, b, e.)

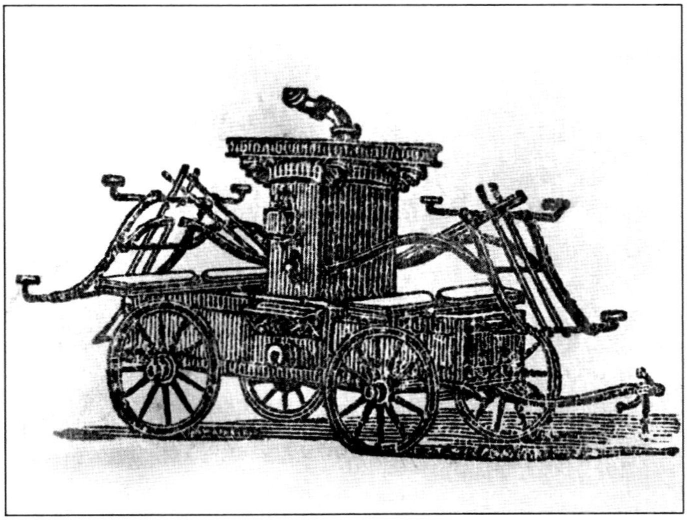

Collinsville purchased this fire hose cart and pumper from the City of St. Louis in 1860. Many years after it had been used for fighting fires, the Missouri Historical Society allegedly had it restored. In about 1910, it became part of an exhibit. (e.)

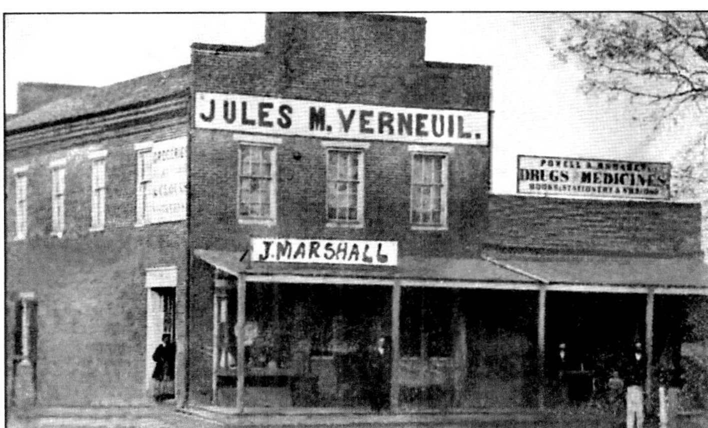

This is a photo of the building owned by Joseph Marshall on the northeast corner of Main and Morrison. In 1867, it housed Marshall's General Store and the Powell and Davison Drug Store. The original photo belonged to Mrs. A.M. Powell. (e.)

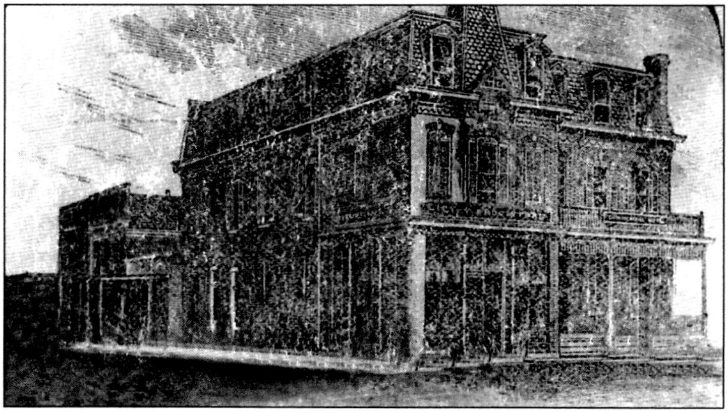

Pictured on the southeast corner of Main and Morrison streets c. 1886 were the Commercial Hotel and the E. Gerding Drug Store facing South Morrison. The furniture store of M. Wilhelm and M. Brede's tin store faced East Main Street. (d, e.)

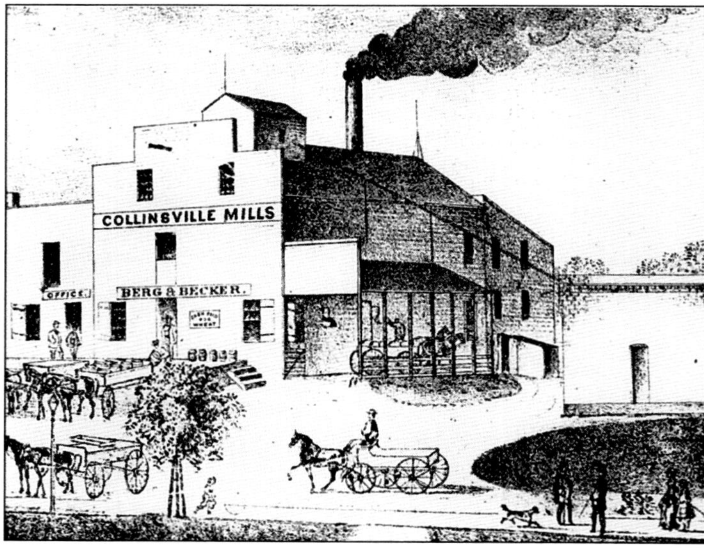

In the early 1870s, the Collinsville Flour Mill, operated by Berg and Becker was located at about 215 West Main Street. John Becker, educated in Perry County, Missouri, was the first mayor of Collinsville. (e.)

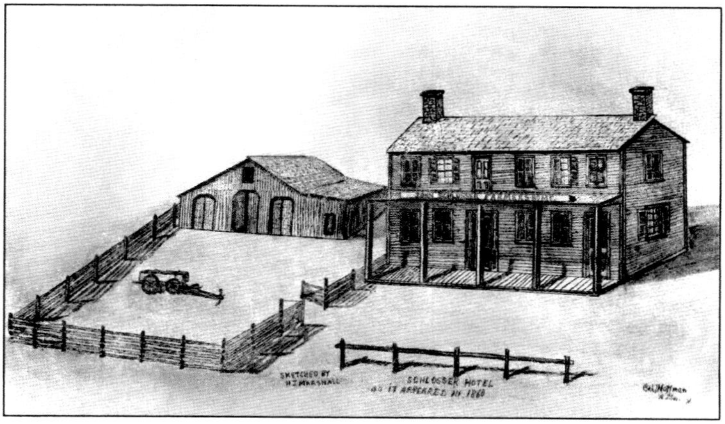

In 1860, the John Schlosser Farmers' Home stood on the northwest corner of Main and Seminary. On their journey to and from St. Louis, farmers from the eastern part of the county, would stop overnight for food and rest for themselves and their horses. (a, b, e.)

Tom White has added missing parts of the image to a deteriorating Marshall postcard. The first City Hall included a jail, an engine house, a police court, and a stock law pen in the rear. Located at about 108 (North) Vandalia Street, it was demolished in 1885 after the present City Hall was constructed. (a, b.)

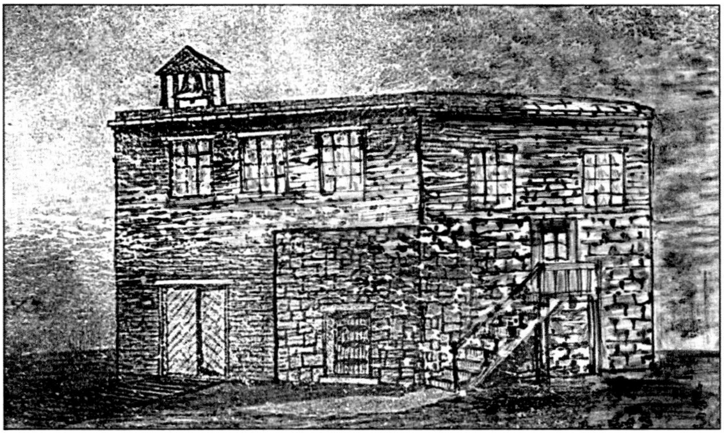

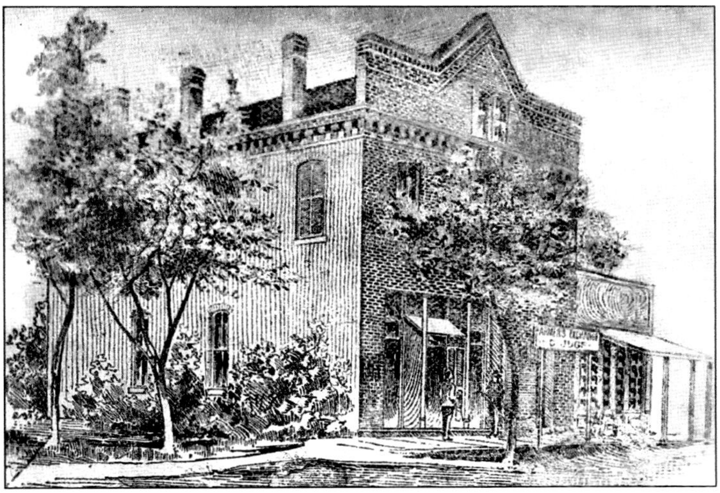

This building was located on the northeast corner of Main and Vandalia streets c. 1886. A saloon, the Farmers Exchange, was owned by C. Juge. (d, e.)

This blacksmith shop, owned by Wm. Johnson, was built in 1878 and was located behind the first City Hall; it faced Chestnut Street. In 1882, it was sold to J. Kalina who had it moved to about 110 North Center. Wieduwilt built a wagon shop adjoining the blacksmith shop. He eventually became the owner of both shops and moved them to the northeast corner of Center and Clay. (e.)

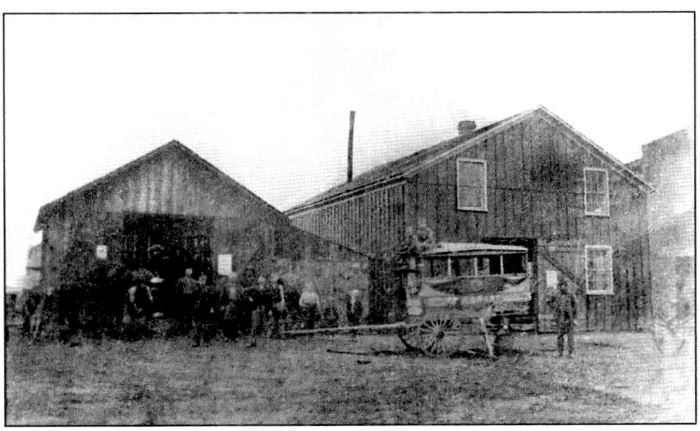

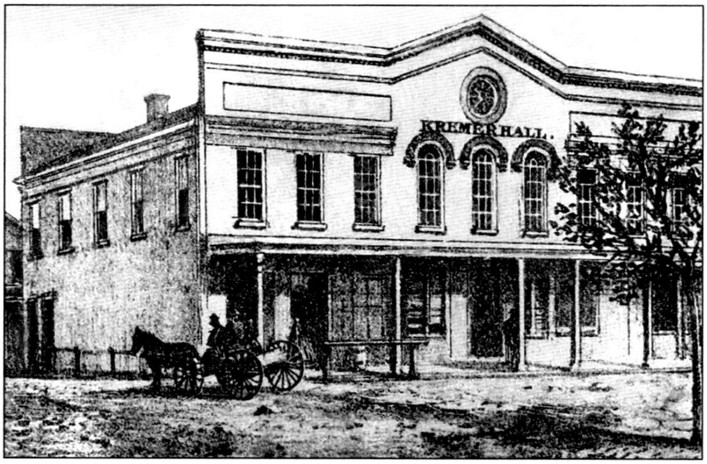

This is Kremer Hall and the J. Kremer General Store as it appeared in the mid-1870s on the southwest corner of Main and Morrison. Town meetings and social activities were held in Kremer Hall. J. Mersinger eventually became the owner of the building, and the area became known as the Mersinger block. (e.)

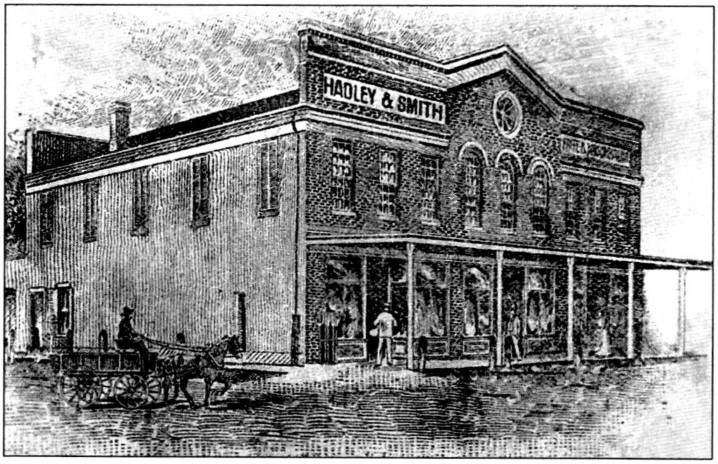

By 1886, the Mersinger building housed the general store of Hadley and Smith and the hardware store of Krite and Kirschbaum. The address was listed as 124-128 East Main Street. (d, e.)

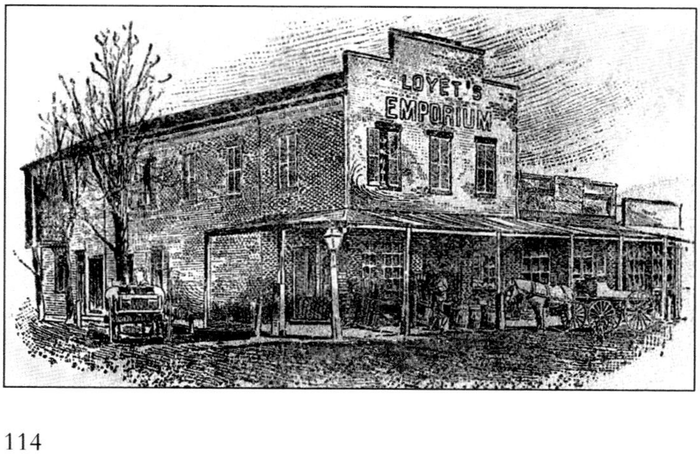

The general store of J.L. Loyet was located on the northeast corner of Main and Morrison, c. 1880. The building was owned by Joseph Marshall and eventually by his son, Henry. (d, e.)

The Valley Flouring Mills was located at the foot of Mill Street facing the Vandalia Railroad in the mid-1880s. It later became the Tiedemann Mill. African-American churches used the nearby mill pond for baptism by immersion. (d, e.)

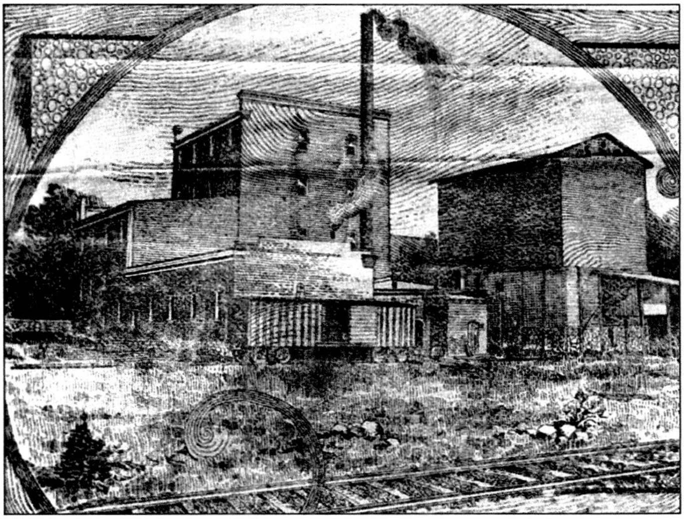

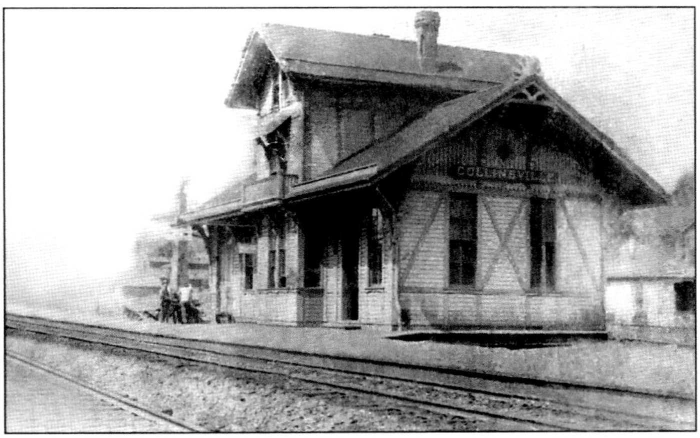

The Vandalia Depot was built in 1871 at the foot of Reed Avenue. For travelers it was within walking distance or a buckboard ride to downtown Collinsville businesses and hotels. The presence of the railroad also expanded business and industry opportunities. (e.)

This is the Illinois Hydraulic Press Brick Works as it appeared in 1886. It was located on the railroad line about a mile east of the depot. It was one of the more successful of the several Collinsville brick manufacturers. (d, e.)

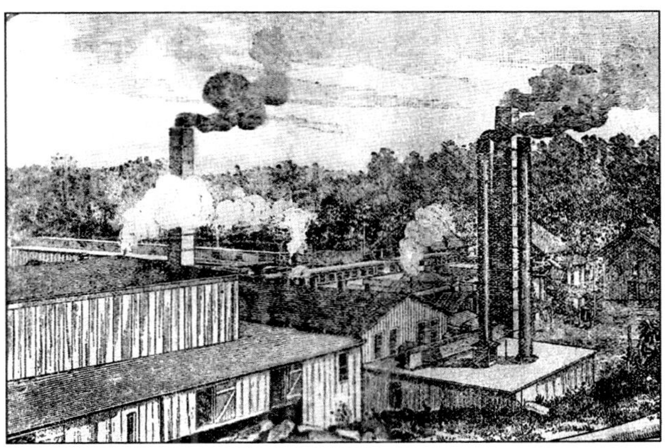

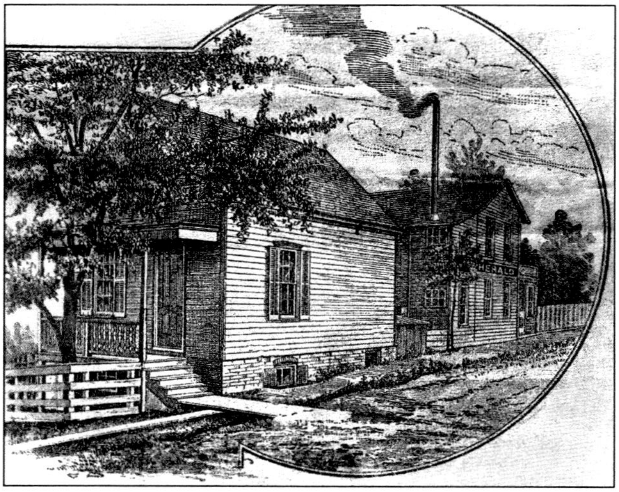

The office and residence of James N. Peers, the first owner and editor of the *Collinsville Herald*, is pictured. Peers' residence faced South Chestnut Street, and the office was directly behind the house facing the alley. The first *Collinsville Herald* was printed here in 1879. (d, e.)

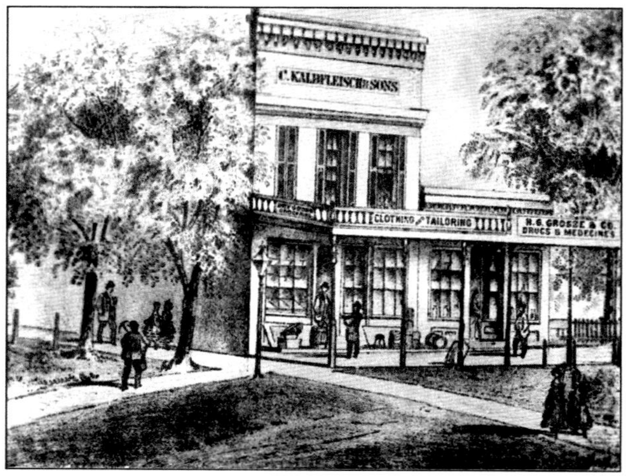

An 1873 photo shows the general store of C. Kalbfleisch and Son and the H.G. Grosse Drug Store. This building was located on the northeast corner of Main and Clinton where Simon Jewelers is currently located. (e.)

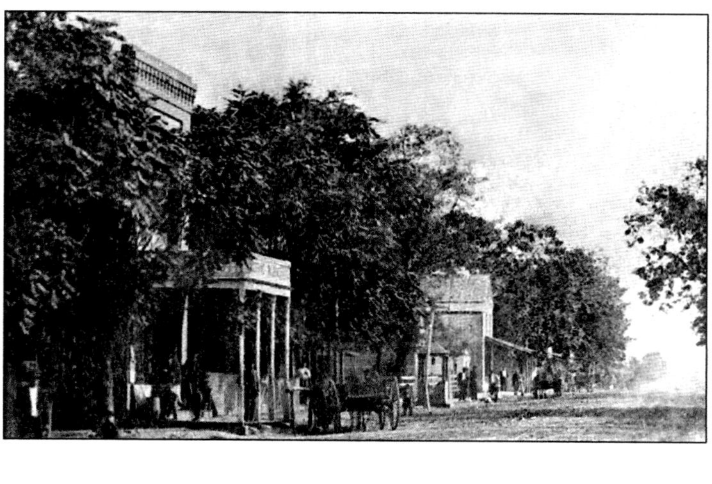

This street scene is from the early 1870s looking east from Clinton Street showing the north side of West Main. The buildings are the Kalbfleisch Store, American Hotel, Dewald Barber Shop, and C. Wacker Saloon. (e.)

One of Collinsville's most successful stores was the Yates and Ambrosius General Store. The business was located on the northwest corner of Main and Morrison in this c. 1886 photo. (d, e.)

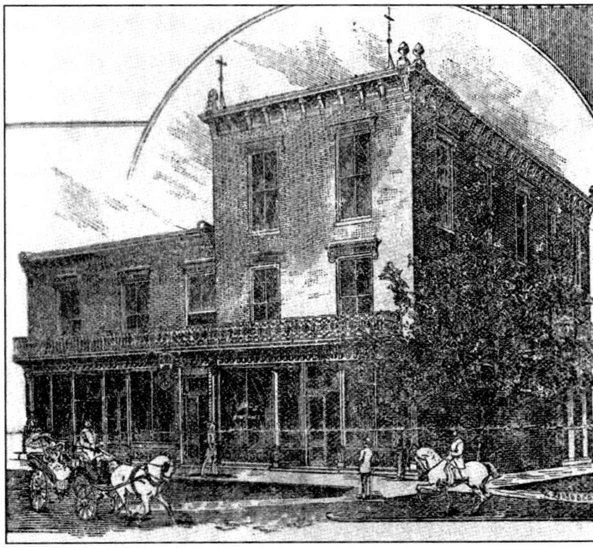

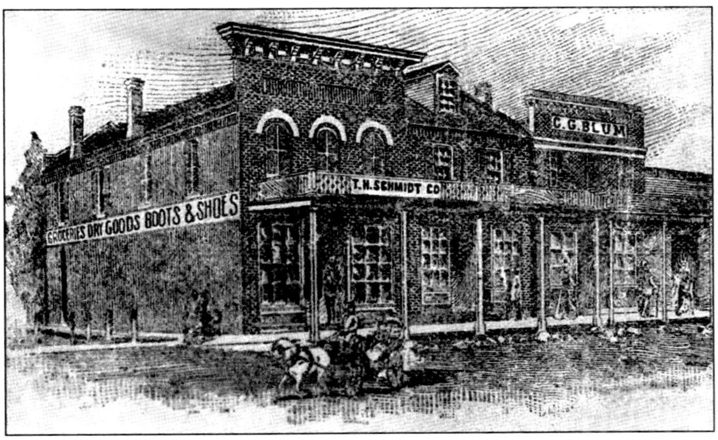

Pictured are the T.H. Schmidt Co. and General Store and the C.G. Blum Tin and Hardware Store as they appeared in the mid-1880s on the southwest corner of Main and Clinton, the present location of Miners Theatre. (d, e.)

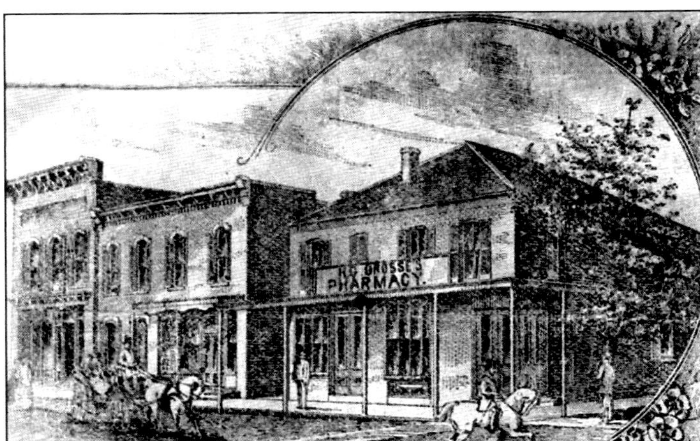

Shown are the buildings on the southeast corner of Main and Seminary streets known as 224-228 West Main in about 1886. They include the John Weber Saloon, H. Holt Butcher Shop, and Grosse Drug Store. (d, e.)

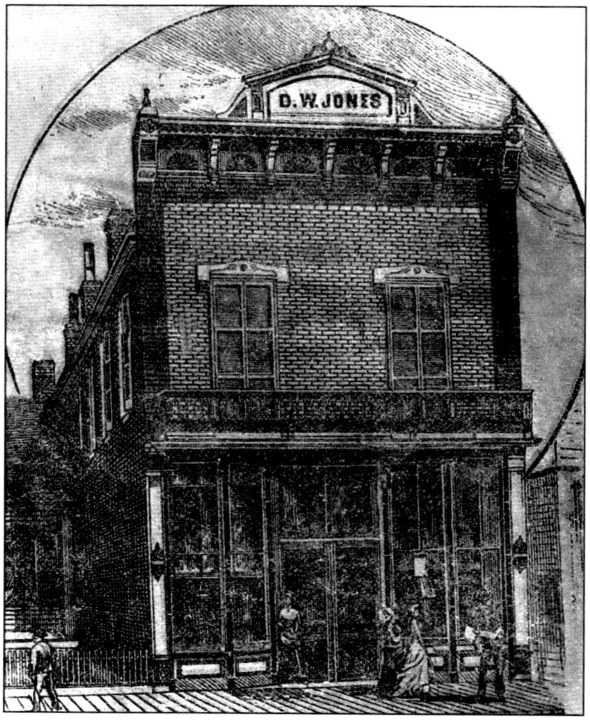

The D.W. Jones Candy and Confectionary Store was located on the north side of Main Street one door east of Center Street, also known as 105 East Main. (d, e.)

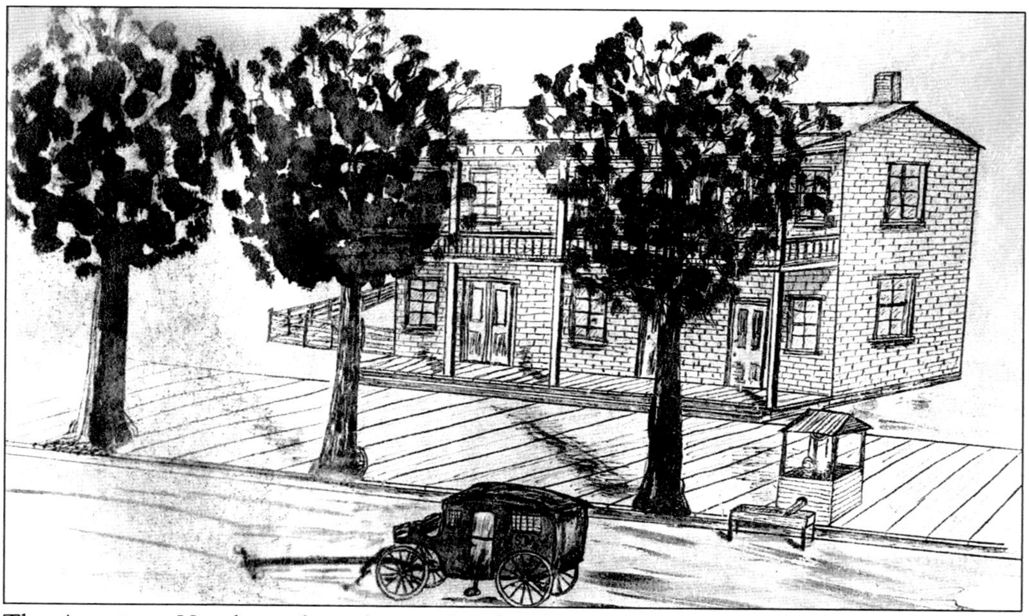

The American Hotel stood on the north side of Main Street between Center and Clinton streets. It was situated between the Kalbfleisch store and the Dewald Barber Shop. The hotel was on the horse-delivered U.S. mail route before Collinsville had a railroad. It is not clear if the 1882 American House (hotel), whose proprietor was Daniel Steele, was the same establishment. (a, b, e.)

The first banking establishment in Collinsville was organized in the early 1880s. The pictured second location was at 123 East Main Street. The bank became the First National Bank in 1902. Remaining at this location for about thirty years, it was extensively remodeled in 1916. Butterfield Jewelers has been located in this building since 1954. (d, e.)

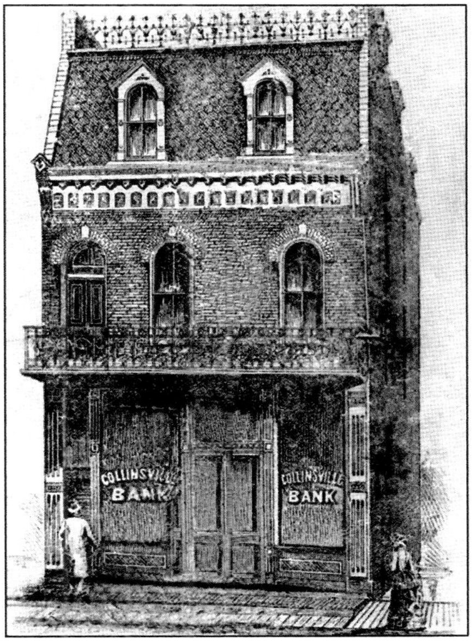

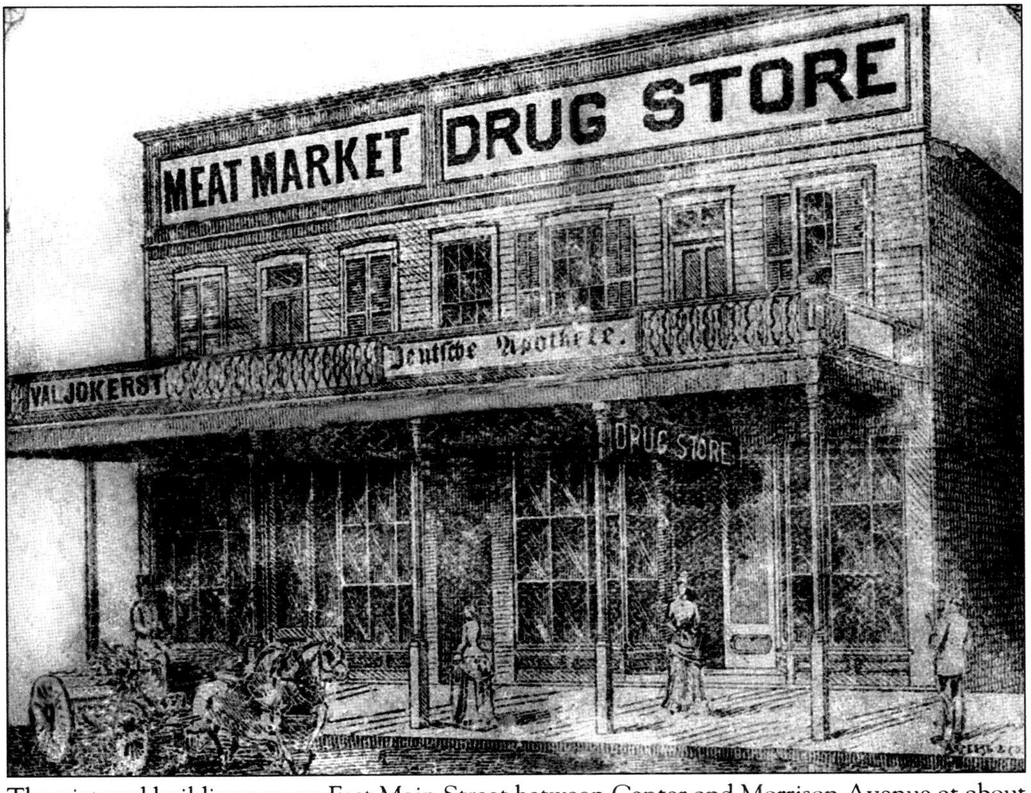

The pictured building was on East Main Street between Center and Morrison Avenue at about 115-119 East Main Street. Shown in an 1886 *Collinsville Herald*, it was occupied by the Val Jokerst Butcher Shop and the Schoettle Drug Store. At some unknown time, the building was destroyed by fire. (d, e.)

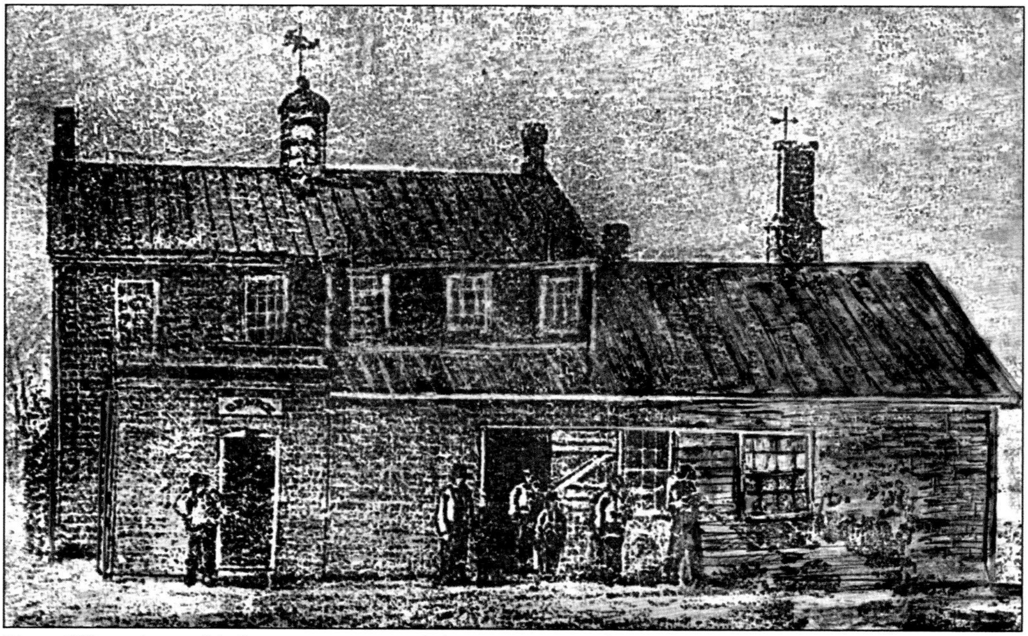

Tom White has added missing parts of the image to a deteriorating Marshall postcard. In the early 1850s, the cowbell factory of Joseph Moore was located on the north side of Main Street about 100 feet west of Aurora or at about 419 East Main. The building in the background was the first public school in the village and stood where Webster School now stands. Moore bought the building when it wasn't needed as a school and had it moved to enlarge his East Main Street factory. The factory was eventually destroyed by fire. (c.)

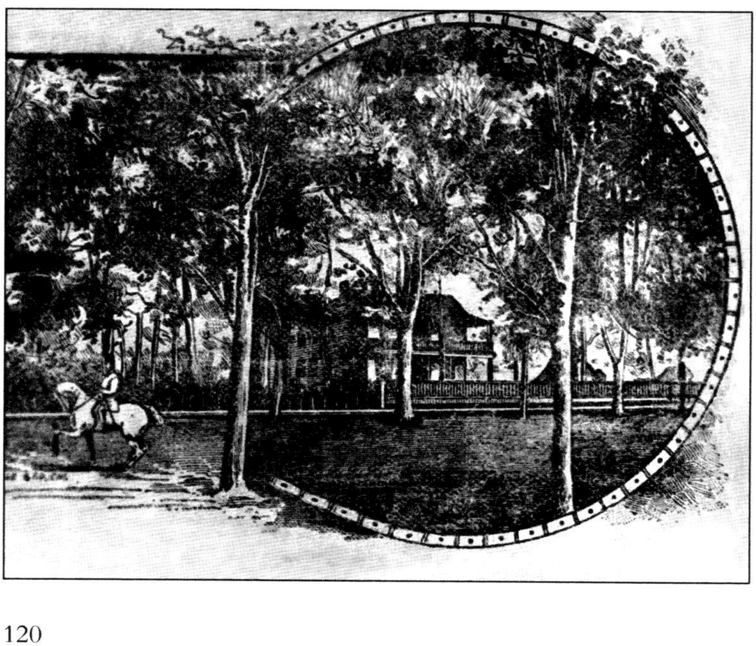

In 1889, this 14-room house became the newly organized Cottage Sanatorium. The private institution was a hospital that had an operating room and facilities to care for the sick and injured. An 1893 newspaper article stated that it had been sold at auction; it had also been remodeled as an apartment building for a time, before being returned to a single dwelling residential unit. (d, e.)

This is the F.C. Metz General Store as it appeared in the mid-1880s. It was located at 118 West Main Street. Metz's store was in business from approximately 1886 to 1911. (d, e.)

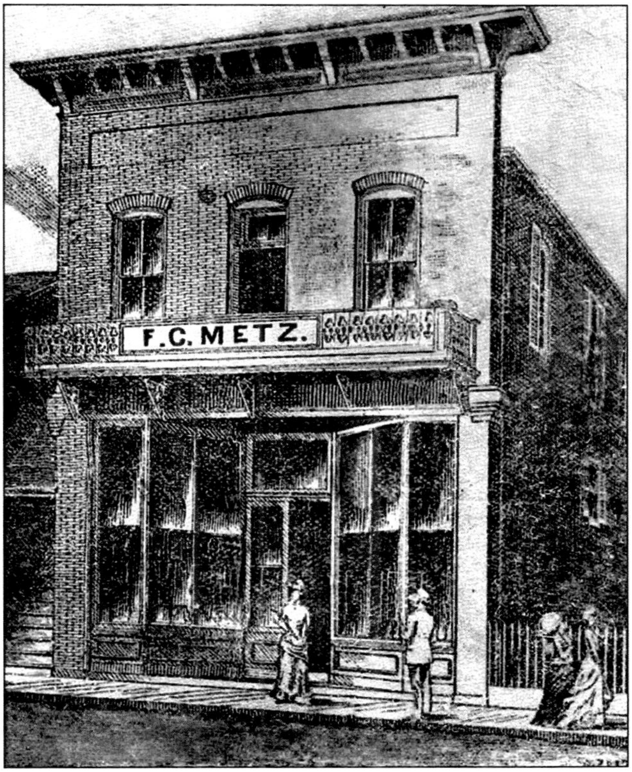

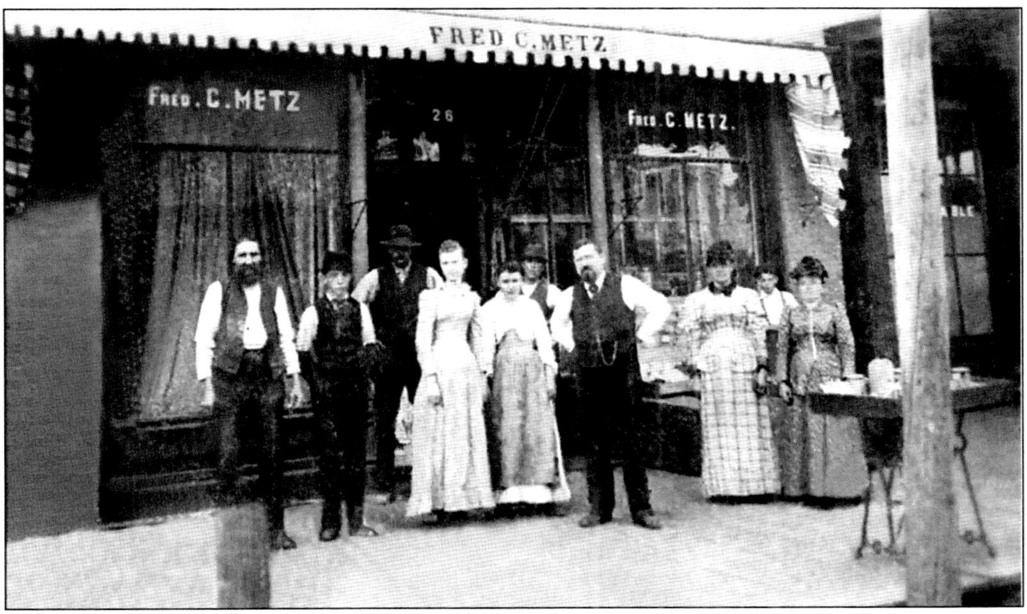

Fred Metz and his employees stand on the wooden sidewalk in front of the store. Fred is pictured with hands on his hips. This location was later the site of Silverblooms. (d, e.)

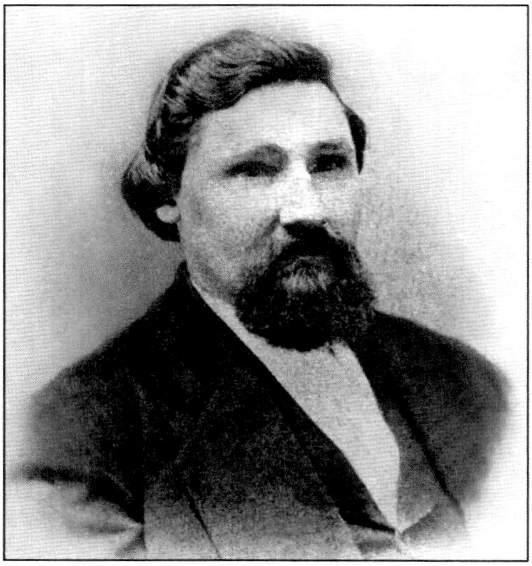

The son of Joseph Moore, I.C. Moore, was the last president of the village board, 1868-72. Beginning in 1872, with the city form of government, mayors were elected. I.C. took over the running of the cowbell factory after his father's death. (e.)

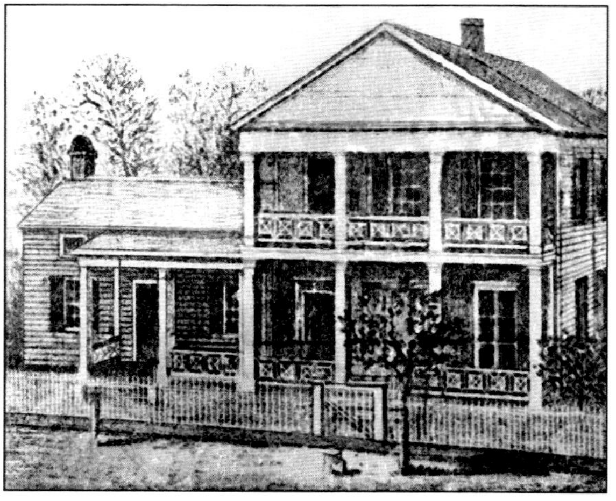

The I.C. Moore residence was located at 214 East Church Street. Public spirited and popular, Moore was presented a gold-headed cane by a group of citizens. (c, e.)

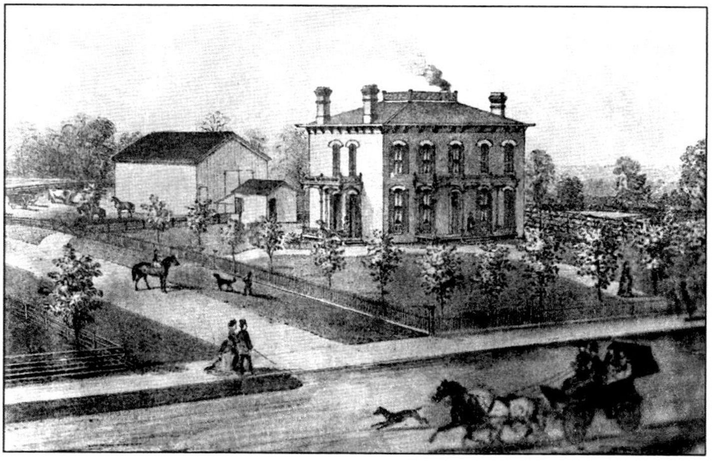

Isaac Harkelford had this Italianate style house built in 1872 at 604 West Main (the southwest corner of Main and Hesperia). He owned farmland in the American Bottom near the present Arlington Golf Course. (c, e.)

The A.W. Brown mansion was located on a prominent downtown corner, the northwest corner of Main and Morrison. This is the same place that the Yates and Ambrosius Store was located at the turn of the century. Currently Home Furniture Co. occupies this area. (c, e.)

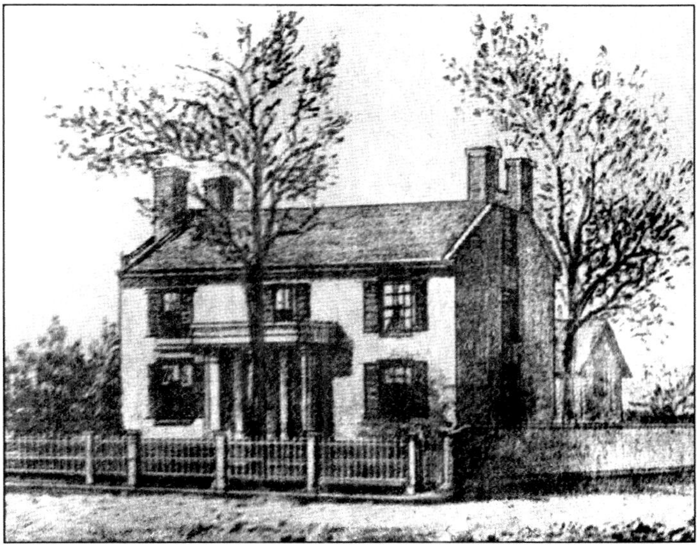

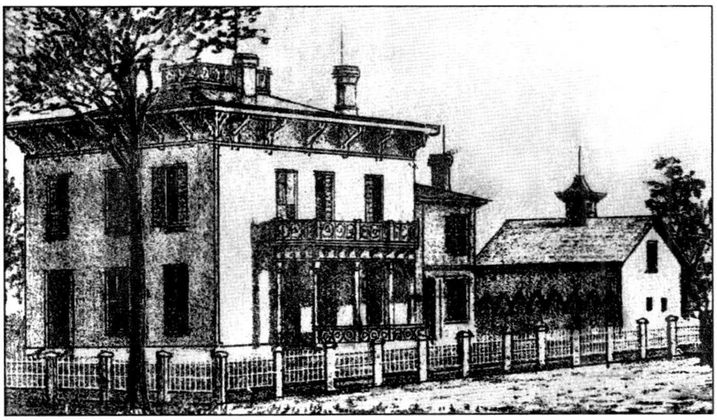

The Morrison home was on the northwest corner of Church and Chestnut streets. This area is now part of the Presbyterian Church parking lot. (c, e.)

The residence of Dr. J.L. Wadsworth stood on the north side of Church Street, 100 feet east of Morrison Street, 207 Church Street. This is approximately where the Presbyterian Church Educational Building now stands. Before becoming the mayor in 1907-08, Wadsworth had served as secretary for the village board. (c, e.)

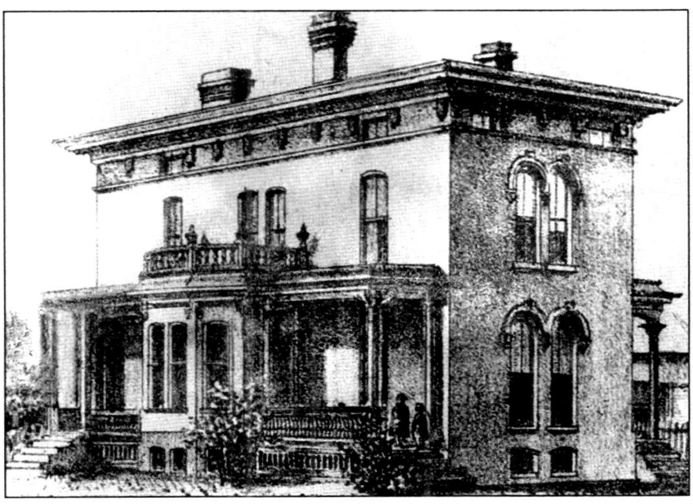

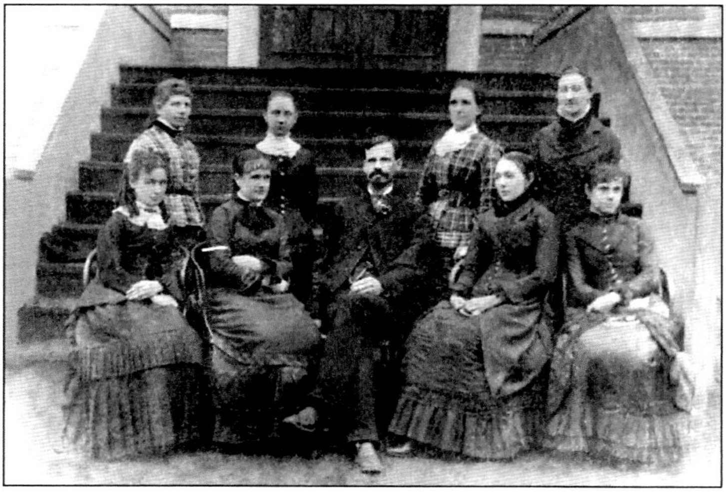

Pictured from left to right are the teachers of the public school that was destroyed by fire in 1870: (seated) Mrs. Bartlett, Mrs. Page, Professor Keebler (the principal), Jennie Kneedler, and Addie Willoughby; (standing) Mattie Peters, Maggie Wilkins, Ellie Stockings, and Kate Evans. (e.)

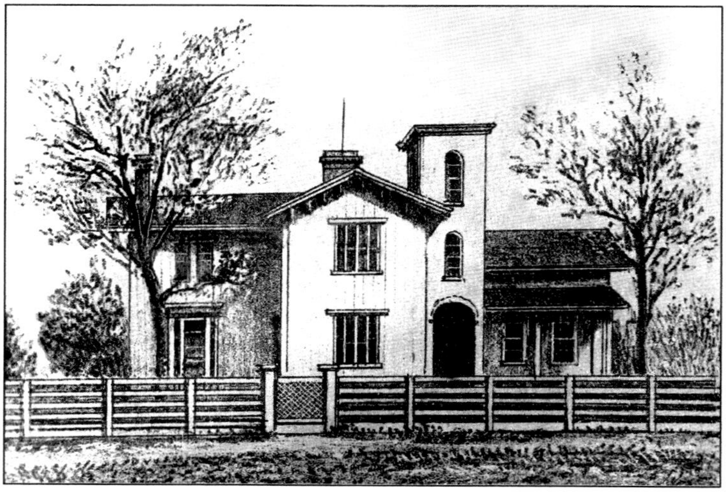

Dr. Henry Wing's home was situated on the northeast corner of Church and Aurora streets on the current Braner Building property. At different times, the Oliver Childs Look, James Dilliard, C.H. Dorris, and Irving Dilliard families had lived here. (c, e.)

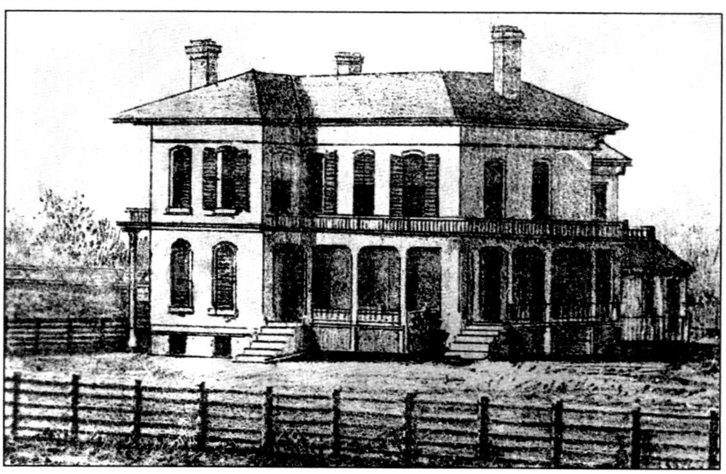

The home of Joseph W. Peers was on the southeast corner of Clay and Aurora. J.W. was the village assessor, tax collector and treasurer in 1853. He also ran a lumber yard on the northwest corner of Church and Morrison. Cynthia and J.W.'s son James began printing the *Herald* in 1870. (c, e.)

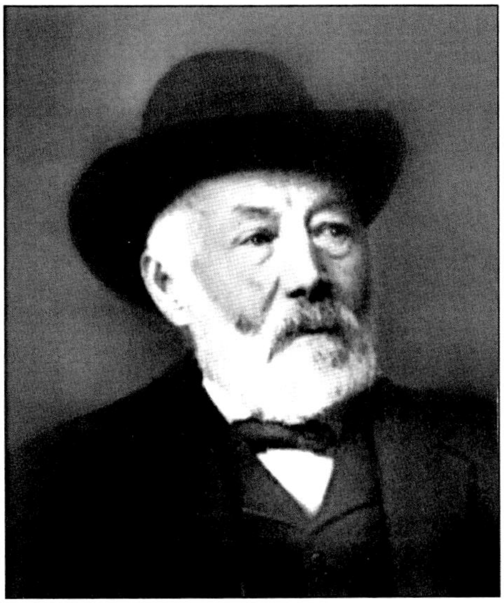

JOHN BECKER
Mayor 1872-74, 1881-82. (e.)

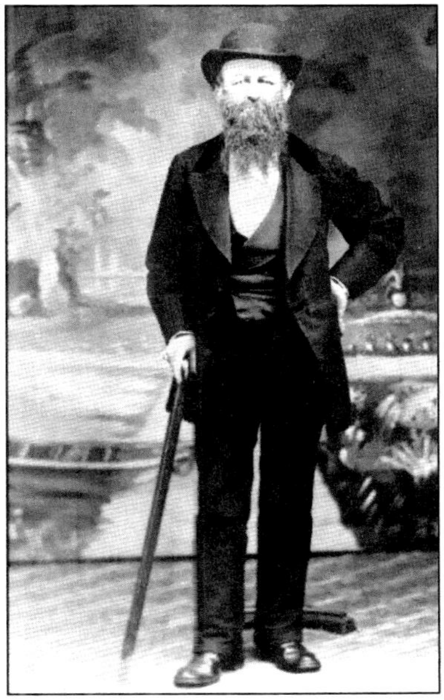

P.B. WONDERLY
Mayor 1875-76, 1879-80. (e.)

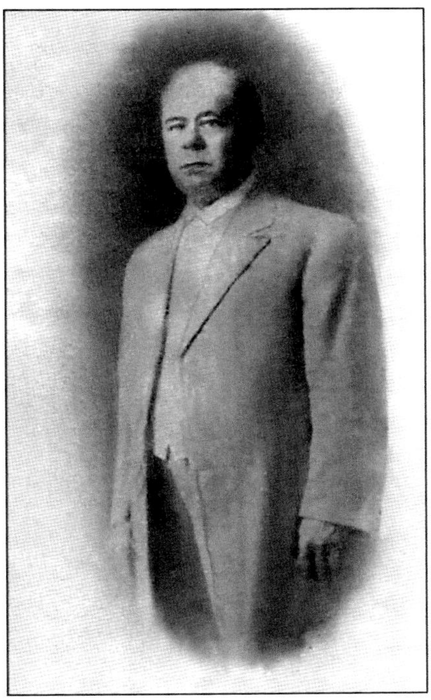

WILLIAM STEVENS
Mayor 1877-78. (e.)

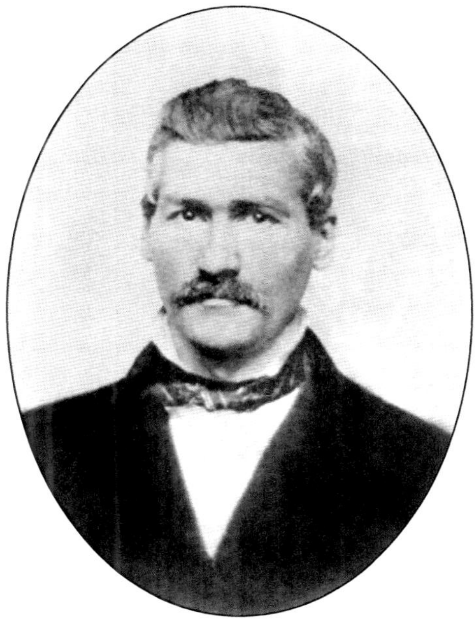

Dr. CHARLES OATMAN
Mayor 1885-86. (e.)

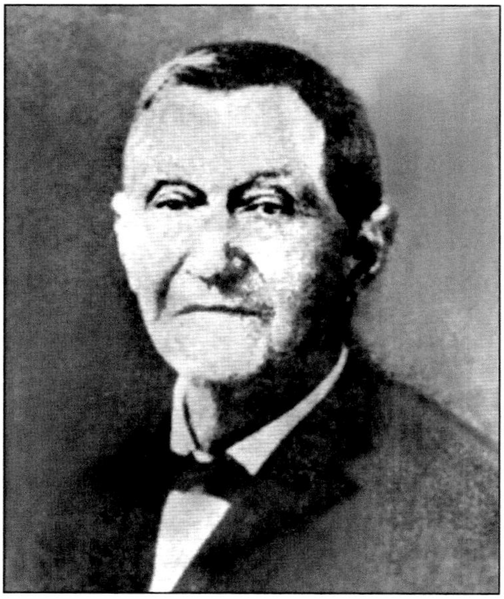

WILLIAM J. MATTHEWS
Mayor 1883-84,1887-94,
1899-1900, 1905-06. (e.)

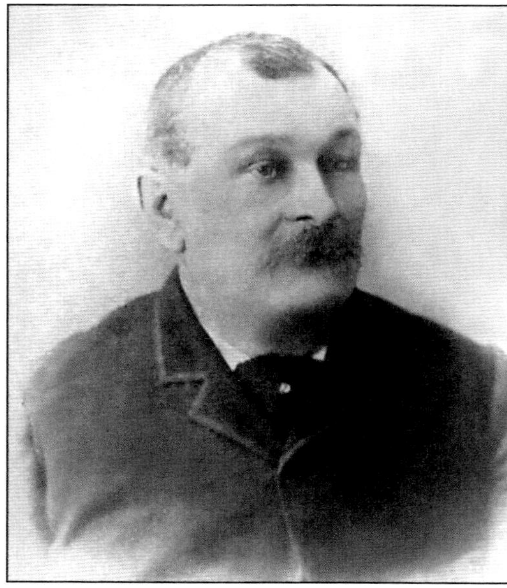

CHRIST KILLINGER
Mayor 1895-96. (e.)

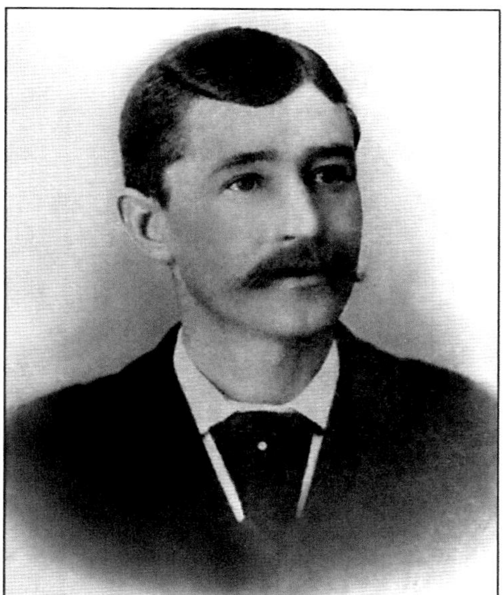

WILLIAM FIELDS
Mayor 1897-98. (e.)

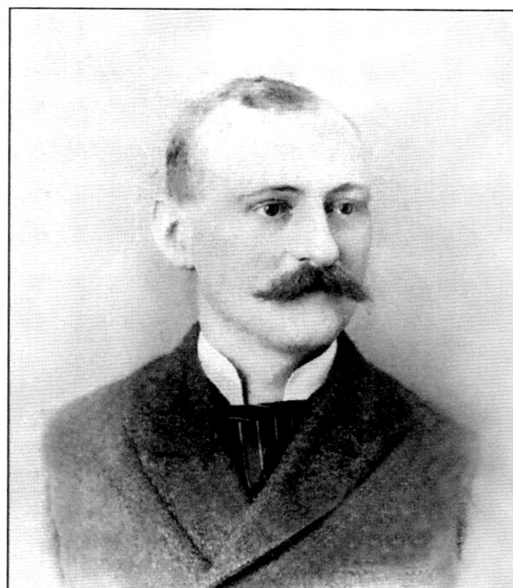

LOUIS LUMAGHI
Mayor 1901-04. (e.)

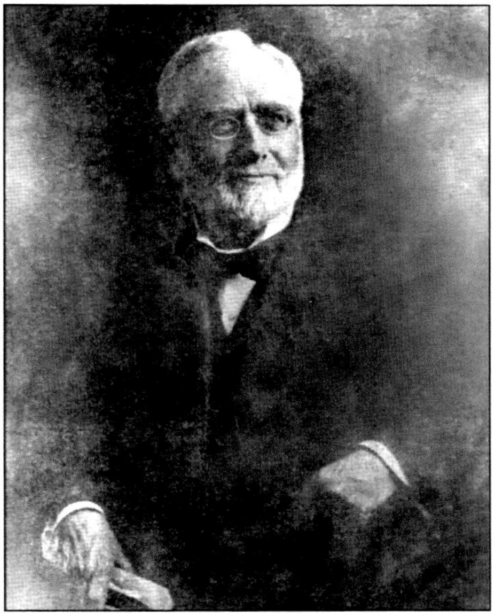

Dr. J.L. WADSWORTH
Mayor 1907-08. (e.)

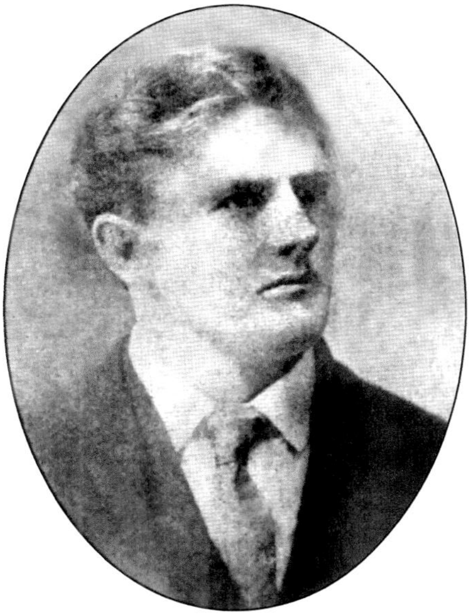

WILLIAM SIMPSON
Mayor 1909-10. (e.)

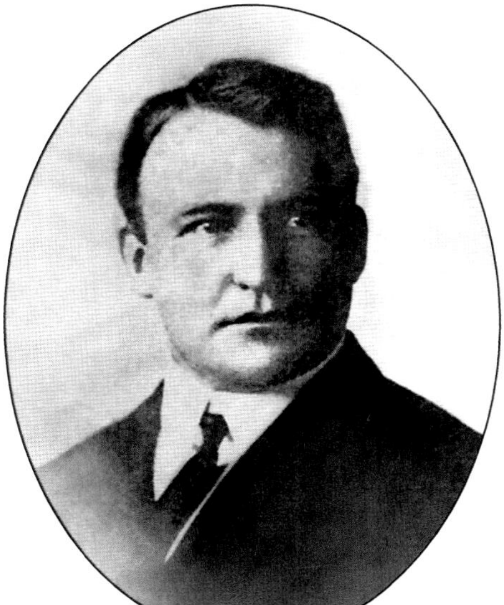

R. GUY KNEEDLER
Mayor 1911-12.(e.)

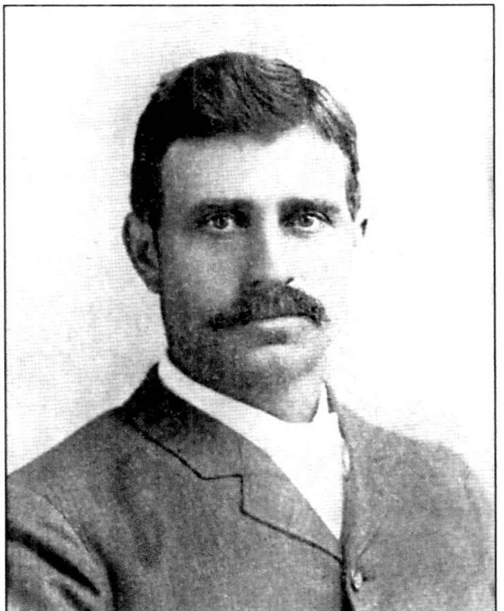

JAMES MATTHEWS
Mayor 1913-14. (e.)

Listed are postcards from the Marshall Collection that are in the Collinsville Historical Museum files but not in this publication because of their deterioration.

Baptist Church
Catholic Church
Episcopal Church
Lutheran Church
Methodist Church (1st)
Methodist Church (2nd)
Presbyterian Church
St. Joseph Society
Public School (2nd)
Dr. Biewend's House
Lumaghi/Greene House
Peter Wonderly
First Printing Press
Marshall Store/Madison Hall
Simon House
Town Hall
Metz & Simons General Store
Small/Tuft/Turner/Penny House
Temperence Hall
Map of Collinsville Cyclone No. 1
Map of Collinsville Cyclone No. 2

Newspapers-Front Pages:

- The *Argus*
- The *Banner of the Cross*
- The *Hustler*
- The *Liberal Democrat*
- The *Mercury*
- The *Monitor*
- The *Press*
- The *Sun*

Listed are items in the 1964 *Collinsville Herald* article that were in the copper box but the whereabouts are unknown.

John Cook Site after 105 years
Public School (1st)
Old Lime House
Old Ox Mill
Berry House
Terry House
Uncle Dick Wither's Plow Shop
Fisher Blacksmith Shop
Grosse's Second Drug Store

Newspapers-Front Pages:

- The *Advertiser*
- The *Collinsville Herald*
- The *Star*
- The *Union Pilot*

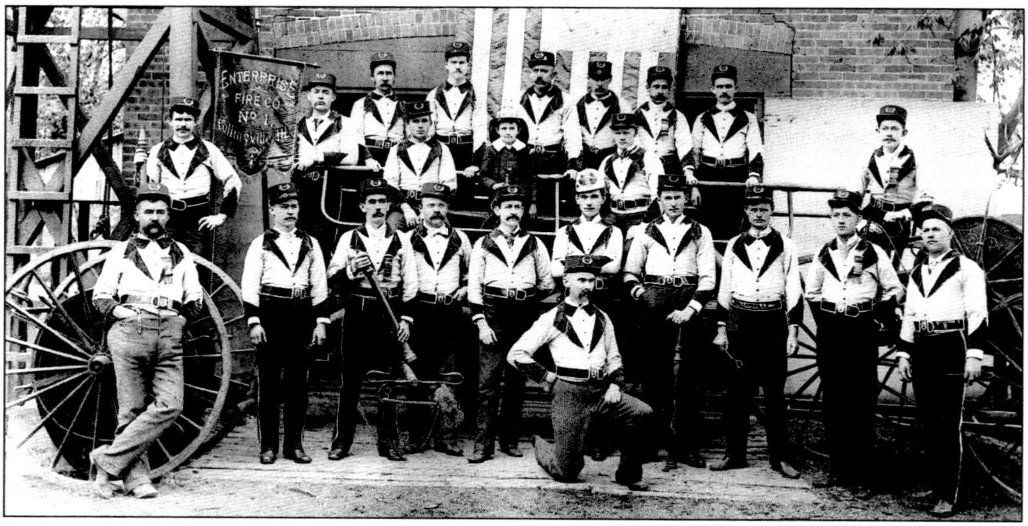

Beginning in 1872, a fire protection organization, The I.C. Moore Enterprise Fire Co. No. 1, was formed by Moore. It originally used a hand pumper donated by Mayor I.C. Moore. The name was later changed to Enterprise Fire Co. No. 1. This photo is believed to have been taken after 1886, when the four-wheel hose cart at right was purchased from Belleville.